FAVORITE BRAND NAME
ITALIAN
COLLECTION

PUBLICATIONS INTERNATIONAL, LTD.

Pictured on the front cover: *Top row, left:* Chicken & Pasta Sicilian (*page 98*); *Center:* Marinated Three Bean Salad (*page 154*); *Right:* Italian Chicken Pasta (*page 54*). *Bottom row, left:* Elegant Antipasto (*page 13*); *Center:* Deli Stuffed Calzone (*page 145*); *Right:* Zucchini Italiano (*page 171*).

Pictured on the back cover: *Top row, left:* Roasted Red Pepper Pasta with Shrimp (*page 46*); *Center:* Chocolate Biscotti (*page 209*); *Right:* Broccoli-Stuffed Shells (*page 49*). *Bottom row, left:* Chicken Pomodoro (*page 110*); *Center:* Pasta Primavera (*page 42*); *Right:* Italian Baked Frittata (*page 18*).

ISBN: 0-7853-0786-9

Manufactured in U.S.A.

8   7   6   5   4   3   2   1

Microwave ovens vary in wattage. The microwave cooking times given in this publication are approximate. Use the cooking times as guidelines and check for doneness before adding more time. Consult manufacturer's instructions for suitable microwave-safe cooking dishes.

Contents

Today's Italian Cooking 4
Helpful hints for successful results every time

Appetizers & Soups 6
Savory appetizers and superb soups to start off any meal

Pasta 38
An abundance of pasta dishes from tortellini to lasagna to fettuccine

Meat 80
Parmesan, florentine, piccata and other ways to dress up beef, pork, veal and lamb

Poultry 98
Versatile regional chicken and turkey meals sure to excite taste buds

Seafood 116
Fabulous fish and shellfish dishes with an Italian flair

Pizza & Breads 130
Crusty homemade focaccia, deep-dish pizzas, calzones and more

Salads & Side Dishes 154
Classic risottos, a variety of salads, and vegetables from artichokes to zucchini

Desserts 192
Tempting sweets from biscotti to chocolate hazelnut pie

Acknowledgments 214

Index 215

TODAY'S ITALIAN COOKING

In the last decade, Italian cuisine has gone from the usual spaghetti and meatballs to becoming a favorite in America's kitchens with diverse dishes, such as tortellini in cream sauce and linguine with seafood and roasted red pepper sauce. In fact, Americans eat almost 3 billion pounds of pasta each year. With pasta popularity at an all time high, more than 150 different shapes are available!

But Italian food is clearly more than just pasta. A true Italian meal is very different from the single, large plate of pasta many of us associate with Italian cooking. In Italy, there is a series of courses rather than a main course as we know it. *Antipasto*, which literally translated means "before the pasta," is the appetizer course and may be served either hot or cold. Soup may sometimes follow or replace the antipasto. The next course—*I Primi* or first course—usually consists of a pasta dish. *I Secondi* is the second course and features meat, poultry or fish. The pasta and meat courses are sometimes combined. The salad course or *Insalata* is served after the main portion of the meal to perk up tired taste buds. *I Dolci,* which translates to "the sweets," is the dessert course and is usually served with an espresso or cappuccino.

Favorite Brand Name Italian Collection includes many traditional dishes in all of the above courses and illustrates the variety of this delicious cuisine. Buon Appetito!

COOKING PASTA

Dry Pasta: For every pound of dry pasta, bring 4 to 6 quarts of water to a full, rolling boil. Add 2 teaspoons salt, if desired. Gradually add pasta, allowing water to return to a boil. The boiling water helps circulate the pasta so that it cooks evenly. Stir frequently to prevent the pasta from sticking. Begin testing for doneness after 5 minutes of cooking. Pasta that is "al dente"—meaning "to the tooth"—is tender, yet firm. Draining the pasta as soon as it is done stops the cooking action and helps prevent overcooking. For best results, toss the pasta with sauce immediately after draining and serve within minutes. If the sauce is not ready, toss the pasta with some butter or oil to prevent it from becoming sticky. Pasta in its dry, uncooked form may be stored almost indefinitely in a cool, dry place.

Fresh Pasta: Homemade pasta and store-bought fresh pasta take less time to cook than dry pasta. Cook fresh pasta in the same manner as dry, except begin testing for doneness after 2 minutes. Some of the recipes in this book include instructions for making fresh pasta, and most supermarkets contain pasta in the refrigerator section. Making pasta is fun and easy, but when time is short, dry pasta is a good substitute. What's important is that the pasta is never overcooked. Fresh pasta lasts several weeks in the refrigerator or may be frozen for up to 1 month.

FROM THE ITALIAN PANTRY

Most of these Italian ingredients can be found in large supermarkets. If you are unable to locate them in your store, look for them in gourmet food stores or Italian markets.

Arborio Rice: Italian-grown short-grain rice that has large, plump grains with a nutty taste. Arborio rice is traditionally used for risotto dishes because its high starch content produces a creamy texture since it absorbs more liquid than long-grain rice. Medium- or regular-grain rice may be substituted.

Cannellini Beans: Large, white Italian kidney beans available both in dry and canned forms. Dried beans need to be soaked in water several hours or overnight before cooking; canned beans should be rinsed and drained. Cannellini beans are often used in Italian soups, such as Minestrone. Great Northern beans make a good substitute.

Capers: Flower buds of a bush native to the Mediterranean. The buds are sun-dried, then pickled in a vinegar brine. Drain before using to remove excess salt.

Eggplant: A cousin of the tomato, the eggplant is actually a fruit, though commonly thought of as a vegetable. Eggplants come in various shapes and sizes and their color can vary from deep purple to creamy ivory. However, these varieties are similar in taste and should be salted to remove their bitter flavor. Choose firm, unblemished eggplants with a smooth, glossy skin. They should feel heavy for their size. Store in a cool, dry place and use within 1 or 2 days. Do not cut in advance as the flesh discolors rapidly.

Fennel: An anise-flavored, bulb-shaped vegetable with celerylike stems and feathery leaves. Both the base and stems may be eaten raw in salads or sautéed, and the seeds and leaves may be used for seasoning food. Purchase clean, crisp bulbs with no sign of browning. Greenery should be a fresh bright color. Store in the refrigerator, tightly wrapped in a plastic bag, for up to 5 days.

Italian Plum Tomatoes (also called Roma Tomatoes): A flavorful egg-shaped tomato that comes in red and yellow varieties. As with other tomatoes, they are very perishable. Choose firm tomatoes that are fragrant and free of blemishes. Ripe tomatoes should be stored at room temperature and used within a few days. Canned tomatoes are a good substitute when fresh ones are out of season.

Mascarpone Cheese: A buttery-rich double- to triple-cream cheese made with cow's milk. It is the creamiest of the Italian cheeses. When purchasing cheese, check the expiration date; store tightly covered in the refrigerator.

Olive Oil: Extracted oil from tree-ripened olives used for both salads and cooking. The highest grade is extra virgin olive oil. Exposure to air and heat turns olive oil rancid. Store in a cool, dark place for up to 6 months or refrigerate for up to 1 year. Bring chilled olive oil to room temperature before using.

Pine Nuts (also called Pignolias): Italian pine nuts come from the stone pine tree and are found inside pine cones. They have a delicate flavor and are a well known ingredient in the classic Italian pesto sauce. Store in an airtight container in the refrigerator for up to 3 months or freeze for up to 9 months.

Prosciutto: The Italian word for "ham," prosciutto is seasoned, salt-cured and air-dried (not smoked). Although the imported Parma may now be purchased in America, the less expensive domestic prosciutto is a good substitute. It is usually sold in very thin slices and eaten as a first course with melon slices and figs. It may also be added at the last minute to cooked foods, such as pasta and vegetables. Wrap tightly and refrigerate slices for up to 3 days or freeze for up to 1 month.

Radicchio: A red-leafed Italian chicory with burgundy red leaves and white ribs. It is mainly used as a salad green. Radicchio grows in a small, loose head and has tender, but firm leaves with a slightly bitter flavor. Choose crisp heads with no sign of browning. Refrigerate in a plastic bag for up to 1 week.

APPETIZERS & SOUPS

Bruschetta

1 can (14½ ounces) DEL MONTE®
    Italian Recipe Stewed Tomatoes
1 to 2 cloves garlic, crushed
2 tablespoons chopped fresh basil *or*
    ½ teaspoon dried basil
1 baguette (6 inches) French bread,
    cut into ½-inch slices
1 tablespoon olive oil

Drain tomatoes reserving liquid. In small saucepan, boil reserved liquid with garlic, 5 to 6 minutes, stirring occasionally. Remove from heat. Chop tomatoes; combine with garlic mixture and basil. Brush bread with oil. Broil until golden. Top with tomato mixture; serve immediately. Garnish with fresh basil leaves, if desired.
Makes 6 appetizer servings

Prep time: 5 minutes
Cook time: 5 minutes

Tortellini Soup

1 tablespoon margarine
2 cloves garlic, minced
2 cans (13¾ fluid ounces *each*)
    COLLEGE INN® Chicken or Beef
    Broth
1 package (8 ounces) fresh or frozen
    cheese-filled tortellini, thawed
1 can (14½ ounces) stewed tomatoes,
    cut up, undrained
1 package (10 ounces) fresh or frozen
    spinach, thawed
Grated Parmesan cheese

In large saucepan, melt margarine over medium-high heat. Add garlic; cook and stir 2 to 3 minutes or until lightly browned. Add broth and tortellini; bring to a boil. Reduce heat to low; simmer 10 minutes, stirring occasionally. Add tomatoes with liquid and spinach; simmer 5 minutes or until heated through. Top individual servings with Parmesan cheese. *Makes 6 servings*

Bruschetta

Hearty Minestrone Gratiné

1 cup diced celery
1 cup diced zucchini
1 can (28 ounces) tomatoes with
    liquid, chopped
2 cups water
2 teaspoons sugar
1 teaspoon dried Italian herb
    seasoning
1 can (15 ounces) garbanzo beans,
    drained
4 (3×½-inch) slices French bread,
    toasted
1 cup (4 ounces) SARGENTO®
    Preferred Light® Fancy Shredded
    Mozzarella Cheese
2 tablespoons SARGENTO® Grated
    Parmesan Cheese
    Chopped fresh parsley

Spray large saucepan or Dutch oven with nonstick cooking spray. Over medium heat, cook and stir celery and zucchini until tender. Add tomatoes, water, sugar and herb seasoning. Simmer, uncovered, 15 to 20 minutes. Add garbanzo beans; heat 10 minutes more.

Meanwhile, preheat broiler. Place toasted French bread on broiler pan. Divide Mozzarella on bread slices. Broil until cheese melts. Ladle soup into bowls and top with Mozzarella French bread. Sprinkle Parmesan cheese over each bowl and garnish with parsley. Serve immediately. *Makes 4 servings*

Baked Garlic Bundles

½ of 16-ounce package frozen phyllo
    dough, thawed to room
    temperature
¾ cup butter, melted
3 large heads fresh garlic,* separated
    into cloves and peeled
½ cup finely chopped walnuts
1 cup Italian-style bread crumbs

Preheat oven to 350°F. Remove phyllo from package; unroll and place on large sheet of waxed paper. Use scissors to cut phyllo crosswise into 2-inch-wide strips. Cover with large sheet of waxed paper and damp kitchen towel. (Phyllo dries out quickly if not covered.)

Lay 1 strip at a time on a flat surface and brush immediately with melted butter. Place 1 clove of garlic at 1 end. Sprinkle about 1 teaspoon walnuts along length of strip. Roll up garlic clove and walnuts in strip, tucking in side edges as you roll. Brush bundle with more butter; roll in bread crumbs. Repeat with remaining phyllo strips, garlic cloves, walnuts, butter and bread crumbs until all but smallest garlic cloves are used. Place bundles on rack in shallow roasting pan. Bake 20 minutes or until crispy.
      Makes 24 to 27 appetizers
*The whole garlic bulb is called a head.

*Favorite recipe from **Christopher Ranch of Gilroy***

Hearty Minestrone Gratiné

Light Pasta e Fagiole

1 cup dried cannellini beans, covered with 2 inches water and soaked overnight*
1 tablespoon olive oil
3 cloves garlic, minced
2 cups chopped onion (2 medium)
1 cup chopped celery (optional)
1 carrot, chopped (optional)
3 cans (14½ ounces *each*) low salt chicken or vegetable broth
2 bay leaves
1 tablespoon dried oregano leaves, crushed
1 teaspoon black pepper (optional)
1 can (1 pound) stewed tomatoes, sliced
1 tablespoon dried basil leaves, crushed
8 ounces uncooked pasta, such as small shells, ziti, bow ties or any combination, cooked according to package directions and drained
8 ounces Jarlsberg Lite cheese, shredded

Drain beans. Heat oil in large saucepan over medium-high heat until hot. Add garlic, onion, celery and carrot; cook and stir until carrot is tender. Stir in beans, broth, bay leaves, oregano and black pepper. Bring to a boil. Reduce heat to low; cover and simmer 1 hour or until beans are tender.

Add tomatoes and basil. Simmer 15 minutes. Add pasta and heat through. Before serving, remove and discard bay leaves; stir in half the cheese. Serve, passing remaining cheese for topping.
Makes 8 to 10 servings

*Or, cover dried beans with 4 inches of water; bring to a boil. Remove from heat; let stand 1 hour.

Favorite recipe from **Norseland Foods, Inc.**

Shrimp Cocktail Strata Tart

Shrimp Cocktail Strata Tart

2½ cups fresh bread crumbs (5 slices)
1 cup BORDEN® or MEADOW GOLD® Half-and-Half
4 eggs, beaten
2 (4¼-ounce) cans ORLEANS® Shrimp, drained and soaked as label directs
½ cup BENNETT'S® Cocktail or Hot Seafood Sauce
¼ cup chopped green onions
2 tablespoons REALEMON® Lemon Juice from Concentrate
1½ teaspoons WYLER'S® or STEERO® Chicken-Flavor Instant Bouillon
¼ teaspoon pepper
Additional BENNETT'S® Cocktail or Hot Seafood Sauce

Preheat oven to 350°F. In large bowl, combine crumbs and half-and-half; let stand 10 minutes. Add all remaining ingredients except additional cocktail sauce; mix well. Pour into 10-inch oiled quiche dish or tart pan. Bake 30 to 35 minutes or until set. Cool. Garnish as desired. Serve warm or chilled with additional cocktail sauce. Refrigerate leftovers. *Makes 1 (10-inch) tart*

Italian-Style Chili

1 pound lean ground beef
¾ cup chopped onion
1 (26-ounce) jar CLASSICO®
    Di Napoli (Tomato & Basil)
    Pasta Sauce
1½ cups water
1 (14½-ounce) can whole tomatoes,
    undrained and broken up
1 (4-ounce) can sliced mushrooms,
    drained
2 ounces sliced pepperoni (⅓ cup)
1 tablespoon WYLER'S® or
    STEERO® Beef-Flavor Instant
    Bouillon *or* 3 Beef-Flavor
    Bouillon Cubes
1 tablespoon chili powder
2 teaspoons sugar

In large kettle or Dutch oven, brown meat with onion; pour off fat. Add remaining ingredients; bring to a boil. Reduce heat; simmer, uncovered, 30 minutes, stirring occasionally. Garnish as desired. Refrigerate leftovers.

Makes about 2 quarts

Artichoke Puffs

16 to 20 slices small party rye bread
2 tablespoons CRISCO® Shortening,
    melted
1 can (14 ounces) artichoke hearts,
    drained
2 egg whites
⅓ teaspoon salt
¼ cup grated Parmesan cheese
2 tablespoons shredded sharp
    Cheddar cheese
    Dash ground red pepper
    Paprika

1. Preheat oven to 400°F. Brush bread slices with melted Crisco® and place on ungreased cookie sheet.

2. Cut artichoke hearts in half; drain on paper towels. Place 1 artichoke piece, cut side down, on each bread slice.

3. Beat egg whites and salt in medium bowl until stiff, not dry, peaks form. Fold in cheeses and ground red pepper.

4. Spoon about 1 measuring teaspoonful of egg white mixture over each artichoke piece; sprinkle with paprika. Place on baking sheets.

5. Bake at 400°F for 10 to 12 minutes or until golden brown. Serve hot. Garnish tray with celery leaves and carrot curls, if desired.

Makes about 16 puffs

Calico Minestrone Soup

2 cans (14 ounces *each*) chicken broth
¼ cup uncooked small shell pasta
1 can (14½ ounces) DEL MONTE®
    Italian Recipe Stewed Tomatoes
1 can (8¾ ounces) or 1 cup kidney
    beans, drained
½ cup chopped cooked chicken or
    beef
1 carrot, cubed
1 stalk celery, sliced
½ teaspoon dried basil, crushed

In large saucepan, bring broth to boil; stir in pasta and boil 5 minutes. Add remaining ingredients. Reduce heat; cover and simmer 20 minutes. Garnish with grated Parmesan cheese, if desired.

Makes about 6 (1-cup) servings

Prep time: 5 minutes
Cook time: 25 minutes

Tip: This is an easy recipe for kids and parents to make together.

Basil & Vegetable Cheese Spread

2 packages (8 ounces *each*) cream
    cheese, softened
½ cup butter or margarine, softened
1 envelope LIPTON® Recipe
    Secrets™ Vegetable Soup Mix
⅓ cup chopped almonds
¼ cup chopped fresh basil leaves*
2 tablespoons grated Parmesan
    cheese

With electric mixer or food processor, beat cream cheese and butter until smooth. Add remaining ingredients; beat until well blended.

Line 7½×3¾×2¼-inch loaf pan or small bowl with waxed paper. Pack cheese mixture into prepared pan; cover and refrigerate 2 hours or until firm. To serve, unmold onto serving platter; remove waxed paper. Serve, if desired, with bagel chips, dark bread, cucumber slices or assorted crackers, and fresh fruit.

Makes 1 loaf

*Substitution: Use 2 tablespoons dried basil leaves.

Basil & Vegetable Cheese Spread

Elegant Antipasto

1 jar (16 ounces) mild cherry peppers
1 package (9 ounces) frozen artichoke hearts, cooked, drained
½ pound asparagus spears, cooked
½ cup pitted ripe olives
1 medium red onion, cut into wedges
1 green bell pepper, cut into wedges
1 red bell pepper, cut into wedges
1 bottle (8 ounces) KRAFT® House Italian Dressing
1 wedge (4 ounces) KRAFT® Natural Parmesan Cheese, shredded, divided
1 package (8 ounces) OSCAR MAYER® Hard Salami

• Arrange vegetables in rows in 13 × 9-inch glass baking dish.

• Mix dressing and ⅓ cup cheese. Pour over vegetables; cover. Refrigerate 1 to 2 hours to marinate.

• Drain vegetables, reserving marinade. Arrange vegetables and salami on serving platter. Drizzle with marinade; top with remaining cheese.

Makes 6 servings

Prep time: 20 minutes plus refrigerating

Variation: Substitute mushrooms, green beans, cherry tomatoes or broccoli flowerets for any of the vegetables listed.

Crostini

½ cup PROGRESSO® Olive Oil
2 tablespoons minced garlic
1 loaf (1 pound) Italian bread, cut into 3 × 3-inch pieces, ¼ inch thick
2 cups of your favorite topping, chopped*
2 cups (8 ounces) shredded cheese**
2 teaspoons dried oregano leaves, crushed

1. In small skillet, heat olive oil. Add garlic; cook 1 minute.

2. Preheat broiler. Place bread on large baking sheet. Brush one side of each slice generously with olive oil mixture. Broil until lightly toasted.

3. Turn bread slices over; brush untoasted side with remaining olive oil mixture.

4. Spoon topping evenly onto each slice; sprinkle with cheese and oregano.

5. Broil until cheese is melted and edges of bread are golden brown.

Makes about 3 dozen appetizers

Prep time: 10 minutes
Cooking time: 5 minutes

*Topping Suggestions: Any one or combination of Progresso® Marinated Mushrooms, Progresso® Pepper Salad, Progresso® Tuscan Peppers (pepperoncini), Progresso® Roasted Peppers (red), Progresso® Imported Capers, anchovies, pepperoni

**Cheese Suggestions: Any one or combination of mozzarella, provolone, fontinella, Italian sharp

Elegant Antipasto

Hot Artichoke Spread

Hot Artichoke Spread

1 cup MIRACLE WHIP® Salad
    Dressing
1 cup (4 ounces) KRAFT® 100%
    Grated Parmesan Cheese
1 can (14 ounces) artichoke hearts,
    drained, chopped
1 can (4 ounces) chopped green
    chilies, drained
1 garlic clove, minced
2 tablespoons sliced green onions
2 tablespoons seeded, chopped
    tomato

• Heat oven to 350°F.

• Mix all ingredients except onions and
tomatoes until well blended.

• Spoon into shallow ovenproof dish or
9-inch pie plate.

• Bake 20 to 25 minutes or until lightly
browned. Sprinkle with onions and
tomatoes. Serve with toasted bread
cutouts. *Makes 2 cups*

Prep time: 10 minutes
Cooking time: 25 minutes
Microwave: •Mix all ingredients except
onions and tomatoes until well blended.
•Spoon into 9-inch pie plate. •Microwave
at MEDIUM (50%) 7 to 9 minutes or until
mixture is warm, stirring every 4
minutes. Stir before serving. Sprinkle
with onions and tomatoes. Serve with
toasted bread cutouts.

Chicken Fingers Italiano

*Kids of all ages will love these zesty chicken
sticks dipped into their favorite sauce.*

1 pound boneless, skinless chicken
    breast halves, pounded to ¼-inch
    thickness
1 egg, lightly beaten
¾ cup PROGRESSO® Italian Style
    Bread Crumbs
¼ cup PROGRESSO® Olive Oil

1. Cut chicken into strips.

2. Dip chicken into egg; coat with bread
crumbs.

3. In large skillet, heat oil over medium
heat. Cook chicken 6 minutes or until
browned on both sides and no longer
pink in center. Serve with your choice
of dipping sauces.

Makes 8 appetizer servings

Prep time: 20 minutes
Cooking time: 6 minutes

Suggested Dipping Sauces: Progresso®
Marinara Sauce, mayonnaise/mustard,
horseradish, sweet and sour sauce, honey

Two Cheese Pesto Dip

1 cup light sour cream
½ cup light mayonnaise
½ cup finely chopped fresh parsley
¼ cup finely chopped walnuts
1 clove garlic, minced
1½ teaspoons dried basil leaves *or*
  **3 tablespoons minced fresh basil
    leaves**
**½ cup (2 ounces) SARGENTO®
    Preferred Light® Shredded
    Mozzarella Cheese**
**2 tablespoons SARGENTO® Grated
    Parmesan Cheese**
Assorted fresh vegetable dippers

Combine all ingredients. Cover and
refrigerate several hours or overnight.
Serve with vegetable dippers.

Makes 2 cups

Italian Wedding Soup

1 pound ground beef
**1 cup PROGRESSO® Italian Style
    Bread Crumbs**
1 egg, lightly beaten
2 teaspoons Worcestershire sauce
1 teaspoon garlic powder
**2 tablespoons PROGRESSO®
    Olive Oil**
5 cups chicken broth
1 cup water
1½ cups pastina or any miniature pasta
**1 package (10 ounces) frozen
    chopped spinach, cooked
    according to package directions,
    drained**

1. In large bowl, combine ground beef,
bread crumbs, egg, Worcestershire sauce
and garlic powder; mix well.

2. Shape meatballs using 1 rounded
teaspoon meat mixture for each meatball.

3. In large skillet, heat olive oil. Add
meatballs; cook 5 to 7 minutes or to
desired doneness, turning occasionally to
brown on all sides. Drain.

4. In large saucepan, bring chicken broth
and water to a boil. Reduce heat. Add
meatballs, pastina and spinach; cover.
Simmer 10 minutes.

Makes 8 servings

Prep time: 30 minutes
Cooking time: 20 minutes

Italian Wedding Soup

Fried Pasta with Marinara Sauce

These crunchy fried pasta dippers will be the hit at any party.

PROGRESSO® Olive Oil for deep frying
½ cup PROGRESSO® Grated Parmesan Cheese
¼ cup PROGRESSO® Italian Style Bread Crumbs
1 package (7 ounces) spiral-shaped pasta, cooked according to package directions
1 cup PROGRESSO® Marinara Sauce, heated

1. In heavy 2-quart saucepan, heat 1½ inches olive oil (about 3 cups) until oil reaches 350°F on deep-fry thermometer.

2. In medium bowl, combine Parmesan cheese and bread crumbs; set aside.

3. Deep fry pasta, in small batches, 4 minutes or until crunchy and lightly browned. Remove with slotted spoon; drain on paper towels. Add to cheese mixture; toss lightly to coat. Serve immediately with marinara sauce.
Makes 4 appetizer servings

Prep time: 15 minutes
Cooking time: 16 minutes

Fried Pasta with Marinara Sauce

Pesto Pizza

2 loaves (2 ounces *each*) regular size SAHARA® Pita Bread
½ cup HELLMANN'S® or BEST FOODS® Real or Light Mayonnaise or Reduced Fat Mayonnaise Dressing
½ cup grated Parmesan cheese
½ cup chopped fresh basil
¼ cup pine nuts, toasted
1 small clove garlic, minced or pressed
Fresh basil leaves for garnish (optional)

Preheat oven to 375°F. Cut each pita bread around edge, separating halves. Place cut sides up in shallow pan. Bake, turning once, 8 minutes or until slightly crisp.

In small bowl combine mayonnaise, Parmesan, chopped basil, pine nuts and garlic until blended. Spread evenly on pita halves. Bake 8 minutes or until puffed and lightly browned. Cut each into 8 wedges. If desired, garnish with basil leaves. *Makes 32 appetizers*

Winter Pesto Pizza: Follow recipe for Pesto Pizza. Omit fresh basil. Add ½ cup chopped fresh parsley and ½ teaspoon dried basil.

Cioppino

1½ cups chopped onion
1 cup chopped celery
½ cup chopped green bell pepper
1 large clove garlic, crushed
3 tablespoons olive oil
2 cans (14.5 ounces *each*)
    CONTADINA® Recipe Ready
    Diced Tomatoes and Juice
1⅓ cups (two 6-ounce cans)
    CONTADINA® Italian Paste
½ teaspoon Italian seasoning
1 teaspoon salt
½ teaspoon ground black pepper
2 cups water
1 cup dry red wine
3 to 3½ pounds mixed seafood:
    clams, oysters, mussels, shrimp,
    whitefish, scallops, cooked crab,
    cooked lobster, or crawfish

In Dutch oven, cook and stir onion, celery, green pepper and garlic in oil until tender. Add tomatoes and juice, Italian paste, Italian seasoning, salt, black pepper, water and wine. Heat to boiling. Reduce heat; boil gently, uncovered, 30 minutes.

To prepare seafood, scrub clams, oysters and mussels under running water. Place in ½ inch boiling water in saucepan. Cover and boil gently until shells open, about 3 minutes (discard any shellfish that do not open). Set aside. Peel and devein shrimp. Cut fish, scallops, crab and lobster into bite-size pieces.

Add whitefish to tomato mixture; boil gently 5 minutes. Add scallops, shrimp and crawfish; cook additional 5 minutes. Add lobster, crab and reserved shellfish. Heat to serving temperature.

Makes 3½ quarts

Veg-All® Italian Soup

Veg-All® Italian Soup

2 tablespoons butter or margarine
1 cup diced onion
1 cup shredded cabbage
2 cups water
1 (16-ounce) can VEG-ALL® Mixed
    Vegetables, drained
2 (14½-ounce) cans stewed tomatoes
2 tablespoons chopped fresh parsley
½ teaspoon dried basil leaves
½ teaspoon dried oregano leaves
½ teaspoon black pepper

Melt butter in large saucepan over medium-high heat. Stir in onion and cabbage. Heat 2 minutes or until onion is soft. Add water; cover and simmer 10 minutes. Stir in Veg-All® mixed vegetables, tomatoes and seasonings. Reduce heat to low; simmer 10 minutes more or until heated through.

Makes 6 servings

Italian Baked Frittata

1 cup broccoli flowerettes
½ cup sliced mushrooms
½ red pepper, cut into rings
2 green onions, sliced into 1-inch
    pieces
1 tablespoon BLUE BONNET®
    Spread
8 eggs
¼ cup GREY POUPON® Dijon or
    Country Dijon Mustard
¼ cup water
½ teaspoon Italian seasoning
1 cup (4 ounces) shredded Swiss
    cheese

Preheat oven to 375°F. In 10-inch ovenproof skillet, over medium-high heat, cook broccoli, mushrooms, red pepper and green onions in spread until tender-crisp, about 5 minutes. Remove from heat.

In small bowl, with electric mixer, beat eggs, mustard, water and Italian seasoning until foamy; stir in cheese. Pour mixture into skillet over vegetables. Bake 20 to 25 minutes or until set. Serve immediately. *Makes 4 servings*

Pizza Soup

1 medium onion, chopped
2 ounces pepperoni or salami, cut
    into small pieces
½ teaspoon LAWRY'S® Garlic Powder
    with Parsley
½ teaspoon dried oregano leaves,
    crushed
1 envelope LIPTON® Noodle Soup
    Mix with Real Chicken Broth
3 cups water
2 tablespoons tomato paste
½ cup (2 ounces) shredded
    mozzarella cheese

In medium saucepan, cook onion, pepperoni, garlic powder and oregano over medium-high heat, stirring frequently, 3 minutes or until onion is tender. Stir in remaining ingredients except cheese. Bring to a boil. Reduce heat to low and simmer, stirring occasionally, 5 minutes. Sprinkle with cheese before serving.
Makes 7 servings (about 3½ cups)

Felicia Solimine's Neapolitan-Style Calamari

2 pounds fresh or thawed frozen
    squid (calamari)
¼ cup FILIPPO BERIO® Extra Virgin
    Olive Oil
2 cups lemon juice
1 cup dry white wine
2 cloves garlic, cut into halves
½ teaspoon salt
½ teaspoon dried dill weed
    Fresh ground black pepper to taste
    Italian parsley sprigs and lemon
    slices, for garnish

Clean squid (directions on page 126); pat dry with paper towels. Cut squid into ¾-inch-wide slices; cut tentacles into 1-inch pieces.

Heat oil in 5-quart saucepan over medium-high heat; add squid. Cook and stir about 3 minutes or until lightly browned. Add lemon juice, wine, garlic, salt, dill and black pepper. Bring to a boil over high heat. Reduce heat to low; cover and simmer 45 minutes or until squid is tender, stirring occasionally. Remove squid rings with slotted spoon. Divide among 6 individual plates. Garnish with parsley and lemon.
Makes 6 first-course or
4 main-dish servings

Italian Baked Frittata

Antipasto with Marinated Mushrooms

Antipasto with Marinated Mushrooms

1 recipe Marinated Mushrooms
   (recipe follows)
4 teaspoons red wine vinegar
½ teaspoon dried basil leaves
½ teaspoon dried oregano leaves
   Generous dash black pepper
¼ cup olive oil
4 ounces mozzarella cheese, cut into
   ½-inch cubes
4 ounces prosciutto or cooked ham,
   thinly sliced
4 ounces Provolone cheese, cut into
   2-inch sticks
1 jar (10 ounces) pepperoncini
   peppers, drained
8 ounces hard salami, thinly sliced
2 jars (6 ounces *each*) marinated
   artichoke hearts, drained
1 can (6 ounces) pitted ripe olives,
   drained
   Lettuce leaves (optional)
   Fresh basil leaves and chives, for
   garnish

Prepare Marinated Mushrooms; set aside. Combine vinegar, dried basil, oregano and black pepper in small bowl. Whisk in oil until well blended. Add mozzarella cubes; stir to coat. Marinate, covered, in refrigerator at least 2 hours. Wrap ½ of prosciutto slices around Provolone sticks; roll up remaining slices separately.

Drain mozzarella cubes; reserve marinade. Arrange mozzarella cubes, prosciutto-wrapped Provolone sticks, prosciutto rolls, marinated mushrooms, pepperoncini, salami, artichoke hearts and olives on large platter lined with lettuce, if desired. Drizzle reserved marinade over pepperoncini, artichoke hearts and olives. Garnish, if desired. Serve with small forks or wooden toothpicks. *Makes 6 to 8 servings*

Marinated Mushrooms

3 tablespoons lemon juice
2 tablespoons chopped fresh parsley
½ teaspoon salt
¼ teaspoon dried tarragon leaves
   Generous dash black pepper
½ cup olive oil
1 clove garlic
½ pound small or medium fresh
   mushrooms

To prepare marinade, combine lemon juice, parsley, salt, tarragon and black pepper in medium bowl. Whisk in oil until well blended. Lightly crush garlic with flat side of chef's knife or mallet; add to marinade. Slice stems off mushrooms; reserve stems for another use. Wipe mushroom caps clean. Add mushrooms to marinade; mix well. Marinate, covered, in refrigerator 4 hours or overnight, stirring occasionally. To serve, remove and discard garlic. Serve mushrooms on antipasto tray or as relish. Or, add to green salad, using marinade as dressing. *Makes about 2 cups*

Caponata

1 medium eggplant, peeled and
    finely chopped (about 3 cups)
½ cup finely chopped onion
1 clove garlic, minced
1 teaspoon Italian seasoning
⅓ cup olive oil
½ cup finely chopped red or green
    bell pepper
½ cup finely chopped tomato
    TRISCUIT® Wafers

In large skillet, over medium-high heat,
cook and stir eggplant, onion, garlic and
Italian seasoning in hot oil for 5 minutes
or until tender. Stir in pepper and tomato.
Cover; reduce heat. Cook 10 minutes
longer or until pepper is tender, stirring
occasionally. Cover; refrigerate several
hours or overnight to allow flavors to
blend. Serve with Triscuit® wafers.

Makes 2¼ cups

Deep-Fried Stuffed Shells

16 uncooked jumbo pasta shells
2 eggs, divided
1 can (6½ ounces) tuna, drained and
    flaked *or* 1 can (6 ounces)
    crabmeat, drained, flaked and
    cartilage removed
1 cup (4 ounces) shredded Cheddar
    or Swiss cheese
1 medium tomato, peeled, seeded
    and chopped
2 tablespoons sliced green onion
½ teaspoon dried basil leaves,
    crushed
⅛ teaspoon black pepper
1 tablespoon water
1 cup dry bread crumbs
    Vegetable oil, for frying
    Tartar sauce, for serving

Cook shells according to package
directions until tender but still firm;
drain. Rinse under cold running water;
drain again. Set aside to cool.

Slightly beat 1 egg in large bowl. Add
tuna, cheese, tomato, green onion, basil
and black pepper; mix well. Stuff cooked
shells with tuna mixture.

Beat remaining 1 egg with water in small
bowl. Place bread crumbs in large
shallow dish. Dip each stuffed shell in
egg mixture and roll in bread crumbs.
Heat 2 inches oil in large heavy saucepan
over medium-high heat until oil reaches
365°F on deep-fry thermometer; adjust
heat to maintain temperature. Fry shells,
a few at a time, in hot oil 1½ to 2 minutes
until golden brown. Remove with slotted
spoon; drain on paper towels. Serve with
tartar sauce. Garnish as desired.

Makes 8 appetizer servings

*Favorite recipe from **North Dakota Wheat Commission***

Deep-Fried Stuffed Shells

Noodle Soup Parmigiano

1 envelope LIPTON® Noodle Soup
    Mix with Real Chicken Broth
3 cups water
½ pound boneless skinless chicken
    breast halves, cut into ½-inch
    pieces
1 cup chopped fresh tomatoes *or*
    1 can (8 ounces) whole peeled
    tomatoes, undrained and
    chopped
½ teaspoon LAWRY'S® Garlic Powder
    with Parsley (optional)
½ cup shredded mozzarella cheese
    (about 2 ounces)
    Grated Parmesan cheese (optional)

In medium saucepan, combine all
ingredients except cheeses; bring to a
boil. Reduce heat and simmer, uncovered,
stirring occasionally, 5 minutes or until
chicken is tender and no longer pink in
center. To serve, spoon into bowls;
sprinkle with cheeses.

Makes about 5 (1-cup) servings

Noodle Soup Parmigiano

Prosciutto Fruit Bundles in Endive

1 green onion, sliced
1 (4-inch) rib celery, sliced
2 tablespoons rice or white wine
    vinegar
1 tablespoon vegetable oil
1 tablespoon light soy sauce
½ teaspoon sugar
½ teaspoon grated lime peel
¼ teaspoon ground ginger
4 (3×½-inch) slices *each:* cantaloupe,
    pineapple, honeydew melon
8 (2×¼-inch) julienned strips *each:*
    celery, green and red bell pepper
3 ounces thinly sliced domestic
    prosciutto ham
24 Belgian endive leaves

For dressing, place first 8 ingredients in
blender or food processor; cover and
blend until fairly smooth. Place fruits and
vegetables in plastic bag. Add dressing;
turn to coat. Close bag securely and
marinate in refrigerator 30 minutes.
Meanwhile, trim excess fat from ham and
discard; cut ham lengthwise into ½-inch-
wide strips. Remove fruits and vegetables
from dressing. Wrap ham strips around the
following combinations: cantaloupe/
2 strips celery; pineapple/2 strips
green pepper; honeydew melon/2 strips
red pepper. Place each bundle on endive
leaf. Cover with plastic wrap and
refrigerate until serving.

Makes 24 appetizers

Favorite recipe from **National Live Stock & Meat Board**

Classic Meatball Soup

2 pounds beef bones
3 ribs celery
2 carrots
1 medium onion, cut in half
1 bay leaf
6 cups cold water
1 egg
4 tablespoons chopped fresh parsley, divided
1 teaspoon salt, divided
½ teaspoon dried marjoram leaves, crushed
¼ teaspoon black pepper, divided
½ cup soft fresh bread crumbs
¼ cup grated Parmesan cheese
1 pound ground beef
1 can (14½ ounces) whole peeled tomatoes, undrained and chopped
½ cup uncooked rotini or small macaroni

Classic Meatball Soup

To prepare stock, rinse bones. Combine bones, celery, carrots, onion and bay leaf in 6-quart stockpot. Add water. Bring to a boil; reduce heat to low. Cover partially and simmer 1 hour, skimming foam occasionally.

Preheat oven to 400°F. Spray 13×9-inch baking pan with nonstick cooking spray. Combine egg, 3 tablespoons parsley, ½ teaspoon salt, marjoram and ⅛ teaspoon black pepper in medium bowl; whisk lightly. Stir in bread crumbs and cheese. Add beef; mix well. Place meat mixture on cutting board; pat evenly into 1-inch-thick square. With sharp knife, cut meat into 1-inch squares; shape each square into a ball. Place meatballs in prepared pan; bake 20 to 25 minutes until brown on all sides and cooked through, turning occasionally. Drain on paper towels.

Strain stock through sieve into medium bowl. Slice celery and carrots; set aside. Discard bones, onion and bay leaf. To degrease stock, let stand 5 minutes to allow fat to rise. Holding paper towel, quickly pull across *surface only*, allowing towel to absorb fat. Discard. Repeat with clean paper towels as many times as needed to remove all fat. Return stock to stockpot. Add tomatoes with liquid to stock. Bring to a boil; uncover and boil 5 minutes. Stir in rotini, remaining ½ teaspoon salt and ⅛ teaspoon black pepper. Cook 6 minutes, stirring occasionally. Add reserved vegetables and meatballs. Reduce heat to medium; cook 10 minutes until heated through. Stir in remaining 1 tablespoon parsley. Season to taste.

Makes 4 to 6 servings (about 7 cups)

Chilled Seafood Lasagna with Herbed Cheese

2 cups Wisconsin ricotta cheese
1½ cups Wisconsin mascarpone cheese
2 tablespoons lemon juice
1 tablespoon minced fresh basil leaves
1 tablespoon minced fresh dill
1 tablespoon minced fresh tarragon leaves
¼ teaspoon white pepper
8 lasagna noodles (2 inches wide), cooked and drained
1 pound lox, divided
4 ounces whitefish caviar, gently rinsed
Fresh tarragon sprigs, for garnish (optional)

Place ricotta cheese, mascarpone cheese, lemon juice, basil, dill, minced tarragon and white pepper in food processor or blender; process until well combined. Line terrine mold* with plastic wrap, allowing wrap to come 5 inches over sides of mold. Layer 1 noodle, ½ cup cheese mixture, 2 ounces lox and 2 rounded teaspoons caviar in mold. Repeat layers 6 times. Top with remaining noodle. Set aside remaining 2 ounces lox for garnish. Cover; refrigerate several hours or until firm.

Turn mold over onto serving platter. Carefully lift mold from lasagna and remove plastic wrap. Garnish with strips of lox rolled to look like roses and tarragon sprigs, if desired. Slice with warm knife. *Makes 24 first-course or 8 main-dish servings*

*You may prepare lasagna without terrine mold. Layer as directed on plastic wrap. Cover and wrap with foil.

*Favorite recipe from **Wisconsin Milk Marketing Board** © 1994*

Chilled Seafood Lasagna with Herbed Cheese

Almonds Italiano

These snack almonds could become your house specialty. You may make these ahead and store in the freezer.

1½ tablespoons butter
1 teaspoon salt
1 teaspoon dried oregano leaves, crushed
1 teaspoon dried basil leaves, crushed
2 cloves garlic, finely chopped
2 cups BLUE DIAMOND® Whole Natural Almonds

Preheat oven to 375°F. Melt butter in 8-inch square baking dish in oven. Stir in salt, oregano, basil and garlic. Add almonds, stirring until coated. Bake 15 to 20 minutes, stirring occasionally, until almonds are crisp. *Makes 2 cups*

Minestrone

1 tablespoon WESSON® Oil
1 small zucchini, diced
1 cup chopped onion
2 (14½-ounce) cans low-salt chicken broth
1 (15-ounce) can HUNT'S® Ready Tomato Sauces Original Italian
1 (8-ounce) can mixed vegetables, drained
1 (8-ounce) can kidney or garbanzo beans, drained
¼ cup uncooked small elbow macaroni
⅛ teaspoon *each* black pepper and dried thyme leaves

In large saucepan, in hot oil, cook and stir zucchini and onion until tender. Stir in *remaining* ingredients. Simmer, covered, 15 minutes or until heated through.
Makes 7 cups

Zesty Bruschetta

Zesty Bruschetta

1 envelope LIPTON® Recipe
   Secrets™ Savory Herb with
   Garlic or Italian Herb with
   Tomato Soup Mix
3 tablespoons olive or vegetable oil
1 loaf French or Italian bread (about
   18 inches long), sliced
   lengthwise
2 tablespoons shredded or grated
   Parmesan cheese

Preheat oven to 350°F. Blend savory herb
with garlic soup mix and oil. Brush onto
bread, then sprinkle with cheese. Bake 3
minutes or until golden. Slice, then serve.
Makes 1 loaf, about 18 pieces

Creamy Roasted Red Pepper Dip

1 (7-ounce) jar roasted red peppers,
   well drained
1 teaspoon dried basil leaves
1 teaspoon liquid hot pepper sauce
1 large clove garlic, crushed
1 cup part-skim ricotta cheese
   Fresh basil sprig, for garnish
   Original, Low Salt, Sesame or Fat
   Free MR. PHIPPS® Pretzel Chips

In electric blender or food processor,
blend red peppers, dried basil, liquid hot
pepper sauce and garlic until chopped.
Add ricotta cheese; blend until smooth.
Refrigerate for 1 hour to blend flavors.
Garnish with basil sprig. Serve as a dip
with pretzel chips. *Makes 1¾ cups*

Zucchini Frittata

6 eggs
⅓ cup PROGRESSO® Grated
    Romano Cheese
⅓ cup chopped PROGRESSO®
    Roasted Peppers (red)
1 teaspoon dried basil leaves
¼ teaspoon salt
⅛ teaspoon ground black pepper
3 tablespoons PROGRESSO®
    Olive Oil
½ cup chopped zucchini
⅓ cup chopped onion

1. In medium bowl, beat eggs, Romano cheese, roasted peppers, basil, salt and black pepper until blended.

2. In large nonstick skillet, heat olive oil. Add zucchini and onion; cook 3 minutes or until tender, stirring occasionally.

3. Pour egg mixture over vegetables. Cook on low heat until egg mixture begins to set around outer edge. With spatula gently lift edge and tip skillet to allow uncooked egg to flow to bottom. Cook 4 minutes or until bottom is golden brown. Loosen edge with spatula; slide onto plate.

4. Return frittata to skillet, top side down. Cook 4 minutes or until bottom is golden brown. Cut into wedges to serve.

Makes 8 appetizer servings

Prep time: 20 minutes
Cooking time: 15 minutes
Microwave: In microwave-safe 10-inch quiche dish or pie plate, combine olive oil, zucchini and onion; cover. Microwave on HIGH (100% power) 2 minutes. In medium bowl, beat eggs, Romano cheese, roasted peppers, basil, salt and black pepper until blended; pour over vegetables. Microwave on MEDIUM (50% power) 6 minutes, stirring cooked portions toward center every 2 minutes. Continue microwaving 3 to 4 minutes or until almost set. Let stand 5 minutes before serving.

Cream of Artichoke Soup

1 jar (6 ounces) marinated artichoke
    hearts
3 large cloves fresh California garlic
½ cup chopped onion
2 tablespoons all-purpose flour
2 cans (10¾ ounces *each*) condensed
    chicken broth, divided
1 cup half-and-half or milk
    Finely chopped fresh parsley

Drain marinade from artichoke hearts into 2-quart saucepan. Set aside artichoke hearts. Crush garlic with press; add to marinade. Add onion; cook, covered, over low heat until onion is soft, about 10 minutes. Blend in flour. Slowly stir in 1 can broth. Cook over high heat until mixture comes to a boil, stirring constantly. Boil 1 minute or until mixture thickens.

Place artichoke hearts in blender or food processor; process until smooth. Strain through sieve into saucepan. Add remaining can of broth and half-and-half. Heat just to serving temperature; *do not boil.* Sprinkle each serving with parsley.

Makes 4 (1-cup) servings

*Favorite recipe from **Christopher Ranch of Gilroy***

Quick Veal and Pasta Soup

    2 teaspoons olive oil
    1 small onion, chopped (about
        ⅔ cup)
    ½ cup *each* thinly sliced carrots and
        celery
    2¼ cups water
    1 can (14½ ounces) Italian-style
        stewed tomatoes
    1 bay leaf
    ¼ teaspoon salt
    ⅛ teaspoon black pepper
    ⅓ cup uncooked small pasta shells or
        bow ties
    Veal Meatballs (recipe follows)

Heat oil in large saucepan over medium
heat. Add onion, carrots and celery; cook
and stir about 5 minutes or until tender.
Stir in water, tomatoes (breaking up with
spoon), bay leaf, salt and black pepper.
Bring to a boil. Stir in pasta. Reduce heat
to low and simmer 10 minutes or until
pasta is tender. Add Veal Meatballs; heat
through. Remove and discard bay leaf
before serving.   *Makes 4 servings*

Prep time: 15 minutes
Cooking time: 20 minutes

Quick Veal and Pasta Soup

Veal Meatballs

    1 pound ground veal
    1 cup fresh bread crumbs
    1 egg, lightly beaten
    2 tablespoons finely chopped fresh
        parsley
    ¼ cup finely chopped onion
    ½ teaspoon *each* salt and minced
        garlic
    ⅛ teaspoon black pepper
    1 teaspoon olive oil

Preheat oven to 350°F. Combine all
ingredients except oil in large bowl; mix
lightly. Shape into 20 meatballs. Brush
15½ × 10½ × 1-inch baking pan with oil.
Arrange meatballs in pan. Bake about 15
minutes or until meatballs are cooked
through, turning once.

Prep time: 15 minutes
Cooking time: 15 minutes

Favorite recipe from **National Live Stock & Meat Board**

Sicilian Eggplant Appetizer

    1 eggplant (about 1 pound), peeled
        and cut into ¼-inch cubes
    1 teaspoon salt
    ¾ cup chopped onion
    ½ cup chopped green bell pepper
    2 cloves garlic, minced
    2 tablespoons vegetable oil
    2 medium tomatoes, peeled and
        chopped
    ¼ cup HEINZ® Chili Sauce
    2 tablespoons HEINZ® Vinegar
    1 tablespoon capers, drained
    ½ teaspoon dried basil leaves,
        crushed
    ½ teaspoon dried oregano leaves,
        crushed
    ¼ teaspoon black pepper
    ⅓ cup sliced ripe olives
        Toasted pocket pita bread or
        crackers

Place eggplant in sieve or colander over bowl; sprinkle with salt. Let stand 30 minutes. Rinse eggplant; drain on paper towels. In large skillet, cook and stir onion, green pepper and garlic in hot oil. Add eggplant; cook and stir until tender, adding more oil if necessary. Add tomatoes, chili sauce, vinegar, capers, basil, oregano and black pepper; simmer, uncovered, 10 minutes. Stir in olives. Cover; chill overnight to allow flavors to blend. Serve at room temperature with toasted pita bread or crackers.

Makes about 3½ cups

Flounder Ravioli with Mustard-Tomato Sauce

Flounder Ravioli with Mustard-Tomato Sauce

½ **pound fresh flounder, cut into chunks**
1 **egg, separated**
⅓ **cup buttermilk**
2 **tablespoons minced fresh parsley**
   Salt and black pepper to taste
1 **package (16 ounces) wonton wrappers**
2 **tablespoons virgin olive oil, divided**
2 **large tomatoes, seeded and chopped**
¼ **cup minced onion**
1 **clove garlic, minced**
1 **cup *each* white wine and water**
4½ **teaspoons *each* prepared yellow and spicy brown mustard**
4 **tablespoons butter, cut into pieces**
   Lemon slices

Place flounder, egg white and buttermilk in food processor or blender; process until well combined. Stir in parsley; season with salt and black pepper. Place heaping teaspoonful of fish mixture in center of 1 wonton wrapper; moisten edges with beaten egg yolk. Top with

another wonton wrapper and press to seal, working out any air bubbles. Repeat with remaining wrappers and flounder mixture, keeping wrappers covered to prevent drying.

Heat 1 tablespoon oil in large skillet over medium-high heat until hot; add tomatoes and cook briefly to soften. Remove with slotted spoon to small bowl; set aside. Heat remaining 1 tablespoon oil in same skillet; add onion. Cook and stir until tender. Add garlic; cook and stir about 2 minutes. Add wine, scraping up any brown bits. Add water; bring to a boil. Reduce heat to low; simmer until reduced to ½ cup. Whisk mustards into wine mixture until well blended. Gradually whisk in butter. Season with salt and pepper; add reserved tomatoes. Cook until heated through.

Cook flounder ravioli, a few at a time, in boiling salted water for 5 minutes; drain. Top with sauce mixture. Serve with lemon.

Makes 4 first-course servings

*Favorite recipe from **New Jersey Department of Agriculture***

Minestrone alla Milanese

¼ pound green beans
2 medium zucchini
1 large potato
½ pound cabbage
⅓ cup olive oil
3 tablespoons butter or margarine
2 medium onions, chopped
3 medium carrots, coarsely chopped
3 ribs celery, coarsely chopped
1 clove garlic, minced
1 can (28 ounces) Italian plum
    tomatoes, undrained
3½ cups beef broth
1½ cups water
½ teaspoon salt
½ teaspoon dried basil leaves,
    crushed
¼ teaspoon dried rosemary leaves,
    crushed
¼ teaspoon black pepper
1 bay leaf
1 can (16 ounces) cannellini beans
    Freshly grated Parmesan cheese
    (optional)

Trim green beans; cut into 1-inch pieces. Trim zucchini; cut into ½-inch cubes. Peel potato; cut into ¾-inch cubes. Coarsely shred cabbage. Heat oil and butter in 6-quart stockpot or Dutch oven over medium heat. Add onions; cook and stir 6 to 8 minutes until onions are soft and golden but not brown. Stir in carrots and potato; cook and stir 5 minutes. Stir in celery and green beans; cook and stir 5 minutes. Stir in zucchini; cook and stir 3 minutes. Stir in cabbage and garlic; cook and stir 1 minute more.

Drain tomatoes, reserving juice. Add broth, water and reserved juice to stockpot. Chop tomatoes coarsely; add to stockpot. Stir in salt, basil, rosemary, black pepper and bay leaf. Bring to a boil over high heat; reduce heat to low. Cover and simmer 1½ hours, stirring occasionally.

Rinse and drain cannellini beans; add beans to stockpot. Uncover and cook over medium-low heat 30 to 40 minutes more until soup thickens, stirring occasionally. Remove and discard bay leaf. Serve with cheese.

Makes 8 to 10 servings (about 12 cups)

Florentine Crescents

1 package (10 ounces) frozen
    chopped spinach, thawed, well
    drained
½ pound VELVEETA® Pasteurized
    Process Cheese Spread, cubed
¼ cup dry bread crumbs
3 slices OSCAR MAYER® Bacon,
    crisply cooked, crumbled
2 cans (8 ounces each) refrigerated
    crescent dinner rolls
1 egg, beaten (optional)

• Heat oven to 375°F.

• Stir spinach, process cheese spread, crumbs and bacon in saucepan on low heat until process cheese spread is melted.

• Separate dough into 16 triangles; cut each lengthwise in half, forming 32 triangles. Spread each triangle with rounded teaspoonful spinach mixture. Roll up, starting at wide end. Place on greased cookie sheet; brush with egg.

• Bake 11 to 13 minutes or until golden brown.   *Makes 32 appetizers*

Prep time: 20 minutes
Cooking time: 13 minutes

Minestrone alla Milanese

Mediterranean Frittata

Mediterranean Frittata

¼ cup olive oil
5 small yellow onions, thinly sliced
1 can (14½ ounces) whole peeled
    tomatoes, drained and chopped
¼ pound prosciutto or cooked ham,
    chopped
¼ cup grated Parmesan cheese
2 tablespoons chopped fresh parsley
½ teaspoon dried marjoram leaves
¼ teaspoon dried basil leaves
¼ teaspoon salt
    Generous dash black pepper
6 eggs
2 tablespoons butter or margarine
    Italian parsley leaves, for garnish

Heat oil in medium skillet over medium-high heat. Cook and stir onions in hot oil 6 to 8 minutes until soft and golden. Add tomatoes. Cook and stir over medium heat 5 minutes. Remove tomatoes and onions to large bowl with slotted spoon; discard drippings. Cool tomato-onion mixture to room temperature.

Stir prosciutto, cheese, parsley, marjoram, basil, salt and black pepper into cooled tomato-onion mixture. Whisk eggs in small bowl; stir into prosciutto mixture.

Preheat broiler. Heat butter in large *broilerproof* skillet over medium heat until melted and bubbly; reduce heat to low. Add egg mixture to skillet, spreading evenly. Cook over low heat 8 to 10 minutes until all but top ¼ inch of egg mixture is set; shake pan gently to test. *Do not stir.*

Broil egg mixture about 4 inches from heat 1 to 2 minutes until top of egg mixture is set. (Do not brown or frittata will be dry.) Frittata can be served hot, at room temperature or cold. To serve, cut into wedges. Garnish, if desired.

Makes 6 to 8 appetizer servings

Chilled Zucchini-Basil Soup

2 cups chicken broth
3 medium zucchini, sliced
2 medium onions, chopped
1 tablespoon minced fresh basil *or*
    1 teaspoon dried basil leaves,
    crushed
1 clove garlic, sliced
½ cup HELLMANN'S® or BEST
    FOODS® Real or Light
    Mayonnaise or Reduced Fat
    Mayonnaise Dressing
2 tablespoons lemon juice
⅛ teaspoon hot pepper sauce

In 3-quart saucepan, combine chicken broth, zucchini, onions, basil and garlic. Bring to a boil over high heat. Reduce heat to low; cover and simmer 10 minutes or until zucchini is tender. Cool.

In blender or food processor container, place zucchini mixture, half at a time. Process until smooth. Pour into large bowl. Stir in mayonnaise, lemon juice and hot pepper sauce until well blended. Cover; refrigerate several hours or overnight. *Makes about 4 cups*

Beef and Bean Soup with Pesto

1 pound beef strips for stir-fry*
2 teaspoons olive oil
1 can (28 ounces) plum tomatoes, broken up
1 cup ready-to-serve beef broth
Pesto Sauce (recipe follows)
1 can (15 ounces) Great Northern beans, drained

Cut beef strips for stir-fry into 1-inch pieces. Heat oil in Dutch oven or large saucepan over medium heat. Brown half the beef. Remove with slotted spoon; set aside. Brown remaining beef. Pour off drippings, if necessary.

Stir in tomatoes, beef broth and reserved beef. Bring to a boil over high heat. Reduce heat to low. Cover and simmer, stirring occasionally, 35 to 40 minutes until beef is fork-tender.

Meanwhile, prepare Pesto Sauce; set aside. Add beans to beef mixture; heat through. Serve hot with dollops of Pesto Sauce. *Makes 4 servings*

*For stir-fry beef strips, cut 1-inch-thick beef sirloin or top round steak into ⅛- or ¼-inch-wide strips.

Prep time: 5 minutes
Cooking time: 50 minutes

Pesto Sauce: Place ½ cup fresh parsley sprigs (stems removed), ¼ cup grated Parmesan cheese and 1 or 2 cloves garlic in blender or food processor; cover. Process until finely chopped. Add 2 tablespoons olive oil; process until paste forms.

Favorite recipe from **National Live Stock & Meat Board**

Basil-Vegetable Soup

1 can (15 ounces) cannellini or Great Northern beans, undrained
1 package (9 ounces) frozen cut green beans
3 medium carrots, thinly sliced
3 medium zucchini or yellow squash, cut into thin slices
2 quarts beef broth
2 cloves garlic, minced
Salt and black pepper to taste
2 to 3 ounces uncooked vermicelli or spaghetti
½ cup tightly packed fresh basil leaves, finely chopped
Grated Romano cheese

Combine beans, vegetables, broth and garlic in stockpot or Dutch oven. Bring to a boil over high heat. Reduce heat to low. Cover and simmer until carrots are tender. Season with salt and black pepper. Add vermicelli; bring to a boil over high heat. Reduce heat to low. Simmer until pasta is tender but still firm. (Pasta may be cooked separately; add to soup just before serving.) Add basil; simmer until basil is tender. Sprinkle with cheese just before serving. *Makes 10 to 12 servings*

Basil-Vegetable Soup

Cocktail Meatballs Italian-Style

A hearty appetizer with a wonderful Italian flavor. You can make and brown the meatballs ahead, then simmer them in the sauce just before the party.

1 pound ground beef
¾ cup PROGRESSO® Italian Style Bread Crumbs, divided
½ cup chopped onion
¼ cup PROGRESSO® Grated Parmesan Cheese
½ cup water
1 egg, lightly beaten
1 clove garlic, minced
½ teaspoon salt
⅛ teaspoon ground black pepper
¼ cup PROGRESSO® Olive Oil
1 can (15 ounces) PROGRESSO® Tomato Sauce
⅓ cup packed brown sugar
½ cup PROGRESSO® Red Wine Vinegar

1. In large bowl, combine ground beef, ¼ cup bread crumbs, onion, Parmesan cheese, water, egg, garlic, salt and pepper.

2. Shape meatballs using 1 level tablespoon meat mixture for each meatball; coat with remaining ½ cup bread crumbs.

Cocktail Meatballs Italian-Style

3. In large skillet, heat olive oil. Add meatballs. Cook 5 to 7 minutes or to desired doneness, turning occasionally to brown on all sides. Drain.

4. In small bowl, combine tomato sauce, brown sugar and vinegar; pour over meatballs. Cover; simmer 20 minutes, stirring occasionally.

Makes about 3 dozen appetizers

Prep time: 45 minutes
Cooking time: 30 minutes

Microwave: Omit olive oil. Prepare meatballs as directed in Steps 1 and 2. In shallow 2-quart microwave-safe casserole, place meatballs in single layer. Microwave on HIGH (100% power) 7 to 8 minutes or to desired doneness, rotating dish after 4 minutes; drain. In small bowl, combine tomato sauce, brown sugar and vinegar; pour over meatballs. Cover. Microwave on MEDIUM (50% power) 9 minutes or until thoroughly heated, stirring every 4 minutes.

Spicy Cheese and Cappicola Appetizers

3 ounces Neufchâtel or light cream cheese, softened
2 teaspoons spicy brown mustard
½ teaspoon prepared horseradish, undrained
4 ounces thinly sliced ham cappicola
12 bread sticks, each 6 inches long

Combine Neufchâtel cheese, mustard and horseradish in small bowl until well blended. Spread equal amount of cheese mixture evenly on each cappicola slice; wrap each slice, cheese mixture side in, around 1 bread stick.

Makes 1 dozen appetizers

Prep time: 10 minutes

*Favorite recipe from **National Live Stock & Meat Board***

Antipasto Platter

¼ cup GREY POUPON® Dijon
    Mustard
¼ cup dairy sour cream
¼ cup buttermilk
¼ cup grated Parmesan cheese
1 teaspoon coarsely ground black
    pepper
½ head leaf lettuce, separated into
    leaves
2 ounces radicchio leaves
1 bunch endive, separated into
    leaves
½ pound sliced ham
¼ pound sliced Swiss cheese
2 ounces sliced Genoa salami
1 medium tomato, cut into wedges
¼ cup ripe olives

In small bowl, whisk mustard, sour
cream, buttermilk, Parmesan cheese and
pepper until well blended. Refrigerate
until serving time.

Place lettuce, radicchio and endive on
large platter; top with ham, Swiss cheese,
salami, tomato and olives. Serve with
prepared dressing.

Makes 4 appetizer servings

Tomato Soup

1 tablespoon vegetable oil
1 cup chopped onion
2 cloves garlic, coarsely chopped
½ cup chopped carrot
¼ cup chopped celery
2 cans (28 ounces *each*) crushed
    tomatoes in tomato purée
3½ cups chicken broth
1 tablespoon Worcestershire sauce
½ to 1 teaspoon salt
½ teaspoon dried thyme leaves
¼ to ½ teaspoon black pepper
2 to 4 drops hot pepper sauce

Tomato Soup

Heat oil in large Dutch oven over
medium-high heat. Add onion and garlic;
cook and stir 1 to 2 minutes until onion is
soft. Add carrot and celery; cook 7 to 9
minutes until tender, stirring frequently.
Stir in tomatoes, broth, Worcestershire
sauce, salt, thyme, black pepper and hot
pepper sauce. Reduce heat to low. Cover
and simmer 20 minutes, stirring
frequently.

Remove from heat. Let cool about 10
minutes. Process soup, in food processor
or blender, in small batches until smooth.
Return soup to Dutch oven; simmer 3 to 5
minutes until heated through.

Makes 6 servings

Substitution: 2 cans (10½ ounces *each*)
condensed chicken broth and 1 cup water
for 3½ cups chicken broth.

Venetian Canapés

12 slices firm white bread
5 tablespoons butter or margarine, divided
2 tablespoons all-purpose flour
½ cup milk
3 ounces fresh mushrooms (about 9 medium), finely chopped
6 tablespoons grated Parmesan cheese, divided
2 teaspoons anchovy paste
¼ teaspoon salt
⅛ teaspoon black pepper
Green and ripe olive slices, red and green bell pepper strips and rolled anchovy fillets, for garnish

Preheat oven to 350°F. Cut circles out of bread slices with 2-inch round cutter. Melt 3 tablespoons butter in small saucepan. Brush both sides of bread circles lightly with butter. Bake bread circles on ungreased baking sheet 5 to 6 minutes per side until golden. Remove to wire rack. Cool completely. *Increase oven temperature to 425°F.*

Melt remaining 2 tablespoons butter in same small saucepan. Stir in flour; cook and stir over medium heat until bubbly. Whisk in milk; cook and stir 1 minute or until sauce thickens and bubbles. (Sauce will be very thick.) Place mushrooms in large bowl; stir in sauce, 3 tablespoons cheese, anchovy paste, salt and black pepper until well blended.

Spread heaping teaspoonful mushroom mixture on top of each toast round; place on ungreased baking sheets. Sprinkle remaining 3 tablespoons cheese over canapés, dividing evenly. Garnish, if desired. Bake 5 to 7 minutes until tops are light brown. Serve warm.

Makes 8 to 10 appetizer servings (about 2 dozen)

Meatless Italian Minestrone

1 tablespoon CRISCO® Vegetable Oil
1⅓ cups chopped celery
½ cup chopped onion
2 to 3 cloves garlic, minced
2 cans (14½ ounces *each*) no salt added tomatoes, undrained and chopped
4 cups chopped cabbage
1⅓ cups chopped carrots
1 can (46 ounces) no salt added tomato juice
1 can (19 ounces) white kidney beans (cannellini), drained
1 can (15½ ounces) red kidney beans, drained
1 can (15 ounces) garbanzo beans, drained
¼ cup chopped fresh parsley
1 tablespoon *plus* 1 teaspoon dried oregano leaves
1 tablespoon *plus* 1 teaspoon dried basil leaves
¾ cup (4 ounces) uncooked small elbow macaroni, cooked (without salt or fat) and well drained
¼ cup grated Parmesan cheese
Salt and pepper (optional)

1. Heat Crisco® Oil in large saucepan on medium heat. Add celery, onion and garlic. Cook and stir until crisp-tender. Stir in tomatoes with liquid, cabbage and carrots. Reduce heat to low. Cover. Simmer until vegetables are tender.

2. Stir in tomato juice, beans, parsley, oregano and basil. Simmer until beans are heated. Stir in macaroni just before serving. Serve sprinkled with Parmesan cheese. Season with salt and pepper, if desired.

Makes 16 servings

Venetian Canapés

PASTA

Spaghetti alla Bolognese

2 tablespoons olive oil
1 medium onion, chopped
1 pound ground beef
½ small carrot, finely chopped
½ rib celery, finely chopped
1 cup dry white wine
½ cup milk
⅛ teaspoon ground nutmeg
1 can (14½ ounces) whole peeled
    tomatoes, undrained
1 cup beef broth
3 tablespoons tomato paste
1 teaspoon salt
1 teaspoon dried basil leaves,
    crushed
½ teaspoon dried thyme leaves,
    crushed
⅛ teaspoon black pepper
1 bay leaf
1 pound spaghetti, cooked according
    to package directions and
    drained
1 cup freshly grated Parmesan cheese
    (about 3 ounces)
    Fresh thyme sprig, for garnish

Heat oil in large skillet over medium heat. Cook and stir onion in hot oil until soft. Crumble beef into onion mixture. Brown 6 minutes or until meat just loses its pink color, stirring to separate meat. Spoon off and discard fat. Stir carrot and celery into meat mixture; cook 2 minutes over medium-high heat. Stir in wine; cook 4 to 6 minutes until wine has evaporated. Stir in milk and nutmeg; reduce heat to medium and cook 3 to 4 minutes until milk has evaporated. Remove from heat.

Press tomatoes and juice through sieve into meat mixture; discard seeds. Stir beef broth, tomato paste, salt, basil, thyme, pepper and bay leaf into tomato-meat mixture. Bring to a boil over medium-high heat; reduce heat to low. Simmer, uncovered, 1 to 1½ hours until most of liquid has evaporated and sauce thickens, stirring frequently. Remove and discard bay leaf.

To serve, combine hot spaghetti and meat sauce in serving bowl; toss lightly. Sprinkle with cheese. Garnish, if desired.
Makes 4 to 6 servings

Spaghetti alla Bolognese

Grape and Hazelnut Pasta

2 teaspoons olive oil
2 tablespoons chopped onion
1 clove garlic, minced
2 tablespoons all-purpose flour
½ cup *each* milk and chicken broth
¼ cup dry vermouth
2 cups California seedless grapes
¼ cup chopped fresh basil leaves
3 tablespoons hazelnuts, skins
    removed
½ teaspoon *each* salt and ground dry
    mustard
    Black pepper and ground nutmeg
    to taste
8 ounces tubular pasta, cooked
    according to package directions
    and drained

Heat oil in large nonstick skillet. Add
onion and garlic; cook and stir until
onion is tender. Add flour; mix well.
Gradually whisk in milk and chicken
broth until smooth. Stir in vermouth,
grapes, basil and hazelnuts. Add
seasonings; pour over hot pasta and toss
to coat. Serve immediately.

Makes 4 servings

Favorite recipe from **California Table Grape Commission**

Grape and Hazelnut Pasta

Neapolitan Lasagna

1 pound lean ground beef
2 tablespoons olive or vegetable oil
2 cups sliced zucchini (about
    ½ pound)
1 cup chopped onion
2 cloves garlic, finely chopped
1 (26-ounce) jar CLASSICO®
    Di Napoli (Tomato & Basil) or
    Di Parma (Four Cheese) Pasta
    Sauce
1 tablespoon WYLER'S® or
    STEERO® Beef-Flavor Instant
    Bouillon
2 teaspoons dried oregano leaves
½ teaspoon sugar
1 (16-ounce) container BORDEN® or
    MEADOW GOLD® Small Curd
    Cottage Cheese
3 cups (12 ounces) shredded
    mozzarella cheese, divided
2 eggs
¼ cup grated Parmesan cheese
¼ cup unsifted flour
½ (1-pound) package CREAMETTE®
    Lasagna, cooked according to
    package directions and drained
Parsley flakes

In large saucepan, brown beef in oil. Add
zucchini, onion and garlic; cook until
tender. Add pasta sauce, bouillon,
oregano and sugar; simmer uncovered 20
minutes. Meanwhile, in medium bowl,
combine cottage cheese, *1 cup* mozzarella,
eggs, Parmesan and flour; mix well.

Preheat oven to 350°F. In 13×9-inch
baking dish, layer half each of the lasagna
and meat mixture, all the cottage cheese
mixture and *1 cup* mozzarella. Repeat
layers with remaining lasagna and meat
mixture. Top with *1 cup* mozzarella;
sprinkle with parsley. Cover; bake 35 to
40 minutes or until bubbly. Uncover. Let
stand 10 minutes before serving.
Refrigerate leftovers.

Makes 9 to 12 servings

Dijon Fettuccine

**3 tablespoons GREY POUPON®
 COUNTRY DIJON® Mustard
2 eggs
1 tablespoon olive oil
1½ cups all-purpose flour**

Using food processor fitted with steel blade, combine mustard, eggs and olive oil; process 5 seconds. Add flour; process 30 seconds. If dough forms ball immediately and is wet, add flour by tablespoonfuls until dough feels soft, but not sticky. On well-floured board, divide dough into 3 pieces; cover with damp towel to prevent drying.

Using pasta machine, set rollers for widest setting. Lightly flour first piece of dough. Run through rollers once. Flour lightly, fold into thirds and run through rollers again. Repeat folding and rolling, lightly flouring as necessary and pulling dough gently to stretch as it comes out of machine, until smooth.

Reset rollers for next thinner setting. Lightly flour pasta, but do not fold. Run pasta through machine. Repeat on each thinner setting until as thin as desired. Repeat with remaining dough pieces. Place pasta on towel and let rest until taut but not dry.

Cut pasta on fettucine setting. Separate strands; allow to dry completely on cloth.

Place pasta in 4 quarts rapidly boiling water; return to a boil and cook pasta until tender but still firm, about 30 seconds.   *Makes 4 servings*

Savory Zucchini & Olive Sauce

Savory Zucchini & Olive Sauce

**2 tablespoons olive oil
1 cup chopped onion
1 clove garlic, minced
1¾ cups (14-ounce can) CONTADINA®
 Recipe Ready Diced Tomatoes
 and Juice
⅔ cup (6-ounce can) CONTADINA®
 Tomato Paste
1 cup water or chicken broth
1 cup sliced, quartered zucchini
½ cup sliced ripe olives, drained
2 tablespoons capers, drained
½ teaspoon salt**

In 3-quart saucepan, heat oil; cook and stir onion and garlic until tender. Add tomatoes and juice, tomato paste, water, zucchini, olives, capers and salt. Bring to a boil. Reduce heat; simmer, uncovered, for 15 to 20 minutes. Serve over cooked pasta or omelets.   *Makes 4 cups*

Pasta Primavera

Pasta Primavera

1 medium onion, finely chopped
1 clove garlic, minced
2 tablespoons butter or margarine
¾ pound asparagus, cut diagonally
    into 1½-inch pieces
½ pound mushrooms, sliced
1 medium zucchini, sliced
1 carrot, sliced
1 cup half-and-half or light cream
½ cup chicken broth
1 tablespoon all-purpose flour
2 teaspoons dried basil leaves
1 pound uncooked fettuccine
¾ cup (3 ounces) SARGENTO® Fancy
    Supreme® Shredded Parmesan &
    Romano Cheese

In large skillet, cook onion and garlic in melted butter over medium heat until onion is tender. Add asparagus, mushrooms, zucchini and carrot; cook, stirring constantly, 2 minutes. *Increase heat to high.* Combine half-and-half, broth, flour and basil in small bowl; add to skillet. Allow mixture to boil, stirring occasionally, until thickened. Meanwhile, cook fettuccine according to package directions; drain. In serving bowl, place hot fettuccine, sauce and Parmesan & Romano cheese; toss gently.

Makes 8 servings

Spaghetti Puttanesca

5 tablespoons olive oil
2 cloves garlic, minced
4 anchovy fillets, coarsely chopped
1 can (28 ounces) whole plum
    tomatoes, drained and chopped
2 tablespoons tomato paste
2 tablespoons capers, rinsed and
    drained
¾ teaspoon TABASCO® pepper sauce
¾ teaspoon dried oregano leaves,
    crumbled
½ cup Italian or Greek cured black
    olives, pitted and slivered
2 tablespoons chopped fresh parsley
12 ounces spaghetti, cooked according
    to package directions and
    drained

Heat oil in medium skillet; add garlic and anchovy fillets. Cook and stir 3 minutes. Stir in tomatoes, tomato paste, capers, TABASCO sauce and oregano; simmer 5 minutes, stirring occasionally. Stir in olives and parsley; simmer 2 minutes more. Pour over hot spaghetti in serving bowl; toss gently to coat. Serve with additional TABASCO sauce, if desired.

Makes 4 servings

Fettuccine with Pesto

12 ounces uncooked extra long
    fettuccine
 3 cups (1 ounce) loosely packed fresh
    basil leaves
⅔ cup grated Romano or Parmesan
    cheese
½ cup olive oil
½ cup chopped California walnuts
 2 cloves garlic, peeled
¼ teaspoon *each* salt and black
    pepper

Cook pasta according to package
directions; drain. Meanwhile, place
remaining ingredients in food processor
or blender; process until well blended.
(Sauce thins out on hot pasta.) Place hot
pasta in large bowl; add sauce. Toss until
well coated. Serve immediately.

Makes 4 to 6 servings

Favorite recipe from **Walnut Marketing Board**

Penne with Artichokes

 1 package (10 ounces) frozen
    artichokes
1¼ cups water
 2 tablespoons lemon juice
 2 tablespoons olive oil, divided
 5 cloves garlic
 2 ounces sun-dried tomatoes,
    drained
 2 small dried hot red peppers,
    crushed
 2 tablespoons chopped fresh parsley
¼ teaspoon salt
¼ teaspoon black pepper
¾ cup fresh bread crumbs
 1 tablespoon chopped garlic
12 ounces penne, cooked according to
    package directions and drained
 1 tablespoon grated Romano cheese

Cook artichokes in water and lemon juice
in medium saucepan over medium heat
until tender. Drain, reserving artichoke
liquid. Cool artichokes, then cut into
quarters.

Heat 1½ tablespoons oil in large skillet
over medium-high heat. Add whole
cloves garlic; cook and stir until golden.
Reduce heat to low. Add artichokes and
tomatoes; simmer 1 minute. Stir in
artichoke liquid, red peppers, parsley, salt
and black pepper. Simmer 5 minutes
more.

Meanwhile, heat remaining ½ tablespoon
oil. Add bread crumbs and chopped
garlic; cook and stir until heated through.
Pour artichoke sauce over penne in large
bowl; toss gently to coat. Sprinkle with
bread crumb mixture and cheese.

Makes 4 to 6 servings

Favorite recipe from **National Pasta Association**

Penne with Artichokes

Linguine with Zesty Clam Sauce

2 cans (6½ ounces *each*) minced
    clams, undrained
½ cup WISH-BONE® Classic Olive
    Oil Italian Dressing*
1 large tomato, chopped
½ cup sliced pitted ripe olives
¼ cup grated Parmesan cheese
¼ cup chopped fresh parsley
8 ounces linguine, cooked according
    to package directions and
    drained

In large skillet, bring minced clams and
classic olive oil Italian dressing to a boil;
boil 1 minute. Remove from heat; stir in
tomato, olives, cheese and parsley. Toss
hot linguine with clam sauce. Serve, if
desired, with freshly ground black
pepper. *Makes 2 servings*

*Also terrific with Wish-Bone® Olive Oil
Vinaigrette.

Fettuccine Italiano

8 ounces fettuccine, cooked and
    drained
⅓ cup MIRACLE WHIP® Light
    Reduced Calorie Salad Dressing
1 clove garlic, minced
½ cup milk
5 crisply cooked bacon slices,
    crumbled
⅓ cup (1½ ounces) KRAFT® 100%
    Grated Parmesan Cheese
¼ cup chopped fresh parsley

• Combine salad dressing and garlic in
small saucepan. Gradually stir in milk;
heat thoroughly, stirring occasionally.
• Toss with hot fettuccine until well
coated. Add remaining ingredients; mix
lightly. *Makes 5 servings*

Prep time: 25 minutes
Variations: Substitute spaghetti for
fettuccine.

Substitute Miracle Whip® Salad Dressing
for Reduced Calorie Salad Dressing.

Microwave: • Cook fettuccine as directed
on package; drain. • Combine salad
dressing and garlic in 2-quart microwave-
safe bowl; gradually add milk.
• Microwave on HIGH 1½ to 2 minutes
or until thoroughly heated, stirring after 1
minute. *(Do not boil.)* • Add hot
fettuccine; toss until well coated.
Continue as directed.

Italian Capellini and Fresh Tomato

½ (1-pound) package CREAMETTE®
    Capellini, uncooked
2 cups peeled, seeded and finely
    chopped fresh tomatoes
    (about 3 medium)
2 tablespoons olive oil
1 teaspoon dried basil leaves
½ teaspoon salt
½ teaspoon coarse ground pepper

Prepare Creamette® Capellini according
to package directions; drain. Quickly toss
hot cooked capellini with remaining
ingredients. Serve immediately.
Refrigerate leftovers. *Makes 6 servings*

Linguine with Zesty Clam Sauce

Pasta Marinara

1 pound uncooked fettuccine,
    linguine or other long pasta
    shape
2 cans (28 ounces *each*) peeled plum
    tomatoes, undrained
3 teaspoons olive oil
5 teaspoons finely minced garlic
2 cans (6 ounces *each*) tomato paste
2½ teaspoons dried oregano leaves,
    crushed
   Salt and black pepper to taste
   (optional)
⅔ cup minced fresh parsley

Prepare pasta according to package directions; drain. Place tomatoes with liquid in blender or food processor; process until smooth. Heat oil briefly in medium saucepan; add garlic. Cook and stir 15 seconds (*do not let garlic brown*). Add puréed tomatoes, tomato paste, oregano, salt and black pepper. Bring to a boil; reduce heat and simmer 20 minutes. Remove from heat and stir in parsley. Pour over hot pasta. Serve immediately.

Makes 4 servings

Favorite recipe from **National Pasta Association**

Roasted Red Pepper Pasta with Shrimp

Roasted Red Pepper Pasta with Shrimp

1 jar (7 ounces) roasted red peppers
    packed in oil, undrained
2 tablespoons finely chopped fresh
    basil leaves,* divided
2 teaspoons finely chopped garlic,
    divided
2 tablespoons olive or vegetable oil
1 pound uncooked medium shrimp,
    peeled and deveined
2 tablespoons dry white wine
1½ cups water
½ cup milk
1 package LIPTON® Noodles &
    Sauce–Alfredo
   Black pepper to taste

In food processor or blender, process red peppers, 1 tablespoon basil and 1 teaspoon garlic until smooth; set aside.

In large skillet, heat oil and cook remaining 1 teaspoon garlic with shrimp over medium-high heat, stirring constantly, until shrimp turn pink; remove and set aside. Into skillet, add wine and cook 1 minute. Add water and milk; bring to a boil. Stir in noodles & Alfredo sauce, then simmer, stirring occasionally, 8 minutes or until noodles are tender. Stir in red pepper purée and black pepper; heat through. To serve, arrange shrimp over noodles, then sprinkle with remaining 1 tablespoon basil. Garnish, if desired, with fresh basil.

Makes about 4 servings

*Substitution: Use 1 teaspoon dried basil leaves.

Spinach Pasta Bake

Spinach Pasta Bake

¾ package (12 ounces) spaghetti,
  cooked, drained
1 package (10 ounces) frozen
  chopped spinach, thawed,
  drained
1 cup MIRACLE WHIP® or
  MIRACLE WHIP LIGHT® Salad
  Dressing
1 cup (4 ounces) KRAFT® 100%
  Grated Parmesan Cheese
1 jar (14 ounces) spaghetti sauce

• Heat oven to 375°F.

• Mix all ingredients; spoon into 2-quart
casserole.

• Sprinkle with additional Parmesan, if
desired. Bake 35 to 40 minutes.

Makes 6 servings

Baked Cheesy Rotini

¾ pound lean ground beef
½ cup chopped onion
2 cups cooked rotini, drained
1 (15-ounce) can HUNT'S® Ready
  Tomato Sauces Chunky Italian
¼ cup chopped green bell pepper
¾ teaspoon garlic salt
¼ teaspoon black pepper
1½ cups cubed processed American
  cheese

Preheat oven to 350°F. In large skillet,
brown beef with onions; drain. Stir in
remaining ingredients *except* cheese. Pour
beef mixture into 1½-quart casserole. Top
with cheese. Bake, covered, 20 minutes or
until sauce is bubbly.   *Makes 6 servings*

Spinach Tortellini with Bel Paese®

Spinach Tortellini with Bel Paese®

2 tablespoons butter
4 ounces BEL PAESE® Cheese,* cut
  into small chunks
¾ cup half-and-half
3 ounces chopped GALBANI®
  Prosciutto di Parma (Parma Ham)
  Black pepper
8 ounces spinach tortellini

Melt butter in small saucepan. Add cheese and half-and-half. Cook over low heat until smooth, stirring constantly. Stir in prosciutto. Sprinkle with black pepper to taste. Remove from heat. Set aside.

Cook tortellini in large saucepan of boiling water until tender but still firm. Drain in colander. Place in serving bowl. Pour sauce over pasta. Toss to coat. Serve immediately.   *Makes 4 servings*

*Remove wax coating from cheese.

Tagliatelle

2 ounces sun-dried tomatoes (about
  12 pieces)*
2 cups dry white wine or
  unsweetened apple juice
4 ounces shallots, peeled and thinly
  sliced
2 tablespoons chopped fresh parsley
1 tablespoon dried tarragon leaves,
  crushed *or* 3 tablespoons
  chopped fresh tarragon leaves
1 cup heavy cream
  Hot cooked tagliatelle or extra long
  fettuccine egg noodles
12 ounces shredded Jarlsberg cheese

Microwave: In microwave-safe 1-quart soufflé dish, place tomatoes in white wine. Tightly cover with microwave-safe plastic wrap and microwave on HIGH (100% power) 6 minutes. Let stand 2 minutes. Remove tomatoes, squeezing juice out into dish. Cut into slivers; set aside.

Add shallots, parsley and tarragon to wine mixture in dish. Place dish on 5 microwave-safe paper towels. Microwave on HIGH 15 to 20 minutes or until liquid is nearly evaporated. Add heavy cream. Microwave on HIGH 1 minute more.

Toss hot tagliatelle pasta in bowl with Jarlsberg. Add hot sauce and toss. Serve with slivered sun-dried tomatoes.
*Makes 6 main-dish or
10 first-course servings*

*Variation: Substitute lightly cooked julienned assorted summer vegetables, such as red peppers, zucchini, asparagus, yellow squash or snow peas. Toss with pasta.

Favorite recipe from **Norseland Food, Inc.**

Fettuccine Primavera

2 cups broccoli florets
1 cup sliced zucchini or yellow
    squash
½ cup sliced carrots
½ cup chopped onion
½ teaspoon dried basil leaves
⅓ cup FLEISCHMANN'S® Margarine
½ cup cherry tomatoes, halved
½ cup cooked peas
⅛ teaspoon ground black pepper
1 (12-ounce) package fettuccine,
    cooked according to package
    directions and drained
Grated Parmesan cheese (optional)

In large skillet, over medium-high heat, cook broccoli, zucchini, carrots, onion and basil in margarine until tender. Stir in tomatoes, peas and pepper. Toss vegetable mixture with hot fettuccine; serve with Parmesan cheese if desired.

Makes 8 servings

Broccoli-Stuffed Shells

1 tablespoon butter or margarine
¼ cup chopped onion
1 cup ricotta cheese
1 egg
2 cups chopped cooked broccoli *or*
    1 package (10 ounces) frozen
    chopped broccoli, thawed and
    well drained
1 cup (4 ounces) shredded Monterey
    Jack cheese
20 jumbo pasta shells
1 can (28 ounces) crushed tomatoes
    with added purée
1 package (1 ounce) HIDDEN
    VALLEY RANCH® Milk Recipe
    Original Ranch® Salad
    Dressing Mix
¼ cup grated Parmesan cheese

Preheat oven to 350°F. In small skillet, melt butter over medium heat. Add onion; cook until onion is tender but not browned. Remove from heat; set aside. In large bowl, stir ricotta cheese and egg until well blended. Add broccoli and Jack cheese; mix well. In large pot of boiling water, cook pasta shells 8 to 10 minutes or *just* until tender; drain. Rinse under cold running water; drain again. Stuff each shell with about 2 tablespoons broccoli-cheese mixture.

In medium bowl, combine tomatoes, reserved onion and salad dressing mix; mix well. Pour ⅓ of tomato mixture into 13×9-inch baking dish. Arrange filled shells in dish. Spoon remaining tomato mixture over top. Sprinkle with Parmesan cheese. Cover and bake about 30 minutes or until hot and bubbly.

Makes 4 servings

Broccoli-Stuffed Shells

Fettuccine alla Carbonara

1 recipe Homemade Fettuccine
   (page 74) *or* ¾ pound uncooked
   dry fettuccine or spaghetti
4 ounces pancetta (Italian bacon) or
   lean American bacon, cut into
   ½-inch-wide strips
3 cloves garlic, halved
¼ cup dry white wine
⅓ cup heavy or whipping cream
1 egg
1 egg yolk
⅔ cup freshly grated Parmesan cheese
   (about 2 ounces), divided
   Generous dash ground white
   pepper
   Fresh oregano leaves, for garnish

Prepare and cook Homemade Fettuccine or cook dry fettuccine according to package directions. Drain well; return to dry pot.

Cook and stir pancetta and garlic in large skillet over medium-low heat 4 minutes or until pancetta is light brown. Reserve 2 tablespoons drippings in skillet with pancetta. Discard garlic and remaining drippings. Add wine to pancetta mixture; cook over medium heat 3 minutes or until wine is almost evaporated. Stir in cream; cook and stir 2 minutes. Remove from heat.

Whisk egg and egg yolk in top of double boiler. Place top of double boiler over simmering water, adjusting heat to maintain simmer. Whisk ⅓ cup cheese and pepper into egg mixture; cook and stir until sauce thickens slightly. Pour pancetta-cream mixture over fettuccine in pot; toss to coat. Heat over medium-low heat until heated through. Stir in egg-cheese mixture. Toss to coat evenly. Remove from heat. Serve with remaining ⅓ cup cheese. Garnish, if desired.

Makes 4 servings

Macaroni Italiano

1 can (16 ounces) canned tomatoes,
   undrained
½ teaspoon low sodium baking soda
1 can (8 ounces) tomato sauce
1¼ cups low fat cottage cheese
¼ cup grated Parmesan cheese
1 package (10 ounces) frozen
   chopped spinach, thawed and
   squeezed dry
1½ cups frozen peas, thawed
1 teaspoon dried basil leaves,
   crushed
½ teaspoon black pepper
8 ounces uncooked elbow macaroni,
   cooked according to package
   directions and drained
¾ cup chopped toasted* California
   walnuts
2 tablespoons chopped fresh parsley
   Salt to taste

Preheat oven to 350°F. Place tomatoes and their juice in large bowl. Add baking soda and break up tomatoes into small chunks with fork. Stir in tomato sauce. Add cottage cheese, Parmesan cheese, spinach, peas, basil and black pepper. Toss to combine; set aside. Add macaroni to cheese mixture; toss thoroughly, then pour into oiled 2½-quart baking dish.

Cover with foil and bake 20 minutes. Uncover and bake 10 minutes more. Stir in walnuts and sprinkle with parsley. Season with salt.   *Makes 6 servings*

*Toasting is optional.

Favorite recipe from **Walnut Marketing Board**

Fettuccine alla Carbonara

Lentil Lasagna

This all-vegetable lasagna has a creamy texture and the slightly "nut-like" flavor of lentils.

**1 tablespoon PROGRESSO®
   Olive Oil
½ cup chopped onion
2 cloves garlic, minced
1 can (19 ounces) PROGRESSO®
   Lentil Soup
1 can (8 ounces) PROGRESSO®
   Tomato Sauce
1 can (6 ounces) PROGRESSO®
   Tomato Paste
2 teaspoons Italian seasoning
9 lasagna noodles, cooked according
   to package directions and
   drained
1 container (15 ounces) ricotta cheese
1 package (12 ounces) mozzarella
   cheese slices
¼ cup PROGRESSO® Grated
   Parmesan Cheese**

1. Preheat oven to 350°F.

2. In medium skillet, heat olive oil. Add onion and garlic; cook 2 to 3 minutes or until tender, stirring occasionally.

3. Add soup, tomato sauce, tomato paste and Italian seasoning; cook 10 minutes, stirring occasionally.

4. In greased 12×8-inch baking dish, layer one third each of the lasagna noodles, ricotta cheese, mozzarella cheese, soup mixture and Parmesan cheese; repeat layers two more times. Cover with foil.

5. Bake 35 to 40 minutes or until bubbly. Let stand 15 minutes before serving.

Makes 8 servings

Prep time: 30 minutes
Cooking time: 40 minutes

Apple-Cabbage Ravioli with Bacon & Thyme Broth

Homemade ravioli is a great family project—set up an assembly line with one person rolling, another filling the ravioli, and another (kids preferred) trimming with a speedy pastry wheel. Once made, ravioli can be frozen until minutes before serving.

Ravioli Dough
   **2 cups all-purpose flour
   ½ cup cornstarch
   ½ teaspoon salt
   ¼ cup water
   2 eggs
   2 tablespoons vegetable oil**

Apple-Cabbage Filling
   **2 tablespoons butter or margarine
   1 cup finely chopped onion
   2 cups finely chopped green cabbage
   ½ cup water
   ¼ teaspoon salt
   ¼ teaspoon black pepper
   1 Golden Delicious Apple, peeled,
      cored and grated
   ½ cup ricotta cheese**

   **Additional all-purpose flour
   1 egg white, beaten**

Bacon & Thyme Broth
   **4 ounces thick-cut bacon, coarsely
      chopped
2½ cups water
   1 large cube chicken bouillon
   2 teaspoons fresh thyme leaves *or*
      1 teaspoon dried thyme leaves,
      crushed
4½ teaspoons cornstarch dissolved in
      1 tablespoon cold water**

To prepare ravioli dough, combine flour, cornstarch and salt in large bowl or food processor. Beat together water, eggs and oil in measuring cup. Pour egg mixture into flour mixture; beat or process until dough forms. Divide dough into 4 pieces; wrap in plastic wrap and let rest while preparing filling.

To prepare apple-cabbage filling, heat butter in large skillet. Add onion; cook and stir until golden. Add cabbage, water, salt and black pepper. Cover; simmer 10 minutes, stirring occasionally. Add apple. Cover and cook 7 to 8 minutes until apple softens. Remove from heat; stir in ricotta and set aside until cool enough to handle.

To make ravioli, line 2 baking sheets with clean kitchen towels; dust cloths generously with flour. On lightly floured surface, roll out 1 dough piece to $\frac{1}{16}$-inch-thick 9-inch square. Brush square with egg white and cut square into thirds, creating nine 3-inch squares. Place 2 teaspoons apple-cabbage filling in center of each square. Fold top corner of each square over filling, forming triangle. Pinch seams to seal completely. With knife or pastry wheel, trim edges slightly. Place ravioli on prepared baking sheet.

Repeat rolling, cutting and filling with remaining dough pieces and filling. Dust tops of ravioli with flour. Refrigerate, uncovered, at least 1 hour. (To freeze ravioli, arrange in a single layer on floured baking sheet and place in freezer until frozen; store in sealed plastic bags up to 3 weeks. Increase cooking time 2 to 3 minutes.)

Just before serving, cook bacon in deep skillet until crisp. Remove bacon and set aside. Drain fat from skillet; add water and bring to a boil. Stir in bouillon and thyme; reduce heat and simmer 5 minutes. Stir in cornstarch mixture. Bring to a boil, stirring constantly, until mixture thickens. Remove from heat and add reserved bacon; set aside. Bring 3 quarts water to a boil in large pot; add ravioli and cook 5 to 7 minutes until tender. Drain. Serve immediately with bacon and thyme broth. Garnish with fresh thyme sprigs, if desired.   *Makes 6 servings*

Prep time: 2 hours, plus refrigerating
Cooking time: 15 minutes

Note: To make this recipe more quickly, substitute wonton wrappers for ravioli dough.

Favorite recipe from **Washington Apple Commission**

Apple-Cabbage Ravioli with Bacon & Thyme Broth

Italian Chicken Pasta

Italian Chicken Pasta

1 pound boneless skinless chicken,
    cut into cubes
All-purpose flour
Salt and black pepper
2 tablespoons vegetable oil
1 can HUNT'S® Chunky Italian
    Ready Sauce
Hot cooked pasta

Place chicken in resealable plastic food
storage bag. Cover with flour. Add salt
and black pepper to taste. Seal bag; shake
until well coated. Heat oil in large skillet
over medium heat until hot. Add chicken.
Cook until browned on all sides, stirring
occasionally. Stir in Hunt's® sauce. Cook
until heated through. Serve over pasta.
Garnish as desired.   *Makes 4 servings*

Classic Pesto with Linguine

¼ cup *plus* 1 tablespoon olive oil,
    divided
2 tablespoons pine nuts
1 cup tightly packed fresh (not dried)
    basil leaves, rinsed, drained and
    stemmed
2 cloves garlic
¼ teaspoon salt
¼ cup freshly grated Parmesan cheese
1½ tablespoons freshly grated Romano
    cheese
¾ pound linguine, cooked according
    to package directions and
    drained
2 tablespoons butter or margarine
Fresh basil leaves, for garnish

Heat 1 tablespoon oil in small saucepan
or skillet over medium-low heat. Add
pine nuts; cook and stir 30 to 45 seconds
until light brown, shaking pan constantly.
Remove with slotted spoon; drain on
paper towels. Place toasted pine nuts,
basil leaves, garlic and salt in food
processor or blender. With processor
running, add remaining ¼ cup oil in slow
steady stream until evenly blended and
pine nuts are finely chopped. Transfer
basil mixture to small bowl. Stir in
Parmesan and Romano cheeses.*

Toss hot linguine with butter and pesto
sauce in large serving bowl until well
coated. Garnish, if desired. Serve
immediately.

Makes 4 servings (about ¾ cup pesto sauce)

*Pesto sauce can be stored at this point in
airtight container; pour thin layer of olive
oil over pesto and cover. Refrigerate up to
1 week. Bring to room temperature.
Proceed as directed.

Tomato Caper Sauce

3 tablespoons olive oil
2 cloves garlic, crushed
2 cans (14.5 ounces *each*)
    CONTADINA® Recipe Ready
    Diced Tomatoes and Juice
½ cup rinsed capers
¼ cup chopped fresh cilantro
1 tablespoon chopped fresh basil
    leaves
1 tablespoon chopped fresh thyme
    leaves
    Dash ground black pepper
1 pound rigatoni, cooked according
    to package directions and
    drained

Heat oil in medium saucepan over medium-high heat. Add garlic; cook and stir 1 to 2 minutes or until lightly browned. Add tomatoes and juice, and capers. Reduce heat to low; simmer, uncovered for 15 to 20 minutes. Stir in cilantro, basil, thyme and pepper; simmer an additional 5 minutes. Serve over hot pasta.

Makes 8 servings

Italian Ham Lasagna

6 lasagna noodles (4 ounces)
1 package (10 ounces) frozen
    chopped spinach
1 cup milk
2 tablespoons cornstarch
1 tablespoon dried minced onion
½ cup DANNON® Plain Nonfat or
    Lowfat Yogurt
1 cup diced fully cooked ham
½ teaspoon Italian seasoning,
    crushed
¼ cup grated Parmesan cheese
1 cup lowfat cottage cheese
1 cup shredded mozzarella cheese

Cook noodles according to package directions; rinse and drain. Set aside. Cook spinach according to package directions; drain well. Set aside.

Preheat oven to 375°F. In a large saucepan combine milk, cornstarch and onion. Cook and stir until thickened and bubbly; cook and stir 2 minutes more. Remove from heat. Stir in yogurt. Spread 2 tablespoons of yogurt sauce evenly on bottom of 10×6-inch baking dish. Stir ham and Italian seasoning into remaining sauce. Place 3 lasagna noodles in dish. (Trim noodles to fit, if necessary.) Spread with ⅓ of sauce. Layer spinach on top. Sprinkle with Parmesan. Layer another ⅓ of sauce, the cottage cheese and ½ of mozzarella cheese. Place remaining noodles on top of cheese layer. Top with remaining sauce and mozzarella. Bake 30 to 35 minutes or until heated through. Let stand 10 minutes before serving.

Makes 6 servings

Italian Ham Lasagna

Pasta Primavera

2 tablespoons vegetable oil
½ cup sliced mushrooms
¼ cup sliced green onions
1 clove garlic, minced
1 cup cherry tomato halves
½ cup half-and-half
½ cup grated Parmesan cheese
1 can (16 ounces) VEG-ALL® Mixed
    Vegetables, drained
2 tablespoons chopped fresh basil
    leaves
    Salt and black pepper to taste
4 ounces uncooked spaghetti, cooked
    according to package directions
    and drained

Heat oil in medium skillet; add
mushrooms, green onions and garlic.
Cook and stir 2 to 3 minutes until
vegetables are tender. Add tomato halves
and cook 1 minute, stirring gently; set
aside.

Combine half-and-half, cheese, Veg-All®
mixed vegetables and basil in medium
saucepan; cook over medium heat until
just heated through. Season with salt and
black pepper. Stir in hot pasta and tomato
mixture; serve immediately.

Makes 4 servings

Light Alfredo

1 pound uncooked fettuccine,
    linguine or other long pasta
    shape
1 cup evaporated skim or nonfat
    milk
½ cup grated Parmesan cheese
½ pound fresh parsley, chopped
¼ pound green onions, tops only,
    chopped
¼ teaspoon white pepper

Cook pasta according to package
directions; drain. Bring evaporated milk
in large saucepan to a boil over medium
heat. Reduce heat; stir in cheese, parsley
and green onions until cheese is melted.
Pour over hot pasta. Season with pepper.

Makes 4 servings

Favorite recipe from **National Pasta Association**

Italian Stuffed Shells

18 CREAMETTE® Jumbo Macaroni
    Shells, cooked according to
    package directions and drained
1 pound lean ground beef
⅔ cup chopped onion
1 clove garlic, chopped
2 cups water
1 (12-ounce) can tomato paste
1 tablespoon WYLER'S® or
    STEERO® Beef-Flavor Instant
    Bouillon *or* 3 Beef-Flavor
    Bouillon Cubes
1½ teaspoons dried oregano leaves
1 (16-ounce) container BORDEN® or
    MEADOW GOLD® Cottage
    Cheese
2 cups (8 ounces) shredded
    mozzarella cheese, divided
½ cup grated Parmesan cheese
1 egg

Preheat oven to 350°F. In large skillet,
brown beef, onion and garlic; pour off fat.
Stir in water, tomato paste, bouillon and
oregano; simmer uncovered 30 minutes.
In medium bowl, combine cottage cheese,
1 cup mozzarella, Parmesan cheese and
egg; mix well. Stuff shells with cheese
mixture; arrange in 13×9-inch baking
dish. Pour sauce over shells. Cover; bake
30 minutes or until hot. Uncover; sprinkle
with remaining *1 cup* mozzarella. Bake 3
minutes longer. Refrigerate leftovers.

Makes 6 to 8 servings

Pasta Primavera

Chunky Pasta Sauce with Meat

8 ounces linguine or spaghetti
6 ounces ground beef
6 ounces mild or hot Italian sausage
   links, sliced
½ medium onion, coarsely chopped
1 clove garlic, minced
2 cans (14½ ounces each)
   DEL MONTE® Pasta Style
   Chunky Tomatoes
1 can (8 ounces) DEL MONTE®
   Tomato Sauce
¼ cup red wine (optional)
   Shredded or grated Parmesan
   cheese

Cook pasta according to package directions; drain. In large saucepan, brown meat and sausage; drain, reserving 1 tablespoon drippings. Add onion and garlic to meat, sausage and reserved drippings. Cook over medium-high heat until tender. Add tomatoes, tomato sauce and wine. Cook, uncovered, 15 minutes, stirring frequently. Serve sauce over hot pasta and top with Parmesan cheese.

Makes 4 servings (4 cups sauce)

Prep & Cook time: 30 minutes

Helpful Hint: Cook pasta ahead; rinse and drain. Cover and refrigerate. Just before serving, heat in microwave or dip in boiling water.

Chunky Pasta Sauce with Meat

Pasta with Sausage and Spicy Tomato Sauce

1 pound uncooked rotini, twists or
   spirals
½ pound Italian-style turkey sausage
1 large onion, chopped
1 medium green bell pepper,
   chopped
2 cloves garlic, minced
1 (28-ounce) can tomatoes, cut up and
   undrained
1 (8-ounce) can tomato sauce
1 (4-ounce) can mushrooms, drained
1½ teaspoons dried basil leaves,
   crushed
1 teaspoon dried thyme leaves,
   crushed
½ teaspoon chili powder
½ cup shredded low fat mozzarella
   cheese

Prepare pasta according to package directions; drain. Remove casing from sausage. Cook sausage, onion, green pepper and garlic in Dutch oven or large skillet over medium heat until sausage is no longer pink. Pour off drippings. Stir in tomatoes with liquid, tomato sauce, mushrooms, basil, thyme and chili powder. Simmer, uncovered, 10 minutes. Pour sauce over pasta and top with cheese. Serve immediately.

Makes 6 servings

*Favorite recipe from **National Pasta Association***

Walnut Pesto Sauce

½ cup broken walnuts
1 clove garlic, chopped
2 cups packed fresh basil leaves
¼ teaspoon salt
1 cup packed Italian flat-leaf parsley
¾ cup FILIPPO BERIO® Olive Oil
⅓ cup grated Parmesan cheese

Finely chop walnuts and garlic in food processor; add half the basil and salt. Coarsely chop. Add remaining basil and parsley. With the processor running, add oil in a slow steady stream through feed tube until mixture is thoroughly blended.

Transfer to medium bowl; fold in cheese. To serve, cook 1½ pounds pasta according to package directions and drain, reserving ½ cup liquid. Toss hot pasta with sauce and reserved liquid. Serve immediately with additional cheese, if desired.
Makes 1½ cups sauce, enough for 1½ pounds pasta

Creamy Chicken Primavera

Creamy Chicken Primavera

2 cups water
1 cup diced carrots
1 cup broccoli flowerets
1 cup uncooked tri-color rotini pasta
½ pound cooked chicken, cut into cubes
½ cup DANNON® Plain Nonfat or Lowfat Yogurt
¼ cup finely chopped green onions (green part only)
2 tablespoons plus 2 teaspoons reduced-calorie mayonnaise
2 tablespoons grated Parmesan cheese
½ teaspoon dried basil, crushed
⅛ teaspoon pepper
Carrot curls (optional)

In a medium saucepan combine water, carrots and broccoli. Cook, covered, 10 to 15 minutes or until tender-crisp; drain. Cook pasta according to package directions; rinse and drain. In a large bowl combine pasta, carrots and broccoli. Toss gently.

In a small bowl combine chicken, yogurt, green onions, mayonnaise, cheese, basil and pepper; mix well. Add to pasta mixture. Toss gently to combine. Cover; chill several hours. If desired, garnish with carrot curls.   *Makes 4 servings*

Spinach Pesto

Spinach Pesto

1 bunch fresh spinach, washed, dried
    and chopped
1 cup fresh parsley leaves, stems
    removed
⅔ cup grated Parmesan cheese
½ cup walnut pieces
6 cloves fresh garlic, crushed
4 flat anchovy filets
1 tablespoon dried tarragon leaves,
    crushed
1 teaspoon dried basil leaves,
    crushed
1 teaspoon salt
½ teaspoon black pepper
¼ teaspoon anise or fennel seed
1 cup olive oil
    Hot cooked pasta twists, spaghetti
    or shells
    Mixed salad (optional)

Place all ingredients except oil, pasta and
salad in covered food processor. Process
until mixture is smooth. With motor
running, add oil in thin stream through
feed tube. Adjust seasonings, if desired.
Pour desired amount over pasta; toss
gently to coat. Serve with mixed salad.
Garnish as desired.   *Makes 2 cups sauce*

Note: Sauce will keep about 1 week in a
covered container in the refrigerator.

*Favorite recipe from **Christopher Ranch of Gilroy***

Creamy Beef and Macaroni

1 pound ground beef
1 jar (30 ounces) spaghetti sauce
½ cup MIRACLE WHIP® or
    MIRACLE WHIP LIGHT®
    Dressing
1 package (7 ounces) elbow
    macaroni, cooked, drained
1 cup (4 ounces) KRAFT® Shredded
    Cheddar Cheese

• Brown ground beef; drain.
• Add spaghetti sauce, Miracle Whip®
and macaroni.
• Heat on medium, stirring occasionally,
until hot. Top with cheese.

Makes 6 servings

Eggplant Pasta Bake

4 ounces bow-tie pasta
1 pound eggplant, diced
1 clove garlic, minced
¼ cup olive oil
1½ cups shredded Monterey Jack
    cheese
1 cup sliced green onions
½ cup grated Parmesan cheese
1 can (14½ ounces) DEL MONTE®
    Pasta Style Chunky Tomatoes

Preheat oven to 350°F. Cook pasta
according to package directions; drain. In
large skillet, cook eggplant and garlic in
oil over medium-high heat until tender.
Toss eggplant with cooked pasta, 1 cup
Jack cheese, green onions and Parmesan
cheese. Place in greased 9-inch square
baking dish. Top with tomatoes and
remaining ½ cup Jack cheese. Bake 15
minutes or until heated through.

Makes 6 servings

Prep & Cook time: 30 minutes

Linguine with Creamy Peppercorn Sauce

½ cup chicken broth
¼ cup light cream
¼ cup GREY POUPON® Specialty Mustard: Peppercorn
8 ounces linguine, cooked according to package directions and drained

In small saucepan, over medium-high heat, heat broth, cream and mustard to a gentle boil, stirring occasionally. Reduce heat and simmer for 5 minutes. In serving bowl, toss linguine with peppercorn sauce to coat well; serve immediately.

Makes 4 servings

Lasagna Primavera

3 quarts water
1 package (8 ounces) lasagna noodles
3 carrots, cut into ¼-inch slices
1 cup broccoli flowerets
1 cup zucchini, cut into ¼-inch slices
1 yellow squash, cut into ¼-inch slices
2 packages (10 ounces *each*) frozen chopped spinach, thawed and squeezed dry
8 ounces ricotta cheese
1 jar (26 ounces) NEWMAN'S OWN® Marinara Sauce with Mushrooms
3 cups (12 ounces) shredded mozzarella cheese
½ cup grated Parmesan cheese

Bring water to a boil in 6-quart saucepan over high heat. Add lasagna noodles; boil 5 minutes. Add carrots; cook 2 minutes more. Add broccoli, zucchini and yellow squash; cook 2 minutes or until pasta is tender. Drain well.

Preheat oven to 400°F. Combine spinach and ricotta cheese in medium bowl. Spread ⅓ of Newman's Own® Marinara Sauce with Mushrooms in 3-quart rectangular baking pan. Place half the lasagna noodles on top of sauce. Layer half the vegetables, spinach mixture and mozzarella cheese on top of noodles. Pour half the remaining Newman's Own® Marinara Sauce with Mushrooms over top. Repeat layers and top with remaining sauce. Sprinkle with Parmesan cheese.

Line 15×10-inch baking sheet with foil. Place baking pan on sheet. Bake, uncovered, 30 minutes or until hot in center and sauce is bubbly. Let stand 10 minutes before serving. (Casserole may be prepared up to 2 days before baking. Cover and store in refrigerator. Remove from refrigerator 1 hour before baking. Or, if cold, bake 1 hour at 350°F.) Serve with Italian bread, a green salad with Newman's Own® Light Italian Dressing and red wine, if desired.

Makes 8 servings

Lasagna Primavera

Chicken Tortellini with Mushroom-Cream Sauce

2 cups *plus* 1 tablespoon all-purpose flour
½ teaspoon salt, divided
4 eggs, divided
1 tablespoon milk
1 teaspoon olive oil
2 small boneless skinless chicken breast halves (about 4 ounces *each*), cooked and minced
2 ounces fresh spinach, cooked, squeezed dry and minced
2 ounces prosciutto or cooked ham, minced
⅓ cup *plus* 2 tablespoons grated Parmesan cheese, divided
2 cups heavy or whipping cream, divided
Dash black pepper
3 tablespoons butter or margarine
½ pound fresh mushrooms, thinly sliced
3 tablespoons chopped fresh parsley

Combine flour and ¼ teaspoon salt on pastry board or cutting board; make well in center. Whisk 3 eggs, milk and oil in small bowl until well blended; gradually pour into well in flour mixture while mixing with fingertips or fork to form ball of dough. Place dough on lightly floured surface; flatten slightly. Knead dough 5 minutes or until smooth and elastic, adding more flour to prevent sticking if necessary. Wrap dough in plastic wrap; set aside. Allow dough to stand at least 15 minutes.

Combine chicken, spinach, prosciutto and remaining egg in medium bowl. Add 2 tablespoons cheese, 1 tablespoon cream, remaining ¼ teaspoon salt and pepper to spinach mixture; mix well.

Unwrap dough and knead briefly on lightly floured surface; divide into 3 pieces. Using lightly floured rolling pin, roll out 1 dough piece to ¹⁄₁₆-inch thickness on lightly floured surface. (Keep remaining dough pieces wrapped in plastic wrap to prevent drying.)

Cut out dough circles with 2-inch round cutter. Cover rolled dough with clean kitchen towel to prevent drying while working. Place ½ teaspoon chicken filling in center of 1 dough circle; brush edge of circle lightly with water. Fold circle in half to enclose filling, making sure all air has been pushed out. Pinch outside edges together firmly to seal. Brush end of half circle with water; wrap around finger, overlapping ends. Pinch to seal. Place tortellini on clean kitchen towel. Repeat with remaining dough circles, rerolling dough scraps as needed. Repeat with remaining 2 dough pieces and chicken filling. Let tortellini dry on towel for 30 minutes.

Heat butter in 3-quart saucepan over medium heat until melted and bubbly; cook and stir mushrooms in hot butter 3 minutes. Stir in remaining cream. Bring to a boil over medium heat; reduce heat to low. Simmer, uncovered, 3 minutes. Stir in remaining ⅓ cup cheese; cook and stir 1 minute. Remove from heat.

Cook tortellini, ⅓ at a time, in large pot of boiling salted water 2 to 3 minutes just until tender. Drain well; add to cream sauce. Bring *just* to a boil over medium heat; reduce heat to low. Simmer 2 minutes. Sprinkle with parsley. Serve immediately. *Makes 6 to 8 servings*

Chicken Tortellini with Mushroom-Cream Sauce

Milano Shrimp Fettuccine

4 ounces egg or spinach fettuccine
½ pound medium shrimp, peeled and
    deveined
1 clove garlic, minced
1 tablespoon olive oil
1 can (14½ ounces) DEL MONTE®
    Pasta Style Chunky Tomatoes
½ cup whipping cream
¼ cup sliced green onions

Cook pasta according to package
directions; drain. In large skillet, cook
shrimp and garlic in oil over medium-
high heat until shrimp are pink and
opaque. Stir in tomatoes; simmer 5
minutes. Blend in cream and green
onions; heat through. *Do not boil.* Serve
over hot pasta.   *Makes 3 to 4 servings*

Prep & Cook time: 20 minutes

Milano Shrimp Fettuccine

Four-Meat Ravioli

Four-Meat Filling (recipe follows)
Plum Tomato Sauce (recipe
    follows)
4 cups all-purpose flour
¼ teaspoon salt
2 eggs
1 tablespoon olive oil
⅔ to 1 cup water
1 egg yolk
1 teaspoon milk
1 tablespoon chopped fresh parsley
    Freshly grated Parmesan cheese
    Fresh rosemary sprig, for garnish

Prepare Four-Meat Filling; refrigerate.
Prepare Plum Tomato Sauce; set aside.

For dough, mix flour and salt in large
bowl. Combine 2 eggs, oil and ⅔ cup
water in small bowl; whisk thoroughly.
Gradually stir egg mixture into flour
mixture with fork. Add enough of
remaining ⅓ cup water, 1 tablespoon at a
time, to form firm but pliable dough.
Place dough on lightly floured surface;
flatten slightly. To knead dough, fold
dough in half toward you and press
dough away from you with heels of
hands. Give dough a quarter turn and
continue folding, pressing and turning.
Continue kneading 5 minutes or until
smooth and elastic, adding more flour to
prevent sticking if necessary. Wrap dough
in plastic wrap; let rest 30 minutes.

Unwrap dough and knead briefly on
lightly floured surface; divide into 4
pieces. Using lightly floured rolling pin,
roll out 1 dough piece to ¹⁄₁₆-inch
thickness on lightly floured surface.
(Keep remaining dough pieces wrapped
in plastic wrap to prevent drying.) Cut
dough into 4-inch-wide strips. Place

teaspoonfuls of Four-Meat Filling along top half of long edge of each strip at 2-inch intervals. Whisk egg yolk and milk in small bowl. Brush dough on bottom half of long edge and between filling with egg-milk mixture. Fold dough over filling; press firmly between filling and along long edge to seal, making sure all air has been pushed out. Cut ravioli apart with fluted pastry wheel. Repeat with remaining 3 dough pieces, filling and egg-milk mixture.

Cook ravioli, ¼ at a time, in large pot of boiling salted water 3 to 5 minutes just until tender. Remove with slotted spoon; drain well. Add ravioli to reserved sauce. Bring sauce and ravioli to a boil over medium-high heat; reduce heat to medium-low. Simmer, uncovered, 6 to 8 minutes until heated through. Sprinkle with parsley and cheese. Garnish, if desired. Serve immediately.

Makes 6 servings

Four-Meat Filling

5 ounces fresh spinach, cooked and squeezed dry
2 small boneless skinless chicken breast halves (about 4 ounces *each*), cooked
3 ounces prosciutto or cooked ham
1½ ounces hard salami
1 clove garlic
6 ounces ground beef
½ cup chopped fresh parsley
2 eggs
¼ teaspoon ground allspice
¼ teaspoon salt

Mince spinach, chicken, prosciutto, salami and garlic; combine in medium bowl with beef, parsley, eggs, allspice and salt. Mix well.

Four-Meat Ravioli

Plum Tomato Sauce

⅓ cup butter or margarine
1 clove garlic, minced
1 can (28 ounces) Italian plum tomatoes, undrained
1 can (8 ounces) tomato sauce
¾ teaspoon salt
½ teaspoon ground allspice
½ teaspoon dried basil leaves, crushed
½ teaspoon dried rosemary leaves, crushed
⅛ teaspoon black pepper

Heat butter in large saucepan over medium heat until melted and bubbly; cook and stir garlic in hot butter 30 seconds. Press tomatoes and juice through sieve into garlic mixture; discard seeds. Stir in tomato sauce, salt, allspice, basil, rosemary and black pepper. Cover and simmer 30 minutes. Uncover and simmer 15 minutes more or until sauce thickens, stirring occasionally.

Fettuccine à la Tuna

Fettuccine à la Tuna

½ cup broccoli florets
½ cup chopped red bell pepper
1 tablespoon sliced green onion
1 clove garlic, minced
1 tablespoon butter or margarine
¼ cup low fat milk
¼ cup low fat ricotta cheese
  Salt and black pepper to taste
1 can (3¼ ounces) STARKIST® Tuna,
  drained and broken into small
  chunks
2 ounces fettuccine or linguine,
  cooked according to package
  directions and drained
1 tablespoon grated Parmesan or
  Romano cheese (optional)

In saucepan with steamer insert, steam broccoli and bell pepper over simmering water for 5 minutes. Drain liquid from vegetables and remove steamer. In same pan, cook and stir onion and garlic in melted butter for 2 minutes. Add milk and ricotta cheese, stirring well with wire whisk. Season with salt and black pepper. Add tuna and vegetables; cook over low heat for 2 minutes more or until heated through. Toss fettuccine with tuna mixture. Spoon onto plate; sprinkle with Parmesan cheese if desired.

Makes 1 serving

Prep time: 15 minutes

Pasta with Rustic Lamb Tomato Sauce

12 ounces boneless American leg of
  lamb or shoulder, sliced in thin
  strips*
1 tablespoon olive oil
1 cup chopped onion
2 cloves garlic, minced
1¼ cups thinly sliced zucchini
1 cup (4 ounces) sliced mushrooms
1 can (14.5 ounces) diced tomatoes
  with juice
3 tablespoons chopped fresh basil
  leaves *or* 1 tablespoon dried basil
  leaves, crushed
½ teaspoon black pepper
¼ teaspoon seasoned salt (optional)
8 ounces pasta, cooked according to
  package directions and drained
¼ cup sliced ripe olives (optional)

Heat oil in large skillet with cover. Add onion and garlic; cook and stir 2 minutes. Add lamb; cook and stir 4 to 5 minutes until meat is tender. Pour off drippings; set aside. Add zucchini, mushrooms, tomatoes and juice, basil, black pepper and salt, if desired. Cover and cook 5

*Or, 12 ounces of lean ground lamb.

minutes until vegetables are crisp-tender. Stir in lamb mixture, hot pasta and olives, if desired. Cook until heated through and serve immediately.　　*Makes 8 servings*

Prep time: 10 minutes
Cooking time: 20 minutes

*Favorite recipe from **American Lamb Council***

Broccoli Lasagna

1 tablespoon CRISCO®
　　Vegetable Oil
1 cup chopped onion
3 cloves garlic, minced
1 can (14½ ounces) no salt added
　　tomatoes, undrained and
　　chopped
1 can (8 ounces) no salt added tomato
　　sauce
1 can (6 ounces) no salt added tomato
　　paste
1 cup thinly sliced fresh mushrooms
¼ cup chopped fresh parsley
1 tablespoon red wine vinegar
1 teaspoon dried oregano leaves
1 teaspoon dried basil leaves
1 bay leaf
½ teaspoon salt
¼ teaspoon crushed red pepper
1½ cups lowfat cottage cheese
1 cup (4 ounces) shredded low
　　moisture part-skim mozzarella
　　cheese, divided
6 lasagna noodles, cooked (without
　　salt or fat) and well drained
3 cups chopped broccoli, cooked and
　　well drained
1 tablespoon grated Parmesan cheese

1. Heat oven to 350°F. Oil 11¾ × 7½ × 2-inch baking dish lightly.

2. Heat 1 tablespoon Crisco® Oil in large saucepan on medium heat. Add onion and garlic. Cook and stir until tender. Stir in tomatoes with liquid, tomato sauce, tomato paste, mushrooms, parsley, vinegar, oregano, basil, bay leaf, salt and crushed red pepper. Bring to a boil. Reduce heat to low. Cover. Simmer 30 minutes, stirring occasionally. Remove and discard bay leaf.

3. Combine cottage cheese and ½ cup mozzarella cheese in small bowl. Stir well.

4. Place 2 lasagna noodles in bottom of baking dish. Layer with 1 cup broccoli, one-third of the tomato sauce mixture and one-third of the cottage cheese mixture. Repeat layers twice. Cover with foil.

5. Bake at 350°F for 25 minutes. Uncover. Sprinkle with remaining ½ cup mozzarella cheese and Parmesan cheese. Bake, uncovered, 10 minutes or until cheese melts. Let stand 10 minutes before serving.　　*Makes 8 servings*

Broccoli Lasagna

Garden Primavera Pasta

6 ounces bow-tie pasta
1 jar (6 ounces) marinated artichoke
   hearts
2 cloves garlic, minced
½ teaspoon dried rosemary, crushed
1 green bell pepper, cut into thin
   strips
1 large carrot, cut into 3-inch
   julienne strips
1 medium zucchini, cut into 3-inch
   julienne strips
1 can (14½ ounces) DEL MONTE®
   Pasta Style Chunky Tomatoes
12 small pitted ripe olives (optional)

Cook pasta according to package directions; drain. Drain artichokes reserving marinade. Toss pasta in 3 tablespoons artichoke marinade; set aside. Cut artichoke hearts into halves. In large skillet, cook garlic and rosemary in 1 tablespoon artichoke marinade. Add remaining ingredients, except pasta and artichokes. Cook, uncovered, over medium-high heat 4 to 5 minutes or until vegetables are tender-crisp and sauce is thickened. Add artichoke hearts. Spoon over pasta. Serve with grated Parmesan cheese, if desired.   *Makes 4 servings*

Prep time: 15 minutes
Cook time: 10 minutes

Tuna in Red Pepper Sauce

2 cups chopped red bell peppers
   (about 2 peppers)
½ cup chopped onion
1 clove garlic, minced
2 tablespoons vegetable oil
¼ cup dry red or white wine
¼ cup chicken broth
2 teaspoons sugar
¼ teaspoon black pepper
1 red bell pepper, slivered and cut
   into ½-inch pieces
1 yellow or green bell pepper,
   slivered and cut into ½-inch
   pieces
½ cup julienned carrot strips
1 can (9¼ ounces) STARKIST® Tuna,
   drained and broken into chunks
Hot cooked pasta or rice

In a skillet cook and stir chopped bell peppers, onion and garlic in hot oil for 5 minutes, or until onion is very tender. In a blender container or food processor bowl place onion mixture; cover and process until smooth. Return to pan; stir in wine, chicken broth, sugar and black pepper. Keep warm. In a 2-quart saucepan steam bell pepper pieces and carrots over simmering water for 5 minutes. Stir steamed vegetables into sauce with tuna; cook for 2 minutes, or until heated through. Serve tuna mixture over pasta.   *Makes 4 to 5 servings*

Prep time: 20 minutes

Garden Primavera Pasta

Lamb and Spinach Manicotti

Sauce

- 1½ pounds ground American lamb
- 1 small onion, chopped
- 1 jar (16 ounces) prepared tomato sauce
- ½ teaspoon salt
- ¼ teaspoon black pepper

Stuffing

- 1 tablespoon butter or margarine
- 1 large onion, finely chopped
- 2 cloves garlic, minced
- 2 packages (10 ounces *each*) frozen chopped spinach, thawed and drained
- 2 eggs, slightly beaten
- 1 cup ricotta cheese
- ½ teaspoon salt
- 1 teaspoon dried oregano leaves
- ½ teaspoon chopped fresh basil leaves

- 1 package (5 ounces) manicotti pasta, cooked according to package directions and drained
- 1 cup grated Monterey Jack cheese
- ½ cup grated Parmesan cheese

Lamb and Spinach Manicotti

To prepare sauce, brown lamb and onion in large skillet. Pour off drippings. Stir in tomato sauce, salt and black pepper. Reduce heat; simmer 15 to 20 minutes.

Preheat oven to 350°F. To prepare stuffing, melt butter in medium skillet; add onion and garlic. Cook and stir until onion is translucent. Add spinach; cook until moisture has evaporated. Remove from heat.

Add eggs, ricotta, salt, oregano and basil. Stuff pasta with spinach mixture. Pour thin layer of sauce in 13×9-inch baking dish. Arrange stuffed manicotti on sauce. Top with remaining sauce. Cover with Jack and Parmesan cheeses. Bake, uncovered, 25 to 30 minutes until bubbly and heated through.   *Makes 8 servings*

Favorite recipe from **American Lamb Council**

Fettuccine with Roasted Red Pepper Sauce

- 3 large red bell peppers*
- ½ cup whipping or heavy cream
- ¼ cup WISH-BONE® Italian Dressing
- 2 tablespoons chopped fresh basil leaves**
- Salt and black pepper to taste
- 1 package fettuccine or medium egg noodles, cooked according to package directions and drained
- Grated Parmesan cheese

In large foil-lined baking pan or on broiler rack, place red peppers. Broil, turning occasionally, 20 minutes or until

*Substitution: Use 2 cups drained roasted red peppers.

**Substitution: Use 2 teaspoons dried basil leaves.

peppers turn almost completely black. Immediately place in paper bag; close bag and let cool about 30 minutes. Under cold running water, peel off skin, then remove stems and seeds.

In food processor or blender, process prepared peppers, cream, Italian dressing, basil, salt and black pepper until blended. Toss with hot fettuccine and serve with cheese.

Makes about 4 servings

Note: Also terrific with Wish-Bone® Robusto Italian or Lite Italian Dressing.

Stuffed Mushrooms with Tomato Sauce and Pasta

Tomato Sauce (recipe follows)
1 pound extra-lean (90% lean) ground beef
¼ cup finely chopped onion
¼ cup finely chopped green or red bell pepper
1 garlic clove, minced
2 tablespoons finely chopped fresh parsley
2 teaspoons finely chopped fresh basil *or* 1 teaspoon dried basil leaves, crushed
1 teaspoon finely chopped fresh oregano *or* ½ teaspoon dried oregano leaves, crushed
½ teaspoon salt
Dash black pepper
12 large mushrooms
¼ cup (1 ounce) grated Parmesan cheese
4½ cups cooked spaghetti

Prepare Tomato Sauce; set aside.

Preheat oven to 350°F. Combine ground beef, onion, bell pepper, garlic, parsley, basil, oregano, salt and black pepper in medium bowl; mix lightly. Remove stems

Stuffed Mushrooms with Tomato Sauce and Pasta

from mushrooms; finely chop stems. Add to ground beef mixture. Stuff into mushroom caps, rounding tops.

Pour Tomato Sauce into shallow casserole dish large enough to hold mushrooms in single layer. Place mushrooms, stuffing sides up, in sauce; cover.

Bake 20 minutes; uncover. Sprinkle with Parmesan cheese. Bake, uncovered, 15 minutes more. Serve with spaghetti. Garnish with additional fresh basil leaves, if desired.

Makes 6 servings

Tomato Sauce

2 cans (14½ ounces *each*) tomatoes, chopped, undrained
Dash hot pepper sauce
1 teaspoon finely chopped fresh marjoram *or* ½ teaspoon dried marjoram leaves, crushed
1 teaspoon fennel seeds, crushed
Salt and black pepper to taste

Combine all ingredients except salt and black pepper in medium saucepan. Bring to a boil. Reduce heat; simmer 5 minutes. Season with salt and pepper.

Pasta Hoppin' John

Pasta Hoppin' John

1 pound uncooked bow ties, spirals, wagon wheels or other medium pasta shape
1 tablespoon vegetable oil
1 medium onion, chopped
1 jalapeño pepper, seeded and chopped *or* ½ teaspoon dried jalapeño flakes
3 cloves garlic, chopped
1 green bell pepper, seeded and chopped
1 can (28 ounces) crushed tomatoes
1 package (10 ounces) frozen black-eyed peas, prepared according to package directions *or* 1 can (16 ounces) black-eyed peas, rinsed and drained
1 tablespoon cider vinegar
3 tablespoons fresh chopped cilantro *or* 1 tablespoon ground coriander
Salt and black pepper to taste

Cook pasta according to package directions; drain. Heat oil in large skillet over medium heat. Add onion, jalapeño, garlic and bell pepper; cook and stir about 3 minutes or until softened. Stir in tomatoes with liquid. Simmer 10 minutes; stir occasionally. Stir in black-eyed peas, vinegar and cilantro. Simmer 10 minutes more. Season with salt and black pepper. Pour over hot pasta; toss to coat. Serve immediately. *Makes 6 to 8 servings*

*Favorite recipe from **National Pasta Association***

Tortellini Bake Parmesano

1 package (12 ounces) fresh or frozen cheese tortellini or ravioli
½ pound lean ground beef
½ medium onion, finely chopped
2 cloves garlic, minced
½ teaspoon dried oregano, crushed
2 cans (14½ ounces *each*) DEL MONTE® Pasta Style Chunky Tomatoes
2 small zucchini, sliced
⅓ cup grated Parmesan cheese

Microwave: Cook pasta according to package directions; rinse and drain. In large skillet, brown meat with onion, garlic and oregano; drain. Season with salt and pepper, if desired. Add tomatoes and zucchini. Cook, uncovered, over medium-high heat 15 minutes or until thickened, stirring occasionally. In oiled 2-quart microwavable dish, arrange ½ of pasta; top with ½ of sauce and ½ of cheese. Repeat layers ending with cheese. Cover and microwave on HIGH 8 to 10 minutes or until heated through, rotating halfway through. *Makes 4 servings*

Prep & Cook time: 35 minutes

Shrimp Linguine

1 pound cleaned uncooked shrimp
1 garlic clove, minced
⅛ teaspoon crushed red pepper
2 tablespoons olive oil
½ pound VELVEETA® Pasteurized
    Process Cheese Spread, cubed
2 tablespoons dry white wine or
    milk
6 ounces linguine, cooked, drained
2 tablespoons chopped fresh basil

• Saute shrimp, garlic and red pepper in olive oil on medium heat 3 to 5 minutes or until shrimp is pink. Reduce heat to low.

• Add process cheese spread and wine; stir on low heat until process cheese spread is melted. Toss with hot pasta. Sprinkle with basil before serving.

Makes 4 servings

Prep time: 10 minutes
Cooking time: 10 minutes

Sausage Pasta Primavera

1 pound fresh Italian sausage, cut
    into 2-inch pieces
1 medium onion, cut into 16 wedges
¼ cup water
1 cup uncooked spiral or wagon
    wheel-shaped pasta
8 ounces asparagus, cut diagonally
    into 1-inch pieces *or* 1 package
    (10 ounces) frozen cut asparagus,
    thawed
1 clove garlic, minced
1 teaspoon dried basil leaves,
    crushed
2 medium tomatoes, coarsely
    chopped
2 tablespoons freshly grated
    Parmesan cheese

Place Italian sausage, onion and water in large skillet. Cover tightly and cook over medium heat 11 to 13 minutes, turning sausage once. Meanwhile, cook pasta according to package directions; drain and keep hot. Uncover sausage mixture and stir in asparagus, garlic and basil. Cook 7 to 9 minutes more or until sausage is cooked through and asparagus is crisp-tender, stirring occasionally. Add tomatoes and hot pasta; toss lightly to combine. Cook 1 minute or just until heated through. Sprinkle with Parmesan cheese.

Makes 4 servings

Prep time: 15 minutes
Cooking time: 19 to 25 minutes

Favorite recipe from **National Live Stock & Meat Board**

Sausage Pasta Primavera

Classic Fettuccine Alfredo

1 recipe Homemade Fettuccine
 (recipe follows) *or* ¾ pound
 uncooked dry fettuccine
6 tablespoons unsalted butter
⅔ cup heavy or whipping cream
½ teaspoon salt
 Generous dash ground white
 pepper
 Generous dash ground nutmeg
1 cup freshly grated Parmesan cheese
 (about 3 ounces)
2 tablespoons chopped fresh parsley
 Fresh Italian parsley sprig, for
 garnish

Prepare and cook Homemade Fettuccine or cook fettuccine according to package directions. Drain well; return to dry pot.

Place butter and cream in large heavy skillet over medium-low heat. Cook and stir until butter melts and mixture bubbles. Cook and stir 2 minutes more. Stir in salt, pepper and nutmeg. Remove from heat. Gradually stir in cheese until thoroughly blended and smooth. Return briefly to heat to completely blend cheese if necessary. (Do not let sauce bubble or cheese will become lumpy and tough.) Pour sauce over fettuccine in pot. Toss over low heat 2 to 3 minutes until sauce is thickened and fettuccine is evenly coated. Sprinkle with chopped parsley. Garnish, if desired. Serve immediately.

Makes 4 servings

Homemade Fettuccine

2 cups all-purpose flour
¼ teaspoon salt
3 eggs
1 tablespoon milk
1 teaspoon olive oil

Combine flour and salt on pastry board or cutting board; make well in center. Whisk eggs, milk and oil in small bowl until well blended; gradually pour into well in flour mixture while mixing with fork or fingertips to form ball of dough. Place dough on lightly floured surface; flatten slightly. Knead dough 5 minutes or until smooth and elastic, adding more flour to prevent sticking if necessary. Wrap dough in plastic wrap; let stand 15 minutes.

Unwrap dough and knead briefly on lightly floured surface. Using lightly floured rolling pin, roll out dough to ⅛-inch-thick circle on lightly floured surface. Let rest until dough is slightly dry but can be handled without breaking. Lightly flour dough circle; roll loosely on rolling pin. Slide rolling pin out; press dough roll gently with hand and cut into ¼-inch-wide strips with sharp knife. Carefully unfold strips.* Cook fettuccine in large pot of boiling salted water 1 to 2 minutes just until tender. Drain well.

Makes about ¾ pound

*Fettuccine can be dried and stored at this point. Hang fettuccine strips over pasta rack or clean broom handle covered with plastic wrap and propped between two chairs. Dry at least 3 hours; store in airtight container at room temperature up to 4 days. To serve, cook fettuccine in large pot of boiling salted water 3 to 4 minutes just until tender. Drain well.

Classic Fettuccine Alfredo

Fresh Tomato, Basil and Ricotta Sauce

Ravioli and Chicken Parmesano

1 package (12 ounces) fresh or frozen
    cheese ravioli or tortellini
2 cans (14½ ounces *each*)
    DEL MONTE® Italian Style
    Stewed Tomatoes
½ pound boneless skinless chicken
    breasts or thighs, cut into strips
2 small zucchini, sliced
½ cup chopped onion
2 cloves garlic, crushed
½ teaspoon dried oregano leaves,
    crushed
⅓ cup grated Parmesan cheese

Cook pasta according to package
directions; rinse and drain. In large
skillet, cook tomatoes, chicken, zucchini,
onion, garlic and oregano over medium-
high heat 15 minutes or until sauce is
thickened and chicken is no longer pink
in center, stirring occasionally. Stir in
pasta and top with cheese; heat through.
Makes 4 to 6 servings

Prep & Cook Time: 23 minutes

Fresh Tomato, Basil and Ricotta Sauce

3 cups chopped ripe tomatoes
½ cup chopped fresh basil leaves
2 tablespoons minced red onion
1 clove garlic, chopped
1 cup ricotta cheese
¼ cup FILIPPO BERIO® Olive Oil
    Salt and black pepper to taste
1 pound pasta, such as rotelle, fusilli,
    ziti, penne or tubetti, cooked
    according to package directions
    and drained

Combine tomatoes, basil, onion and
garlic in large bowl. Stir in ricotta, olive
oil, salt and pepper. Add hot cooked
pasta; toss well. Serve immediately.
Makes 3 cups sauce, enough
for 1 pound pasta

Vegetarian Lasagna

½ cup chopped onion
1 teaspoon dried oregano leaves,
    crushed
1 clove garlic, minced
1 tablespoon olive oil
1 can (15 ounces) tomato sauce
¼ cup water
¼ cup tomato paste
¼ cup grated Parmesan cheese
9 lasagna noodles, cooked according
    to package directions and
    drained
4 cups sliced zucchini
1 container (1 pound) low fat part-
    skim ricotta cheese
1½ cups shredded Jarlsberg or
    Nokkelost cheese

Preheat oven to 375°F. In saucepan, cook
onion, oregano and garlic in oil until
tender. Add tomato sauce and water.

Blend in tomato paste and Parmesan. Spoon small amount of sauce into 13×9-inch baking dish. Top with 3 lasagna noodles. Top with ⅓ *each* of zucchini, ricotta cheese, Jarlsberg cheese and sauce. Repeat layers twice with remaining ingredients. Bake 30 minutes or until zucchini is tender. If desired, sprinkle with additional ½ cup Nokkelost. Bake several minutes until cheese melts. Let stand 10 minutes before serving. *Makes 8 servings*

Favorite recipe from **Norseland Foods, Inc.**

Veal-Almond Shells with Quick Basil-Tomato Sauce

        2 teaspoons vegetable oil
        1 cup chopped onion
        1 small zucchini, shredded
            (about 1 cup)
        1 pound ground veal
        8 ounces ground pork (75% lean)
        1 cup fresh bread crumbs
        1 teaspoon salt
        ¾ teaspoon garlic powder
        ¼ to ½ teaspoon ground allspice
            Quick Basil-Tomato Sauce
            (recipe follows)
        ⅓ cup slivered almonds, toasted
        1 cup (4 ounces) shredded
            mozzarella cheese
        18 large pasta shells for filling, cooked
            according to package directions
            and drained
        2 tablespoons chopped fresh Italian
            parsley

Preheat oven to 350°F. Heat oil in heavy nonstick skillet over medium heat. Add onion; cook 3 minutes or until crisp-tender, stirring occasionally. Add zucchini; cook 1 minute. Add ground veal and ground pork; cook 3 to 4 minutes or just until no longer pink,

stirring occasionally to break up veal and pork. Remove from heat. Using slotted spoon, remove veal mixture to large bowl. Add bread crumbs, salt, garlic powder and allspice to taste; stir lightly to combine. Cool 10 minutes. Meanwhile, prepare Quick Basil-Tomato Sauce. Stir almonds and cheese into veal mixture. Fill shells with equal amounts of veal mixture; arrange shells in 13×9-inch baking pan. Pour sauce over shells. Cover tightly with foil. Bake 30 minutes or until heated through. Sprinkle with Italian parsley. *Makes 6 servings*

Prep time: 35 minutes
Cooking time: 40 minutes

Quick Basil-Tomato Sauce

        1 can (14½ to 16 ounces) peeled
            whole tomatoes, undrained
        1½ teaspoons dried basil leaves,
            crushed
        1 teaspoon garlic powder

Combine tomatoes with liquid, basil and garlic powder in food processor or blender. Cover and process until almost smooth. *Makes about 2 cups*

Prep time: 5 minutes

Favorite recipe from **National Live Stock & Meat Board**

Veal-Almond Shells with Quick Basil-Tomato Sauce

Caponata-Style Fettuccine

Caponata is a Sicilian eggplant dish that may be served cold as an appetizer or on lettuce as a salad. Here it is made into a vegetarian sauce for pasta.

1 medium eggplant (about 1 pound)
1¼ teaspoons salt, divided
3 medium tomatoes (about 1 pound)
⅓ cup olive oil, divided
1 small green bell pepper, sliced
1 medium onion, coarsely chopped
2 cloves garlic, minced
⅓ cup *each* raisins and halved pitted green olives
¼ cup balsamic or red wine vinegar
2 tablespoons drained capers (optional)
¼ teaspoon *each* ground cinnamon and black pepper
10 ounces fresh spinach fettuccine, hot cooked and drained
Fresh basil leaves, for garnish

Cut eggplant into ¼-inch-thick slices, discarding cap and stem ends. Place in large colander over bowl; sprinkle with 1 teaspoon salt. Drain 1 hour. Cut tomatoes in half. Remove stems and seeds; discard. Coarsely chop tomatoes.

Place oven rack in lowest position. Preheat oven to 450°F. Place eggplant slices in single layer on baking sheet; brush both sides lightly with some of oil.

Caponata-Style Fettuccine

Bake slices 10 minutes or until lightly browned on bottoms. Turn over; bake about 5 minutes more or until other sides are lightly browned and slices are soft. Set aside.

Heat remaining oil in large skillet over medium-high heat. Add bell pepper; cook and stir 5 minutes or until pepper turns bright green. Transfer to plate; set aside. Add onion and garlic to same skillet; cook and stir 5 minutes or until onion is soft. Add tomatoes, raisins, olives, vinegar, capers, cinnamon, black pepper and remaining ¼ teaspoon salt. Cook until most of the liquid has evaporated.

Cut roasted eggplant slices into quarters; add to tomato mixture. Add reserved bell pepper; cook until heated through. Serve over fettuccine. Garnish, if desired.

Makes 4 main-dish or 8 first-course servings

Linguine with White Clam Sauce

1 pound uncooked linguine
1 tablespoon olive oil
2 cloves garlic, minced
1 tablespoon all-purpose flour
4 cans (6.5 ounces *each*) chopped clams with juice
1½ cups chopped fresh parsley

Cook linguine according to package directions; drain. Heat oil in large skillet over medium-high heat; add garlic. Cook and stir until garlic is golden brown; stir in flour. Gradually add clams and parsley. Cook, stirring constantly, over medium heat until sauce is thickened and smooth. Serve clam sauce over hot linguine.

Makes 4 to 6 servings

*Favorite recipe from **National Pasta Association***

Chicken and Spinach Manicotti

Manicotti filled with the earthy flavors of Italy is baked as a casserole. A pastry bag with a large plain tip is an easy way to stuff manicotti.

1½ cups shredded cooked chicken
1 container (15 ounces) ricotta cheese
1 package (10 ounces) frozen chopped spinach, cooked according to package directions and well drained
1¼ cups half and half, divided
½ cup PROGRESSO® Plain Bread Crumbs
1 teaspoon garlic powder
½ teaspoon dried basil leaves
½ teaspoon dried oregano leaves
½ teaspoon salt
¼ teaspoon ground black pepper
1 package (8 ounces; 14 count) manicotti noodles, cooked according to package directions and drained
1 jar (14 ounces) PROGRESSO® Marinara Sauce
1½ cups (6 ounces) shredded mozzarella cheese

1. Preheat oven to 350°F.

2. In large bowl, combine chicken, ricotta cheese, spinach, ½ cup half and half, bread crumbs, garlic powder, basil, oregano, salt and black pepper; mix well.

3. Stuff chicken mixture into manicotti; place in 13×9-inch baking dish.

4. Combine marinara sauce and remaining ¾ cup half and half; pour over manicotti. Top with mozzarella cheese.

5. Bake 30 minutes or until thoroughly heated. *Makes 7 servings*

Prep time: 30 minutes
Cooking time: 30 minutes

Microwave: Prepare chicken mixture and fill manicotti as directed in Steps 2 and 3. Place in 13×9-inch microwave-safe baking dish. Combine marinara sauce and remaining ¾ cup half and half; pour over manicotti. Cover with plastic wrap, cutting a few slits in center of wrap to vent. Microwave on HIGH (100% power) 5 minutes; top with mozzarella cheese. Microwave on MEDIUM (50% power) 15 minutes, rotating dish every 5 minutes. Let stand 5 minutes before serving.

Creamy Pasta Primavera

1 tablespoon olive oil
1 medium zucchini, cut into julienned strips
2 plum tomatoes, chopped
1 bunch green onions, diced
⅓ cup pea pods, ends removed
⅓ cup chicken broth or water
1 package (6½ ounces) ALOUETTE® Garlic and Spices
12 ounces spinach or egg pasta (linguine or fettucine), cooked according to package directions and drained
Salt and black pepper to taste
2 tablespoons chopped fresh parsley

Heat olive oil in stockpot over medium-high heat. Add zucchini, tomatoes, green onions and pea pods; cook and stir 2 to 3 minutes. Stir in chicken broth and cheese; reduce heat. When cheese has melted, add pasta to pot. Toss to coat; season with salt and black pepper. Top with parsley. Serve immediately. *Makes 4 servings*

*Favorite recipe from **Bongrain Cheese U.S.A.***

MEAT

Italian Pork Cutlets

1 teaspoon CRISCO® Vegetable Oil
6 (4 ounces *each*) lean, boneless, center-cut pork loin slices, ¾ inch thick
1 can (8 ounces) tomato sauce
1½ cups sliced fresh mushrooms
1 small green bell pepper, cut into strips
½ cup sliced green onions with tops
1 teaspoon Italian herb seasoning
½ teaspoon salt
⅛ teaspoon black pepper
¼ cup water
1 tablespoon cornstarch
½ cup (2 ounces) shredded low moisture part-skim mozzarella cheese
2⅔ cups hot cooked rice (cooked without salt or fat)

1. Heat Crisco® Oil in large skillet on medium heat. Add meat. Cook until browned on both sides.

2. Add tomato sauce, mushrooms, green pepper, onions, Italian herb seasoning, salt and black pepper. Reduce heat to low. Cover. Simmer 30 minutes or until meat is tender.

3. Combine water and cornstarch in small bowl. Stir until well blended. Add to juices in skillet. Cook and stir until thickened.

4. Sprinkle cheese over meat mixture. Cover. Heat until cheese melts. Serve with rice.   *Makes 6 servings*

Veal Cutlets Parma Style

2 eggs
2 tablespoons water
½ teaspoon garlic salt
8 thin veal cutlets (about 1 pound)
2 cups plain dry bread crumbs
½ cup butter or margarine
2 tablespoons olive oil
1 (26-ounce) jar CLASSICO® Di Sicilia (Ripe Olives & Mushrooms) or Di Parma (Four Cheese) Pasta Sauce
½ (1-pound) package CREAMETTE® Linguine, cooked according to package directions and drained
Grated Parmesan cheese

In medium bowl, beat eggs, water and garlic salt. Dip veal in bread crumbs, then in egg mixture and again in crumbs. In large skillet, over medium heat, melt butter with oil; brown veal on both sides. In medium saucepan, heat pasta sauce. Arrange veal on *hot* linguine; top with pasta sauce. Garnish with Parmesan cheese. Refrigerate leftovers.

Makes 4 servings

Italian Pork Cutlets

Saucy Meatballs

1 pound lean ground beef
⅔ cup grated Parmesan cheese
½ cup seasoned dry bread crumbs
½ cup milk
1 egg, slightly beaten
1 tablespoon vegetable oil
2 cans (14½ ounces *each*) stewed
    tomatoes, cut into bite-sized
    pieces
⅓ cup HEINZ® 57 Sauce
½ teaspoon salt
⅛ teaspoon pepper
    Hot buttered noodles

Combine first 5 ingredients in large bowl until well blended. Form into 20 meatballs using 1 rounded tablespoon for each. Brown meatballs in oil; drain excess fat. Combine tomatoes, 57 Sauce, salt and pepper in small bowl; pour over meatballs. Simmer, uncovered, 15 to 20 minutes or until sauce is desired consistency, stirring occasionally. Serve meatballs and sauce over noodles.

Makes 5 servings (about 3 cups sauce)

Saucy Meatballs

Beef Italienne

¼ cup olive oil
30 cloves garlic, peeled
2 cups chopped onions, divided
1½ pounds ground beef
2 tablespoons *plus* 1 teaspoon
    CHEF PAUL PRUDHOMME'S
    MEAT MAGIC®, divided
2 tablespoons all-purpose flour
1 can (5½ ounces) unsweetened
    apple juice
2 cups canned crushed tomatoes
1 cup canned tomato puree
1 cup chopped celery
4 cups beef stock or water,* divided
½ teaspoon salt
1 pound pasta, cooked according to
    package directions and drained

In 3½-quart saucepan, heat olive oil over high heat about 3 minutes or until it just starts to smoke. Add garlic and stir to coat with oil. Cook about 2 minutes or until garlic is lightly browned. Remove garlic with slotted spoon; set aside.

Add 1 cup onions to saucepan; stir well. Cook and stir about 8 minutes or until onions are golden brown. Remove onions with slotted spoon; set aside.

Add ground beef and 1 tablespoon Meat Magic®. Cook, stirring occasionally to break up meat chunks, about 6 minutes or until meat is browned. Pour off drippings. Stir in flour and cook about 4 minutes, stirring occasionally. Stir in apple juice, stirring and scraping up browned bits. Cook another 6 minutes, stirring occasionally. Stir in crushed tomatoes, tomato puree, reserved onion and garlic, celery and remaining 1 cup onions. Cook about 10 minutes, stirring

*If using canned broth, use no salt variety.

occasionally. Stir in 2 cups stock and remaining Meat Magic®. Cook about 5 minutes or until sauce is boiling. Reduce heat to low; cover. Simmer, stirring occasionally, about 18 minutes. Stir in remaining 2 cups stock and salt; increase heat to high. Cook, stirring occasionally, about 5 minutes or until sauce is boiling. Reduce heat to low and cook, stirring occasionally, 11 minutes. Stir in pasta and simmer about 2 minutes or until heated through. *Makes 6 servings*

Classic Veal Florentine

6 ounces fresh spinach
6 tablespoons butter or margarine, divided
2 cloves garlic, minced
1 can (14½ ounces) whole peeled tomatoes, undrained
¼ cup dry white wine
¼ cup water
1 tablespoon tomato paste
½ teaspoon sugar
¾ teaspoon salt, divided
¼ teaspoon black pepper, divided
¼ cup all-purpose flour
4 veal cutlets, cut ⅜ inch thick (about 4 ounces *each*)
1 tablespoon olive oil
4 ounces mozzarella cheese, shredded
  Hot cooked angel hair pasta (optional)

To steam spinach, rinse spinach thoroughly in large bowl of lukewarm water; drain but do not squeeze dry. Trim and discard stems. Stack leaves; cut crosswise into coarse shreds. Place in large saucepan over medium heat. Cover and steam 4 minutes or until tender, stirring occasionally. Add 2 tablespoons butter; cook and stir until butter is absorbed. Remove from pan; set aside.

Classic Veal Florentine

Heat 2 tablespoons butter in medium saucepan over medium heat until melted and bubbly. Add garlic; cook and stir 30 seconds. Press tomatoes and juice through sieve into garlic mixture; discard seeds. Add wine, water, tomato paste, sugar, ½ teaspoon salt and ⅛ teaspoon black pepper to tomato mixture. Bring to a boil; reduce heat to low. Simmer, uncovered, 10 minutes, stirring occasionally. Remove from heat; set aside.

Mix flour, remaining ¼ teaspoon salt and ⅛ teaspoon black pepper in small plastic bag. Pound veal with meat mallet to ¼-inch thickness. Pat dry with paper towels. Shake veal, 1 cutlet at a time, in seasoned flour to coat evenly. Heat oil and remaining 2 tablespoons butter in large skillet over medium heat until bubbly. Add veal to skillet; cook 2 to 3 minutes per side until light brown. Remove from heat. Spoon off excess fat. Top veal with reserved spinach, then cheese. Pour reserved tomato mixture into skillet, lifting edges of veal to let sauce flow under. Cook over low heat until bubbly. Cover and simmer 8 minutes or until heated through. Serve with pasta. Garnish as desired. *Makes 4 servings*

Johnnie Marzetti

Johnnie Marzetti

1 tablespoon CRISCO®
   Vegetable Oil
1 cup chopped celery
1 cup chopped onion
1 medium green bell pepper,
   chopped
1 pound ground beef round
1 can (14½ ounces) Italian style
   stewed tomatoes
1 can (8 ounces) tomato sauce
1 can (6 ounces) tomato paste
1 cup water
1 bay leaf
1½ teaspoons dried basil leaves
1¼ teaspoons salt
¼ teaspoon black pepper
1 package (12 ounces) cholesterol
   free, yolk free, noodle style
   pasta, cooked (without salt or fat)
   and well drained
½ cup plain dry bread crumbs
1 cup (4 ounces) shredded (⅓ less fat)
   sharp Cheddar cheese

1. Heat oven to 375°F. Oil 12½ × 8½ × 2-inch baking dish lightly.

2. Heat 1 tablespoon Crisco® Oil in large skillet on medium heat. Add celery, onion and green pepper. Cook and stir until tender. Remove vegetables from skillet. Set aside. Add meat to skillet. Cook until browned, stirring occasionally. Return vegetables to skillet. Stir in tomatoes, tomato sauce, tomato paste, water, bay leaf, basil, salt and black pepper. Reduce heat to low. Simmer 5 minutes, stirring occasionally. Remove bay leaf.

3. Place pasta in baking dish. Spoon meat mixture over pasta. Sprinkle with bread crumbs and cheese.

4. Bake at 375°F for 15 to 20 minutes or until cheese melts. Garnish, if desired.

Makes 8 servings

Pork Chops Roma

½ cup WISH-BONE® Olive Oil
   Classics Vinaigrette Dressing*
6 pork chops, ½ inch thick
   (about 2 pounds)
2 medium green bell peppers, sliced
¼ pound mushrooms, sliced

In large shallow baking dish, pour dressing over pork chops. Cover and marinate in refrigerator, turning occasionally, at least 3 hours or overnight. Remove chops, reserving marinade.

In large skillet, heat 2 tablespoons reserved marinade and cook peppers and mushrooms over medium heat, stirring occasionally, until tender; remove. Brown pork chops; drain. Add remaining marinade and simmer, covered, 15 minutes. Return peppers and mushrooms to skillet; simmer, covered, an additional 10 minutes or until chops are tender.

Makes about 6 servings

*Also terrific with Wish-Bone® Italian, Lite Italian or Robusto Italian Dressing.

Confetti Risotto

1 tablespoon olive oil
1 pound lean fresh American lamb leg, cut into ¾-inch cubes
2 cups unpeeled ¼-inch Japanese eggplant slices (about ½ pound)
1 medium onion, chopped
2 cloves garlic, minced
½ cup diced green bell pepper
½ cup diced yellow bell pepper
2 teaspoons ground cumin
2 teaspoons ground turmeric
1 teaspoon salt (optional)
½ teaspoon black pepper
3 cups cooked rice
1 can (14½ ounces) chopped peeled tomatoes, drained
¾ to 1¼ cups homemade or reduced sodium canned chicken or vegetable broth
Chopped fresh Italian parsley or cilantro

Heat olive oil in 3-quart Dutch oven or casserole over medium-high heat until hot. Add lamb; cook and stir until browned. Remove and set aside. Add eggplant, onion and garlic; cook and stir 3 to 4 minutes. Add bell peppers; cook and stir 2 to 3 minutes more. Stir in cumin, turmeric, salt and black pepper. Add reserved lamb. Gently stir in rice, tomatoes and enough broth to make mixture soft and creamy; heat through, stirring frequently. Add more broth as needed. Garnish with parsley.

Makes 6 servings

Prep time: 15 minutes
Cooking time: 15 minutes

*Favorite recipe from **American Lamb Council***

Veal Piccata

8 ounces veal cutlets, cut ⅛ to ¼ inch thick
4 teaspoons all-purpose flour
¼ teaspoon salt
⅛ teaspoon black pepper
1 tablespoon olive oil
1 clove garlic, minced
¼ cup dry white wine
1 tablespoon fresh lemon juice
2 teaspoons drained capers (optional)

Place veal cutlets on flat surface; cover with waxed paper and flatten with bottom of saucepan, mallet or cleaver to ⅛-inch thickness or less. Combine flour, salt and black pepper in shallow dish; coat cutlets with flour mixture. Heat oil in large nonstick skillet; add cutlets. Cook 1 to 1½ minutes, turning once. Remove cutlets to warm serving platter; cover and keep warm. Add garlic to skillet and cook 30 seconds, stirring constantly. Add wine and lemon juice; cook until slightly reduced. Pour sauce over cutlets; sprinkle with capers, if desired.

Makes 2 servings

Prep time: 10 minutes
Cooking time: 2 minutes

*Favorite recipe from **National Live Stock & Meat Board***

Veal Piccata

Sausage, Peppers & Onions with Grilled Polenta

5 cups canned chicken broth
1½ cups Italian polenta or yellow
    cornmeal
1½ cups cooked fresh corn or thawed
    frozen corn
2 tablespoons butter or margarine
1 cup (4 ounces) freshly grated
    Parmesan cheese
6 Italian-style sausages
2 small to medium red onions, sliced
    into rounds
1 *each* medium red and green bell
    pepper, cored, seeded and cut
    into 1-inch-wide strips
½ cup Marsala or sweet vermouth
    (optional)
    Olive oil

To make polenta, bring chicken broth to a boil in large pot. Add polenta; reduce heat and simmer, stirring frequently, about 30 minutes. If polenta starts to stick and burn on bottom, add up to ½ cup water. During last 5 minutes of cooking, stir in corn and butter. Remove from heat; stir in Parmesan cheese. Transfer polenta to greased 13 × 9-inch baking pan; let cool until firm and set enough to cut. (Polenta may be prepared a day ahead; keep refrigerated.)

Prick each sausage in 4 or 5 places with fork. Place sausages, red onions and bell peppers in large shallow glass dish or heavy plastic bag. Pour Marsala over food, if desired; cover dish or close bag. Marinate in refrigerator up to 4 hours, turning sausages and vegetables several times. (Marinating is optional.)

Oil hot grid to help prevent sticking. Cut polenta into squares; cut into triangles, if desired. Brush one side with oil. Grill polenta, oil sides down, on a covered grill, over medium KINGSFORD® briquets, about 4 minutes until lightly toasted. Halfway through cooking time, brush top with oil, then turn and continue grilling. Move polenta to edge of grill to keep warm.

Drain sausages and vegetables from Marsala; discard Marsala. Grill sausages on a covered grill, over medium-low coals 15 to 20 minutes until cooked through, turning several times. After sausage has cooked 10 minutes, place vegetables in center of grid. Grill vegetables 10 to 12 minutes until tender, turning once or twice. *Makes 6 servings*

Italian Marinated Steak

1 can (19 ounces) PROGRESSO®
    Tomato Soup, drained, reserving
    broth and soup pieces separately
2 tablespoons Burgundy wine
1 tablespoon Worcestershire sauce
¾ teaspoon Italian seasoning
½ teaspoon dry mustard
1¼ pounds boneless sirloin steak

1. In shallow 2-quart baking dish, combine reserved soup broth, wine, Worcestershire sauce, Italian seasoning and dry mustard; mix well.

2. Add steak to marinade; cover. Refrigerate 2 hours, turning steak occasionally. Remove steak from marinade, reserving marinade.

3. Bake, broil or grill steak to desired doneness, brushing frequently with reserved marinade.

4. In small saucepan, combine remaining marinade and soup pieces; bring to a boil. Serve over steak. *Makes 4 servings*

Prep time: 10 minutes
Chilling/cooling time: 2 hours
Cooking time: 10 minutes

Sausage, Peppers & Onions with Grilled Polenta

Veal Shanks Braised in Herb-Tomato Sauce

2 tablespoons *plus* 2 teaspoons olive
   or vegetable oil, divided
4 pounds veal cross cut shanks, cut
   1½ inches thick*
   Salt to taste
1 cup chopped onion
½ cup *each* finely chopped celery and
   carrot
3 cloves garlic, crushed
1½ cups dry white wine
1 can (14½ ounces) whole peeled
   tomatoes, drained
1 teaspoon *each* dried basil leaves
   and dried thyme leaves, crushed
   Gremolata (recipe follows)

Heat 1 tablespoon oil in Dutch oven over
medium heat. Brown veal shanks, ⅓ at a
time, using additional 1 tablespoon oil as
necessary. Sprinkle veal with salt; set
aside. Heat remaining 2 teaspoons oil in
Dutch oven over medium-low heat. Add
onion, celery, carrot and garlic; cook 10
minutes or until tender, stirring
occasionally. Add wine and tomatoes,
breaking up tomatoes with spoon. Bring
to a boil over high heat, stirring to
dissolve browned meat juices; stir in basil
and thyme. Return veal to pan; reduce
heat. Cover tightly and simmer 1½ hours
or until veal is tender.

Meanwhile, prepare Gremolata. Remove
veal to warm platter; cover and keep
warm. Skim and discard fat from cooking
liquid, if necessary. Cook over high heat
to reduce as desired, stirring occasionally.
Spoon about ¾ cup sauce over veal.
Sprinkle with Gremolata; serve with
remaining sauce.   *Makes 6 servings*

*Veal cross cut shanks may be tied with
string to help retain shape, if desired.

Gremolata: Combine 1 tablespoon
chopped fresh parsley, 2 teaspoons grated
lemon peel and ½ teaspoon minced
garlic.

Prep time: 30 minutes
Cooking time: 1 hour 50 minutes

Favorite recipe from **National Live Stock & Meat Board**

Pork Medallions Piccata

*If you like lemons, you'll love this quick and
flavorful dish.*

1 pound boneless pork tenderloin
2 tablespoons all-purpose flour
1½ teaspoons LAWRY'S® Lemon
   Pepper Seasoning
2 tablespoons IMPERIAL®
   Margarine
¼ cup dry sherry wine
2 to 3 tablespoons lemon juice

Slice pork into ½-inch medallion slices.
Flatten each between sheets of waxed
paper to ⅛-inch thickness. In pie plate,
combine flour and Lemon Pepper
Seasoning. Dredge pork slices in flour
mixture. In large skillet, melt margarine
over medium heat; add medallions. Cook
and stir 5 to 6 minutes, turning once. Stir
in wine and lemon juice. Shake pan
gently and cook 2 to 3 minutes more until
sauce is slightly thickened.

Makes 4 servings

Presentation: Serve 3 to 4 medallions on
each plate; garnish each with 2 lemon
slices and 2 to 3 teaspoons capers. Perfect
with herbed bread and seasoned
potatoes.

Hint: For a sweeter variation, substitute
orange juice for lemon juice.

Left to right: Hearty Veal Stew and Veal Shanks Braised in Herb-Tomato Sauce

Hearty Veal Stew

4 teaspoons olive or vegetable oil, divided
1½ pounds veal for stew, cut into 1½-inch pieces
1 large onion, coarsely chopped (about 1¼ cups)
2 cups water, divided
½ cup dry white wine
2 teaspoons Italian seasoning, crushed
¾ teaspoon salt
1½ cups uncooked medium pasta shells*
½ cup *each* chopped green, red and yellow bell pepper
1 tablespoon cornstarch
1 cup whole pitted ripe olives
1 tablespoon balsamic vinegar

Heat 2 teaspoons oil in Dutch oven or large deep skillet over medium heat. Brown veal, ½ at a time, using remaining oil as needed. Return all veal to pan. Add onion, 1¾ cups water, wine, Italian seasoning and salt. Bring to a boil; reduce heat to low. Cover and simmer 1 hour or until veal is tender. Meanwhile, cook pasta according to package directions; drain and set aside. Stir bell peppers into stew. Dissolve cornstarch in remaining ¼ cup water; stir into veal mixture. Cook over medium-high heat 2 minutes or until thickened, stirring constantly. Stir in pasta, olives and vinegar; heat through.

Makes 6 servings

Prep time: 20 minutes
Cooking time: 1 hour 15 minutes

*Elbow macaroni, ziti, mostaccioli, bow ties or radiatore may be substituted for medium pasta shells.

Favorite recipe from **National Live Stock & Meat Board**

Fillet of Beef Andrea

A sprightly sauce of garlic, olives and chick peas complements beef.

- **5 tablespoons PROGRESSO® Olive Oil, divided**
- **4 tablespoons PROGRESSO® Red Wine Vinegar, divided**
- **¾ teaspoon PROGRESSO® Garlic Puree, divided**
- **4 (1½-inch-thick) beef fillets or strip steaks (about ½ to ¾ pound *each*)**
- **1 can (19 ounces) PROGRESSO® Chick Peas, drained**
- **¾ cup sliced ripe olives**

1. In small bowl, combine 2 tablespoons olive oil, 2 tablespoons wine vinegar and ¼ teaspoon garlic puree.

2. Place beef fillets in glass baking dish. Pour olive oil mixture over fillets; cover. Refrigerate 2 hours, turning frequently.

3. In hot 12-inch skillet, cook fillets on both sides to desired doneness. Remove from skillet; keep warm.

4. Add remaining 3 tablespoons olive oil, 2 tablespoons wine vinegar and ½ teaspoon garlic puree to skillet; simmer 3 minutes, stirring occasionally.

5. Stir in chick peas and olives; simmer 1 minute. Serve over fillets.

Makes 4 servings

Prep time: 5 minutes
Chilling/cooling time: 2 hours
Cooking time: 10 minutes

Fillet of Beef Andrea

Steak di Sicilia

- **2 tablespoons olive or vegetable oil, divided**
- **1½ cups fresh bread crumbs (3 slices)**
- **1 clove garlic, finely chopped**
- **1 teaspoon dried oregano leaves**
- **1¼ cups CLASSICO® Di Sicilia (Ripe Olives & Mushrooms) Pasta Sauce**
- **¼ cup freshly grated Parmesan cheese**
- **4 to 6 anchovy fillets, drained and chopped**
- **4 (4- to 6-ounce) beef tenderloin filets, lightly seasoned with salt and pepper**

In large skillet, heat *1 tablespoon* oil; add bread crumbs, garlic and oregano. Over medium-high heat, cook and stir until crumbs are golden. In medium bowl, combine crumb mixture, pasta sauce, cheese and anchovies; mix well. In same skillet, heat remaining *1 tablespoon* oil. Over medium-high heat, brown filets on both sides; reduce heat. Top each filet with one-fourth crumb mixture; cover. Cook 5 minutes or until heated through and filets are desired doneness. Refrigerate leftovers. *Makes 4 servings*

Lamb Chops with Herbed Peppercorn Sauce

4 loin lamb chops (about 1 pound)
1 teaspoon vegetable oil
½ cup beef broth
¼ cup GREY POUPON® Specialty
    Mustard: Peppercorn
1 teaspoon dried basil leaves

In large skillet, over medium-high heat, brown lamb chops in oil. Mix broth, mustard and basil; pour over lamb chops. Cover; cook over medium heat for 5 to 10 minutes until lamb is tender. Serve immediately.   *Makes 4 servings*

Citrus Veal Majorca

1 to 1½ pounds veal cutlets
4 to 6 very thin slices mild cured
    ham
2 Florida oranges, peeled and
    sectioned
1 egg, lightly beaten
½ cup milk
½ cup fine dry bread crumbs
1 teaspoon salt
½ teaspoon ground black pepper
6 tablespoons olive oil
1 small onion, chopped
1 cup Florida orange juice, divided
2 tablespoons cornstarch
½ cup dry sherry
½ teaspoon grated orange peel
1 Florida orange, peeled and sliced
    (optional)

Pound veal slices to ¼-inch thickness. (Ham and veal slices should be about the same size.) Place 1 slice ham on each veal slice. Place 3 orange sections in center of each; roll up and fasten with wooden picks.

Beat together egg and milk in small bowl. Combine bread crumbs, salt and black pepper in shallow dish. Dip each veal roll in egg mixture; roll in bread crumb mixture to coat.

Heat oil in large skillet over medium heat; cook veal rolls 20 to 25 minutes until lightly browned on all sides. Remove to paper towels; drain. Place on warm serving dish; cover and keep warm.

Cook and stir onion in same skillet until translucent; add ¾ cup orange juice. Bring to a boil. Stir cornstarch into remaining ¼ cup orange juice; stir into onion mixture until blended. Bring to a boil. Add dry sherry and orange peel; mix well. Serve sauce over veal rolls. Garnish platter with orange slices, if desired.   *Makes 4 to 6 servings*

*Favorite recipe from **Florida Department of Citrus***

Pork Cutlets Genovese

Spicy mustard adds a burst of flavor to these easy-to-prepare breaded cutlets.

¼ cup sour cream
2 tablespoons Dijon-style mustard
1 pound pork cutlets
⅔ cup PROGRESSO® Italian Style
    Bread Crumbs
3 tablespoons PROGRESSO®
    Olive Oil

1. In small bowl, combine sour cream and mustard.

2. Dip pork into sour cream mixture; coat with bread crumbs.

3. In large skillet, heat olive oil. Add pork; cook 10 to 15 minutes or until browned on both sides and pork is no longer pink in center.   *Makes 4 servings*

Prep time: 10 minutes
Cooking time: 15 minutes

Veal Parmesan

4 veal cutlets, cut ⅜ inch thick
   (about 4 ounces *each*)
4 tablespoons olive oil, divided
1 small red bell pepper, finely
   chopped
1 medium onion, finely chopped
1 rib celery, finely chopped
1 clove garlic, minced
1 can (14½ ounces) whole peeled
   tomatoes, undrained and finely
   chopped
1 cup chicken broth
1 tablespoon tomato paste
1 tablespoon chopped fresh parsley
1 teaspoon sugar
¾ teaspoon dried basil leaves,
   crushed
½ teaspoon salt
⅛ teaspoon black pepper
1 egg
¼ cup all-purpose flour
⅔ cup fine dry bread crumbs
2 tablespoons butter or margarine
1½ cups shredded mozzarella cheese
   (about 6 ounces)
⅔ cup freshly grated Parmesan cheese
   Fresh basil leaves, for garnish
   Hot cooked pasta (optional)

Pound veal with meat mallet to ¼-inch thickness. Pat dry with paper towels; set aside.

Heat 1 tablespoon oil in medium saucepan over medium heat. Cook and stir bell pepper, onion, celery and garlic in hot oil 5 minutes. Stir in tomatoes and juice, broth, tomato paste, parsley, sugar, dried basil, salt and black pepper. Cover and simmer over low heat 20 minutes. Uncover and cook over medium heat 20 minutes more or until sauce thickens, stirring frequently; set aside.

Beat egg in shallow bowl; spread flour and bread crumbs on separate plates. Dip reserved veal cutlets to coat both sides evenly, first in flour, then in egg, then in bread crumbs. Press crumb coating firmly onto veal. Heat butter and 2 tablespoons oil in large skillet over medium-high heat. Add veal. Cook 3 minutes per side or until browned.

Preheat oven to 350°F. Remove veal with slotted spatula to ungreased 13 × 9-inch baking dish. Sprinkle mozzarella cheese evenly over veal. Spoon reserved tomato mixture evenly over cheese. Sprinkle Parmesan cheese over tomato mixture. Drizzle remaining 1 tablespoon oil over top. Bake, uncovered, 25 minutes or until veal is tender and cheese is golden. Garnish, if desired. Serve with pasta.

Makes 4 servings

Tuscany Sausage and Rice Skillet

¾ pound Italian sausage, cut into
   1-inch slices, casings removed
1 medium onion, cut into thin
   wedges
1 clove garlic, minced
1½ cups thin red and green bell
   pepper strips
1⅓ cups chicken broth
¼ teaspoon salt
1½ cups UNCLE BEN'S®
   CONVERTED® Brand–Fast
   Cooking Rice
2 tablespoons grated Parmesan
   cheese

Cook sausage with onion and garlic in 10-inch skillet until sausage is cooked through. Pour off all but 1 tablespoon drippings. Add pepper strips, broth and salt; bring to a boil. Stir in rice; cover and remove from heat. Let stand 5 minutes or until all liquid is absorbed. Sprinkle with cheese.

Makes 4 servings

Veal Parmesan

Italian Meat Pie

1½ pounds ground beef
1 medium onion, chopped
1 envelope LIPTON® Recipe
   Secrets™ Italian Herb with
   Tomato Soup Mix*
¾ cup water
1 cup fresh bread crumbs
¼ cup grated Parmesan cheese
1 refrigerated pie crust or pastry for
   single-crust pie

Preheat oven to 350°F. In 10-inch skillet, brown ground beef with onion; drain. Blend Italian herb with tomato soup mix with water; stir into beef mixture. Bring to a boil. Remove from heat, then stir in bread crumbs and cheese. Turn into greased 9-inch pie plate; top with crust, sealing edges tightly. Pierce crust with fork. Bake 25 minutes or until crust is golden.   *Makes about 6 servings*

*Also terrific with Lipton® Recipe Secrets™ Onion-Mushroom or Beefy Onion Soup Mix.

Italian Meat Pie

Breaded Veal Piccata

1 pound veal scaloppine, sliced ⅜ inch thick and pounded to ¼-inch thickness
2 eggs, lightly beaten
1¼ cups PROGRESSO® Italian Style Bread Crumbs
6 tablespoons PROGRESSO® Olive Oil, divided
2 tablespoons butter
1½ tablespoons all-purpose flour
¼ teaspoon salt
¼ teaspoon ground black pepper
¾ cup chicken broth
⅔ cup dry white wine
1 tablespoon freshly squeezed lemon juice

1. Dip veal into eggs; coat with bread crumbs. Place veal on platter; freeze 5 minutes or refrigerate 30 minutes.

2. In large skillet, heat 3 tablespoons olive oil over medium heat. Add half of the veal; brown 2 minutes on each side. Remove from skillet; keep warm. Repeat with remaining olive oil and veal.

3. Remove drippings and any remaining oil from skillet. Melt butter in skillet. Stir in flour, salt and pepper; cook 1 minute. Gradually add chicken broth, wine and lemon juice, stirring constantly until mixture comes to a boil and thickens slightly; boil 1 minute.

4. Return veal to skillet; simmer 2 to 3 minutes or until thoroughly heated.
Makes 4 servings

Prep time: 25 minutes
Chilling time: 30 minutes
Cooking time: 15 minutes

Note: 1 pound boneless, skinless chicken breast halves, pounded to ¼-inch thickness, may be substituted for veal.

Lamb Tetrazzini

2 tablespoons butter or margarine
1 small onion, diced (about ¼ cup)
¼ cup all-purpose flour
2¾ cups low fat milk
1 can (4 ounces) sliced mushrooms, undrained
½ teaspoon salt
¼ teaspoon black pepper
¼ cup grated Parmesan cheese
1 package (8 ounces) linguine, cooked according to package directions and drained
2 cups cooked fresh American lamb cubes (leg or shoulder)
Topping (recipe follows)

Melt butter in medium skillet over medium-high heat; add onion. Cook and stir until tender but not brown. Sprinkle flour over onion; stir in milk gradually, stirring constantly. Add mushrooms with liquid, salt and black pepper. Cook over medium heat until slightly thickened. Stir in Parmesan cheese. Remove from heat.

Preheat oven to 350°F. Mix cooked linguine, sauce mixture and lamb in large bowl. Spoon into greased 12 × 8-inch casserole. Sprinkle with Topping. Bake 25 to 30 minutes until bubbling and slightly browned on top.
Makes 8 servings

Topping: Remove crusts from 4 slices bread; crumble bread. Combine bread crumbs with 2 tablespoons melted butter or margarine. (For easy soft bread crumbs, spread softened margarine over bread slices and process briefly in food processor.)

*Favorite recipe from **American Lamb Council***

Veal Scaloppine

Veal Scaloppine

4 veal cutlets, cut ⅜ inch thick (about
    4 ounces *each*)
¼ cup butter or margarine
½ pound fresh mushrooms, thinly
    sliced
2 tablespoons olive oil
1 small onion, finely chopped
¼ cup dry sherry
2 teaspoons all-purpose flour
½ cup beef broth
¼ teaspoon salt
⅛ teaspoon black pepper
2 tablespoons heavy or whipping
    cream
    Fresh bay leaf and marjoram
    sprigs, for garnish
    Hot cooked pasta (optional)

Pound veal with meat mallet to ¼-inch thickness. Pat dry with paper towels; set aside.

Heat butter in large skillet over medium heat until melted and bubbly. Cook and stir mushrooms in hot butter 3 to 4 minutes until light brown. Remove mushrooms with slotted spoon to small bowl; set aside.

Add oil to butter remaining in skillet; heat over medium heat. Add veal; cook 2 to 3 minutes per side until light brown. Remove veal to plate; set aside. Add onion to same skillet; cook and stir 2 to 3 minutes until soft. Stir sherry into onion mixture. Bring to a boil over medium-high heat; boil 15 seconds. Stir in flour; cook and stir 30 seconds. Remove from heat; stir in broth. Bring to a boil over medium heat, stirring constantly. Stir in reserved mushrooms, salt and black pepper. Add reserved veal to sauce mixture; reduce heat to low. Cover and simmer 8 minutes or until veal is tender. Remove from heat. Push veal to one side of skillet. Stir cream into sauce mixture; mix well. Cook over low heat until heated through. Garnish, if desired. Serve immediately with pasta.

Makes 4 servings

Tenderloins with Roasted Garlic Sauce

2 whole garlic bulbs, separated but
    not peeled (about 5 ounces)
⅔ cup A.1.® Steak Sauce, divided
¼ cup dry red wine
¼ cup finely chopped onion
4 (4- to 6-ounce) beef tenderloin
    steaks

Preheat oven to 500°F. Arrange unpeeled garlic cloves on baking sheet. Bake 15 to 20 minutes or until garlic is soft. Cool. Squeeze garlic pulp from skins; chop pulp slightly. In small saucepan, combine garlic pulp, ½ cup steak sauce, wine and onion. Bring to a boil; reduce heat and simmer for 5 minutes. Keep warm.

Grill or broil steaks 4 inches from heat source for 5 minutes on each side for rare or until desired doneness, brushing with remaining steak sauce occasionally. Serve steak with prepared garlic sauce.

Makes 4 servings

Sausage Pizza Rice

1 can (10¾ ounces) condensed
    chicken broth
1 cup UNCLE BEN'S®
    CONVERTED® Brand Rice
1 cup water
1 can (8 ounces) pizza sauce (¾ cup)
1 package (3 to 4 ounces) sliced
    pepperoni
1 can (4 ounces) mushroom stems
    and pieces, drained
½ cup chopped onion
1 teaspoon fennel seeds
½ cup chopped green bell pepper
½ cup (2 ounces) shredded Monterey
    Jack cheese

Combine all ingredients except green
pepper and cheese in 10-inch skillet.
Bring to a boil; reduce heat. Cover and
simmer 20 minutes. Stir in green pepper;
remove from heat. Let stand covered 5
minutes or until all liquid is absorbed.
Sprinkle with cheese. *Makes 5 servings*

Wine & Rosemary Lamb Skewers

1 cup dry red wine
¼ cup olive oil
3 cloves garlic, cut into slivers
1 tablespoon chopped fresh thyme *or*
    1 teaspoon dried thyme leaves,
    crushed
1 tablespoon chopped fresh
    rosemary *or* 1 teaspoon dried
    rosemary leaves, crushed
2 pounds boneless lamb, cut into
    1-inch cubes
   Salt and black pepper to taste
4 or 5 sprigs fresh rosemary
    (optional)
   Grilled Bread (recipe follows)

Combine wine, oil, garlic, thyme and
rosemary in shallow glass dish or large
resealable plastic food storage bag. Add
lamb; cover dish or close bag. Marinate
lamb in the refrigerator up to 12 hours,
turning several times. Remove lamb from
marinade; discard marinade. Thread
lamb onto 6 long metal skewers. Season
with salt and black pepper.

Oil hot grid to help prevent sticking. Grill
lamb, on a covered grill, over medium
KINGSFORD® briquets, 8 to 12 minutes,
turning once or twice. Remove grill cover
and throw rosemary onto coals the last 4
to 5 minutes of cooking, if desired. Move
skewers to side of grid to keep warm
while bread is toasting. Garnish, if
desired. *Makes 6 servings*

Grilled Bread

¼ cup olive oil
2 tablespoons red wine vinegar
1 baguette (about 12 inches long),
    sliced lengthwise, then cut into
    pieces
   Salt and freshly ground black
    pepper

Mix oil and vinegar in cup; brush over
cut surfaces of bread. Season lightly with
salt and black pepper. Grill bread, cut
side down, on an uncovered grill, over
medium Kingsford® briquets until lightly
toasted. *Makes 6 servings*

Wine & Rosemary Lamb Skewers

POULTRY

Chicken & Pasta Sicilian

4 to 6 boneless chicken breast halves
Salt and pepper
Flour
Paprika
3 tablespoons vegetable or olive oil
½ (1-pound) package CREAMETTE®
Spaghetti or Fettuccini, cooked
according to package directions
and drained
⅓ cup chopped walnuts, toasted
¼ cup margarine or butter, melted
1 (26-ounce) jar CLASSICO®
Di Sicilia (Ripe Olives &
Mushrooms) Pasta Sauce, heated

Season chicken lightly with salt and
pepper, then coat with flour and sprinkle
with paprika. In large skillet, heat oil.
Cook chicken breasts until no longer pink
in center and golden on both sides. Slice
crosswise; set aside. Toss together hot
cooked pasta, walnuts and margarine. To
serve, arrange chicken and pasta on plate.
Spoon hot pasta sauce over chicken.
Garnish with fresh basil, if desired. Serve
immediately. Refrigerate leftovers.

Makes 4 to 6 servings

Chicken Cutlets Parmesan

6 broiler-fryer chicken breast halves,
boned and skinned
Salt and black pepper to taste
2 tablespoons olive oil
1 jar (14 ounces) spaghetti sauce with
mushrooms
¼ cup sliced black olives
2 tablespoons grated Parmesan
cheese
Hot cooked spaghetti

With meat mallet, pound chicken breasts
to ½-inch thickness. Sprinkle salt and
black pepper over chicken. In large
skillet, heat oil over medium-high heat
until hot. Add chicken; cook about 8
minutes or until chicken is brown on
both sides. Drain off excess fat. Spoon
spaghetti sauce over chicken; top with
sliced olives. Cook over medium heat
about 5 minutes or until chicken is fork-
tender and sauce is bubbly. Sprinkle
cheese over all. Cover and heat 2 minutes
or until cheese melts. Serve with hot
spaghetti. *Makes 4 servings*

*Favorite recipe from **Delmarva Poultry Industry, Inc.***

Chicken & Pasta Sicilian

Pollo alla Firenze

2 cups *plus* 2 tablespoons dry sherry, divided
3 whole chicken breasts, split and boned
3 tablespoons olive oil
2 cloves garlic, minced
3 cups fresh spinach leaves, shredded
2 cups coarsely chopped mushrooms
1 cup grated carrots
⅓ cup sliced green onions
  Salt and black pepper to taste
1½ cups prepared Italian salad dressing
1 cup Italian seasoned dry bread crumbs
⅓ cup grated Romano cheese
  Steamed fresh asparagus (optional)
  Parsley sprigs and carrot strips, for garnish

Pour 2 cups sherry into large shallow dish. Add chicken, turning to coat. Cover; marinate in refrigerator 3 hours.

Heat oil in large skillet over medium heat. Add garlic, spinach, mushrooms, grated carrots, green onions, salt, black

Pollo alla Firenze

pepper and remaining 2 tablespoons sherry. Cook and stir 3 to 5 minutes or until spinach is completely wilted; cool spinach mixture.

Place dressing in another shallow dish; set aside. Combine bread crumbs with Romano cheese in shallow dish; set aside.

Preheat oven to 375°F. Remove chicken from marinade; discard marinade. Slice a pocket into side of each chicken breast. Fill pockets in chicken with spinach mixture. Secure pockets with wooden picks to enclose mixture.

Coat each filled chicken breast with dressing, shaking off excess. Roll each chicken breast in bread crumb mixture to coat. Place chicken in single layer in greased 13×9-inch baking pan. Drizzle with remaining dressing. Cover; bake 15 minutes. Uncover; bake 10 minutes more or until chicken is no longer pink. Serve with asparagus, if desired, and garnish with parsley and carrot.

Makes 6 servings

Turkey Rolls Italiano

½ cup sliced California ripe olives
2½ cups dried Italian style bread crumbs, divided
¼ cup tomato sauce
1½ cups (6 ounces) shredded mozzarella cheese
1 tablespoon olive oil
½ cup minced onion
¼ cup minced bell pepper
1 teaspoon minced garlic
2 pounds turkey breast slices (about 4 ounces *each*)
2 eggs, beaten
1 cup milk

Combine olives, ½ cup bread crumbs, tomato sauce and cheese in large bowl. Heat oil in small skillet over medium-high heat; add onion, pepper and garlic. Cook and stir until soft. Remove from heat and cool. Add to olive mixture. Toss gently. Pound turkey slices to ¼-inch thickness. Spread olive mixture evenly over top of each slice. Roll tightly. Secure with wooden picks. Cover and refrigerate.

Preheat oven to 350°F. Spread remaining 2 cups bread crumbs on plate. Combine eggs and milk in shallow bowl; dip turkey rolls into egg mixture. Roll in bread crumbs and press firmly to coat. Place in square baking dish. Bake 30 to 40 minutes until turkey is cooked through and no longer pink.   *Makes 6 servings*

*Favorite recipe from **California Olive Industry***

Chicken Scaparella

Chicken Scaparella

2 slices bacon, coarsely chopped
2 tablespoons FILIPPO BERIO®
    Olive Oil
1 large chicken breast, split in half
½ cup quartered mushrooms
1 clove garlic, minced
1 cup *plus* 2 tablespoons chicken
    broth, divided
2 tablespoons red wine vinegar
8 small white onions, peeled
4 small new potatoes, cut into halves
½ teaspoon salt
⅛ teaspoon black pepper
1 tablespoon all-purpose flour
    Chopped fresh parsley

Cook bacon in skillet until crisp. Remove bacon with slotted spoon; set aside. Pour off drippings. Add oil and chicken. Brown well on all sides. Add mushrooms and garlic. Cook and stir several minutes, stirring occasionally. Add 1 cup broth, vinegar, onions, potatoes, salt and black pepper. Cover and simmer 35 minutes until chicken and vegetables are tender.

To thicken sauce, dissolve flour in remaining 2 tablespoons chicken broth. Stir into sauce. Cook, stirring until thickened and smooth. Garnish with reserved bacon and parsley.

Makes 2 servings

Chicken Pesto Mozzarella

Forty-Clove Chicken Filice

1 broiler-fryer chicken, cut into
  serving pieces (3 pounds)
40 cloves fresh garlic, peeled and left
  whole
½ cup dry white wine
¼ cup dry vermouth
¼ cup olive oil
4 ribs celery, thinly sliced
2 tablespoons finely chopped fresh
  parsley
2 teaspoons dried basil leaves,
  crushed
1 teaspoon dried oregano leaves,
  crushed
  Pinch of crushed red pepper
1 lemon
  Salt and black pepper to taste

Preheat oven to 375°F. Place chicken
pieces, skin sides up, in single layer in
shallow baking pan. Combine all
remaining ingredients except lemon, salt
and black pepper in medium bowl; mix
well. Sprinkle garlic mixture over chicken

pieces. Remove peel from lemon in thin
strips; place peel throughout pan.
Squeeze juice from lemon and pour over
top. Season with salt and black pepper.
Cover pan with foil. Bake 40 minutes.
Remove foil and bake 15 minutes more.
Garnish as desired.

Makes 4 to 6 servings

*Favorite recipe from **Christopher Ranch of Gilroy***

Chicken Pesto Mozzarella

6 to 8 ounces linguine or corkscrew
  pasta
4 half boneless chicken breasts,
  skinned
1 tablespoon olive oil
1 can (14½ ounces) DEL MONTE®
  Pasta Style Chunky Tomatoes
½ medium onion, chopped
⅓ cup sliced ripe olives
4 teaspoons pesto sauce*
¼ cup shredded skim-milk
  mozzarella cheese

Cook pasta according to package
directions; drain. Meanwhile, season
chicken with salt and pepper, if desired.
In large skillet, brown chicken in oil over
medium-high heat. Add tomatoes, onion
and olives; bring to boil. Cover and cook
8 minutes over medium heat. Remove
cover; cook over medium-high heat about
8 minutes or until chicken is no longer
pink. Spread 1 teaspoon pesto over each
breast; top with cheese. Cook, covered,
until cheese melts. Serve over pasta.

Makes 4 servings

*Available frozen or refrigerated at the
supermarket.

Prep time: 10 minutes
Cook time: 25 minutes

Pollo Pignoli
(Chicken with Pine Nuts)

½ cup PROGRESSO® Grated
    Parmesan Cheese
½ cup PROGRESSO® Plain Bread
    Crumbs
4 boneless, skinless chicken breast
    halves
    Salt and ground black pepper
2 eggs, lightly beaten
1 tablespoon PROGRESSO®
    Olive Oil
2 jars (7 ounces *each*) PROGRESSO®
    Roasted Peppers (red), drained
    and sliced into strips
⅓ cup PROGRESSO® Imported
    Pignoli (pine nuts)

1. Preheat oven to 375°F.

2. In shallow dish, combine Parmesan cheese and bread crumbs.

3. Season chicken with salt and black pepper.

4. Dip chicken into eggs; coat with cheese mixture. Place chicken on lightly greased baking sheet.

5. Bake 20 to 25 minutes or until chicken is no longer pink in center. Keep warm.

6. In small skillet, heat olive oil over medium heat. Add roasted peppers and pine nuts. Cook until pine nuts begin to brown, stirring frequently; drain. Serve over chicken. *Makes 4 servings*

Prep time: 15 minutes
Cooking time: 20 minutes

Drumsticks Confetti

6 PERDUE® Chicken Drumsticks
½ cup all-purpose flour
¼ teaspoon salt or to taste
⅛ teaspoon black pepper or to taste
3 tablespoons vegetable oil
½ cup dry white wine
1 medium onion, chopped
1 clove garlic, crushed
½ teaspoon dried thyme leaves,
    crushed
2 cups chicken broth
1 container (8 ounces) tomatoes
¾ cup uncooked converted rice
2 tablespoons chopped fresh parsley
    or 1 teaspoon dried parsley flakes

Rinse drumsticks and pat dry. Combine flour, salt and black pepper on waxed paper. Roll drumsticks in mixture to coat.

Heat oil in Dutch oven or deep skillet with cover over medium-high heat. Add drumsticks and brown, turning several times to cook evenly. Add wine, onion, garlic and thyme; bring to a boil. Cover; reduce heat to low and simmer 20 minutes. Add all remaining ingredients except parsley. Stir; cover and simmer 35 minutes more or until chicken and rice are cooked and tender. Sprinkle with parsley. Serve immediately.

Makes 3 to 4 servings

Drumsticks Confetti

Chicken Cacciatore

1 broiler-fryer chicken (3 to
    3½ pounds), cut into 8 pieces
1 tablespoon olive oil
4 ounces fresh mushrooms, finely
    chopped
1 medium onion, chopped
1 clove garlic, minced
½ cup dry white wine
4½ teaspoons white wine vinegar
½ cup chicken broth
1 teaspoon dried basil leaves,
    crushed
½ teaspoon dried marjoram leaves,
    crushed
½ teaspoon salt
⅛ teaspoon black pepper
1 can (14½ ounces) whole peeled
    tomatoes, undrained
8 Italian- or Greek-style black olives
1 tablespoon chopped fresh parsley
  Hot cooked pasta
  Fresh marjoram leaves, for garnish

Rinse chicken; drain and pat dry with paper towels. Heat oil in large skillet over medium heat. Add half the chicken pieces in single layer to hot oil. Cook 8 minutes per side or until chicken is brown; remove chicken with slotted spatula to Dutch oven. Repeat with remaining chicken pieces; set aside.

Add mushrooms and onion to drippings in skillet. Cook and stir over medium heat 5 minutes or until onion is soft. Add garlic; cook and stir 30 seconds. Add wine and vinegar; cook over medium-high heat 5 minutes or until liquid is almost evaporated. Stir in broth, basil, marjoram, salt and black pepper. Remove from heat. Press tomatoes and juice through sieve into onion mixture; discard seeds. Bring to a boil over medium-high heat; boil, uncovered, 2 minutes. Pour tomato-onion mixture over chicken. Bring to a boil; reduce heat to low. Cover and simmer 25 minutes or until chicken is tender and juices run clear when pierced with fork. Remove chicken with slotted spatula to heated serving dish; keep warm. Bring tomato-onion mixture to a boil over medium-high heat; boil, uncovered, 5 minutes. Cut olives in half; remove and discard pits. Add olives and parsley to sauce; cook 1 minute more. Pour sauce over chicken and pasta. Garnish, if desired.

Makes 4 to 6 servings

Venetian Pot Luck

4 medium baking potatoes, cut into
    wedges
2 cloves garlic, minced
½ teaspoon salt
1 *each* red and green bell pepper,
    sliced
1 can (28 ounces) chopped Italian
    tomatoes, drained
1 pound Italian sausage links, cut
    into 2-inch segments
6 HUDSON® split chicken breasts
1 tablespoon oil
½ teaspoon lemon pepper

Preheat oven to 350°F. Arrange potatoes in large roasting pan. Sprinkle with garlic and salt. Layer peppers, tomatoes and sausage over potatoes. Arrange chicken on top. Brush chicken with oil and sprinkle lemon pepper on top. Bake, uncovered, about 45 to 55 minutes until internal temperature of chicken reaches 185°F on meat thermometer.

Makes 6 servings

Chicken Cacciatore

Balsamic Chicken and Peppers

2 small whole chicken breasts, split, boned and skinned
1 tablespoon flour
1 teaspoon ground coriander
½ teaspoon salt (optional)
1 tablespoon olive oil
1 small onion, cut into thin wedges
2 cloves garlic, minced
1 small red bell pepper, cut into short, thin strips
½ cup reduced sodium chicken broth
½ cup no salt added tomato sauce
2 tablespoons balsamic vinegar,* divided
1½ teaspoons dried basil leaves, crushed
1½ cups UNCLE BEN'S® CONVERTED® Brand–Fast Cooking Rice
¼ cup thinly sliced green onions with tops
Freshly ground black pepper

Pound chicken to ½-inch thickness. Combine flour, coriander and salt, if desired, in small bowl. Coat chicken with flour mixture. Brown chicken in oil in 10-inch skillet over medium-high heat 2 minutes per side. Remove and set aside. Add onion, garlic and red pepper to skillet; cook and stir 2 minutes. Add broth, tomato sauce, 1 tablespoon vinegar and basil. Return chicken to skillet; spoon sauce over. Cover and cook over low heat 8 minutes. Meanwhile, cook rice according to package directions, adding green onions with rice. When chicken is cooked through, stir in remaining 1 tablespoon vinegar; cook uncovered over high heat until sauce has thickened. Serve chicken over rice; top with sauce. Sprinkle with black pepper to taste.

Makes 4 servings

*Red wine vinegar may be substituted for balsamic vinegar. Decrease amount to 1 tablespoon; add to skillet with tomato sauce.

Turkey Cannellini Sauté

1½ to 2 pounds smoked turkey breast
2 tablespoons olive oil
1 medium onion, chopped
½ green bell pepper, chopped
1 clove garlic, minced
1 medium head Napa cabbage, thinly sliced
½ medium head red cabbage, thinly sliced
2 tablespoons chopped fresh rosemary *or* ¾ teaspoon dried rosemary leaves, crushed
⅔ cup chicken stock or broth
2 tablespoons red wine
2 cans (15 ounces *each*) cannellini beans, drained (white kidney beans)
1 can (28 ounces) plum tomatoes, drained and chopped
Salt and black pepper to taste

Cut turkey breast into 1-inch cubes. Heat oil in large skillet over medium-high heat. Add onion, green pepper and garlic; cook and stir about 2 minutes or until soft. Add turkey cubes, cabbages and rosemary; cook and stir 3 minutes. Add chicken stock, red wine, beans, tomatoes, salt and black pepper; simmer 5 minutes. Serve with pasta or rice in cabbage leaf cups, if desired. *Makes 8 servings*

*Favorite recipe from **California Poultry Industry Federation***

Chicken Rosemary

2 boneless skinless chicken breast
  halves
1 teaspoon margarine
1 teaspoon olive oil
  Salt and black pepper to taste
½ small onion, sliced
1 clove garlic, minced
½ teaspoon rosemary, crumbled
⅛ teaspoon ground cinnamon
½ cup DOLE® Pine-Orange-Guava
  Juice
1 tablespoon orange marmalade
2 cups sliced DOLE® Carrots

• Pound chicken to ½-inch thickness. Heat margarine and oil in medium skillet over medium-high heat. Add chicken and brown on both sides. Sprinkle with salt and black pepper.

• Stir in onion, garlic, rosemary and cinnamon. Cook until onion is soft.

• Blend in juice and marmalade. Spoon over chicken. Reduce heat; cover and simmer 10 minutes.

• Stir in carrots. Cover; simmer 5 minutes or until carrots are crisp-tender.

Makes 2 servings

Prep time: 10 minutes
Cook time: 20 minutes

Chicken Rosemary

Chicken Parmesan

4 half boneless chicken breasts, skinned
2 cans (14½ ounces *each*) DEL MONTE® Italian Recipe Stewed Tomatoes
2 tablespoons cornstarch
½ teaspoon dried oregano or basil, crushed
¼ teaspoon hot pepper sauce (optional)
¼ cup grated Parmesan cheese

Preheat oven to 425°F. Slightly flatten each chicken breast; place in 11×7-inch baking dish. Cover with foil; bake 20 minutes or until chicken is no longer pink. Remove foil; drain. Meanwhile, in large saucepan, combine tomatoes, cornstarch, oregano and pepper sauce. Stir to dissolve cornstarch. Cook, stirring constantly, until thickened. Pour sauce over chicken; top with cheese. Return to oven; bake, uncovered, 5 minutes or until cheese is melted. Garnish with chopped parsley and serve with rice or pasta, if desired.   *Makes 4 servings*

Prep & Cook time: 30 minutes

Chicken Parmesan

Pollo alla Giardiniera
(Gardener's Style Chicken)

Crisp fried chicken strips add a crunchy touch to this tossed salad.

⅓ cup all-purpose flour
⅛ teaspoon salt
⅛ teaspoon ground black pepper
4 boneless, skinless chicken breast halves
2 eggs, lightly beaten
¾ cup PROGRESSO® Italian Style Bread Crumbs
½ cup butter
6 tablespoons PROGRESSO® Olive Oil, divided
2 cups torn radicchio
2 cups torn romaine lettuce
1 cup chopped tomatoes
¼ cup PROGRESSO® Red Wine Vinegar

1. In shallow dish or pie plate, combine flour, salt and pepper.

2. Roll chicken in flour mixture; dip into eggs. Coat with bread crumbs.

3. In large skillet, heat butter and 2 tablespoons olive oil over medium heat. Add chicken; cook 10 minutes or until browned on both sides and no longer pink in center.

4. Remove chicken from skillet; cut into strips.

5. In large bowl, combine radicchio and lettuce; top with tomatoes and chicken.

6. In small bowl, whisk together remaining ¼ cup olive oil and vinegar; pour over salad. Toss gently.
                              Makes 4 servings

Prep time: 25 minutes

Chicken Marsala

4 boneless, skinless chicken breast
    halves
  Salt and black pepper
¼ cup all-purpose flour
2 tablespoons WESSON® Oil
3 cups sliced mushrooms
1 cup sliced onion
1 teaspoon minced garlic
1 (15-ounce) can HUNT'S® Ready
    Tomato Sauces Chunky Special
⅓ cup Marsala wine
¼ teaspoon sugar
½ teaspoon salt

Season chicken with salt and black pepper; coat lightly with flour. In large skillet, in hot oil, lightly brown chicken on both sides over medium-high heat; remove and set aside. Add mushrooms, onion and garlic to skillet; cook and stir until onion is tender. Stir in *remaining* ingredients. Return chicken to skillet; spoon sauce over to coat. Cover and simmer 15 minutes or until chicken is no longer pink in center.

Makes 4 servings

Turkey Picatta on Grilled Rolls

¼ cup lemon juice
¼ cup olive oil
2 tablespoons capers in liquid,
    chopped
2 cloves garlic, crushed
  Black pepper to taste
1 pound turkey breast slices
4 soft French rolls, cut lengthwise
    into halves
4 thin slices mozzarella or Swiss
    cheese (optional)
  Lettuce (optional)
  Red pepper slivers (optional)
  Additional capers (optional)

Turkey Picatta on Grilled Roll

Combine lemon juice, oil, chopped capers with liquid, garlic and black pepper in shallow glass dish or resealable plastic food storage bag. Add turkey; cover dish or close bag. Marinate in refrigerator several hours or overnight. Remove turkey from marinade; discard marinade.

Oil hot grid to help prevent sticking. Grill turkey, on an uncovered grill, over medium-hot KINGSFORD® briquets, 2 minutes until turkey is cooked through, turning once. Move cooked turkey slices to edge of grill to keep warm. Grill rolls, cut sides down, until toasted. Fill rolls with hot turkey slices, dividing equally. Add mozzarella to sandwiches, if desired. Serve with lettuce, red pepper and additional capers, if desired.

Makes 4 servings

Chicken Pomodoro

2 cloves garlic, finely minced
4 half boneless chicken breasts,
 skinned
⅛ teaspoon crushed red pepper flakes
 (optional)
1 tablespoon olive oil
1 can (14½ ounces) DEL MONTE®
 Italian Recipe Stewed Tomatoes
2 small zucchini, cut in half
 lengthwise and sliced crosswise
2 tablespoons thinly sliced fresh
 basil leaves *or* ½ teaspoon dried
 basil, crushed
⅓ cup whipping cream

Rub garlic over chicken. Sprinkle with
red pepper. Season with salt and black
pepper, if desired. In large skillet, brown
chicken in oil over medium-high heat.
Stir in tomatoes, zucchini and basil. Cook,
uncovered, over medium-high heat 15
minutes or until sauce is thickened and
chicken is no longer pink, stirring
occasionally. Stir in cream; heat through.
Do not boil.   *Makes 4 servings*

Prep time: 8 minutes
Cook time: 23 minutes

Chicken Milano

2 cloves garlic, minced
4 boneless skinless chicken breast
 halves
½ teaspoon dried basil, crushed
⅛ teaspoon crushed red pepper flakes
 (optional)
1 tablespoon olive oil
1 can (14½ ounces) DEL MONTE®
 Italian Style Stewed Tomatoes
1 can (16 ounces) DEL MONTE® Cut
 Green Italian Beans or Blue Lake
 Cut Green Beans, drained
¼ cup whipping cream

Rub garlic over chicken. Sprinkle with
basil and red pepper. Season to taste with
salt and black pepper, if desired. In
skillet, brown chicken in oil. Stir in
tomatoes. Cover and simmer 5 minutes.
Uncover and cook over medium heat, 8
to 10 minutes or until liquid is slightly
thickened and chicken is tender. Stir in
green beans and cream; heat through. *Do
not boil.*   *Makes 4 servings*

Chicken Italiano

1 can (20 ounces) chopped Italian
 peeled tomatoes, drained
½ cup tomato sauce
¼ cup red wine vinegar
1 *each* red and green bell pepper,
 chopped
½ cup onion, diced
1 clove garlic, crushed
½ teaspoon dried oregano leaves
4 to 6 HUDSON® boneless skinless
 chicken breast halves
1 egg, beaten
½ cup ricotta cheese
¼ cup sour cream
¼ cup fresh basil leaves, chopped
2 tablespoons grated Parmesan
 cheese
1 cup shredded mozzarella cheese

Preheat oven to 350°F. In medium
saucepan, combine first 7 ingredients.
Bring to a boil; reduce heat. Simmer 15
minutes, stirring occasionally. Pound
each breast to ¼-inch thickness. Combine
egg, ricotta, sour cream, basil and
Parmesan; spoon ¼ of mixture onto each
breast. Roll up and secure with wooden
picks. Spoon half the tomato mixture into
13×9-inch baking pan. Arrange chicken
on top. Pour remaining sauce over top.
Sprinkle with mozzarella. Bake 30 to 35
minutes until chicken is cooked through.
                Makes 4 to 6 servings

Chicken Pomodoro

Chicken Saltimbocca

Chicken Saltimbocca

**4 boneless, skinless chicken breast
    halves, pounded to ¼-inch
    thickness
4 slices (1 ounce *each*) ham
4 slices (½ ounce *each*) Swiss cheese
2 eggs, lightly beaten
¾ cup PROGRESSO® Italian Style
    Bread Crumbs
5 tablespoons PROGRESSO® Olive
    Oil, divided
¼ cup sliced green onions
1 clove garlic, minced
1 tablespoon all-purpose flour
⅓ cup chicken broth
¼ cup dry white wine**

1. Preheat oven to 350°F.

2. Top each chicken breast with 1 slice of ham and cheese. (If necessary, fold ham and cheese slices in half to fit onto top of each chicken piece.) Roll up each chicken breast, starting at short end; secure with toothpicks.

3. Dip chicken into eggs; coat with bread crumbs.

4. In large skillet, heat 3 tablespoons olive oil. Add chicken; cook 5 to 7 minutes or until browned on both sides.

5. Place chicken in lightly greased 8-inch square baking dish.

6. Bake 20 minutes or until chicken is no longer pink in center; remove toothpicks. Keep warm.

7. In large skillet, heat remaining 2 tablespoons olive oil. Add onions and garlic; cook 2 minutes or until tender, stirring occasionally. Stir in flour. Gradually stir in chicken broth and wine; bring to a boil. Serve over chicken.

Makes 4 servings

Prep time: 25 minutes
Cooking time: 20 minutes

Parmesan Chicken

**1 cup MIRACLE WHIP® Salad
    Dressing
½ cup (2 ounces) KRAFT® 100%
    Grated Parmesan Cheese
2 teaspoons dried oregano leaves
1 broiler-fryer chicken, cut up (3 to
    3½ pounds)**

• Heat oven to 375°F.

• Mix salad dressing, cheese and seasonings.

• Place chicken in 13×9-inch baking dish. Spread with salad dressing mixture.

• Bake 40 to 45 minutes or until cooked through.

Makes 4 servings

Chicken Tetrazzini

8 ounces uncooked long spaghetti,
    broken in half
3 tablespoons butter, divided
¼ cup all-purpose flour
1 teaspoon salt
½ teaspoon paprika
½ teaspoon celery salt
⅛ teaspoon black pepper
2 cups milk
1 cup chicken broth
3 cups chopped cooked chicken
1 can (4 ounces) mushrooms, drained
¼ cup pimiento strips
¾ cup grated Wisconsin Parmesan
    cheese, divided

Cook spaghetti according to package
directions; drain. Add 1 tablespoon
butter; stir until melted. Set aside. Melt
remaining 2 tablespoons butter in 3-quart
saucepan; whisk in flour, salt, paprika,
celery salt and black pepper until smooth.
Remove from heat; gradually stir in milk
and chicken broth. Cook over medium
heat until thickened, stirring constantly.
Add chicken, mushrooms, pimiento,
reserved spaghetti and ¼ cup Parmesan
cheese; heat through. Place chicken
mixture on ovenproof platter or in
shallow casserole; sprinkle remaining
½ cup Parmesan cheese over top. Broil
about 3 inches from heat source until
lightly browned.   *Makes 6 to 8 servings*

*Favorite recipe from **Wisconsin Milk Marketing
Board © 1994***

Sicilian Skillet Chicken

4 half boneless chicken breasts,
    skinned
6 tablespoons grated Parmesan
    cheese
3 tablespoons all-purpose flour
2 tablespoons olive oil
1 cup sliced mushrooms
½ medium onion, finely chopped
½ teaspoon dried rosemary, crushed
1 can (14½ ounces) DEL MONTE®
    Italian Recipe Stewed Tomatoes

Slightly flatten each chicken breast. Coat
breasts with 4 tablespoons cheese and
then flour. Season with salt and pepper, if
desired. Heat oil in large skillet over
medium-high heat. Cook chicken until no
longer pink, turning once. Remove to
serving dish; keep warm. In same skillet,
cook mushrooms, onion and rosemary
until tender. Add tomatoes; cook,
uncovered, over medium-high heat until
thickened. Spoon over chicken; top with
remaining 2 tablespoons cheese. Serve
with pasta and garnish with chopped
parsley, if desired.   *Makes 4 servings*

Prep time: 5 minutes
Cook time: 25 minutes

Sicilian Skillet Chicken

Surprisingly Simple Chicken Cacciatore

4 boneless skinless chicken breasts
  (4 ounces *each*), chunked
Salt and black pepper
Flour
Paprika
4 tablespoons olive oil, divided
2 cloves garlic, minced
1 (26-ounce) jar CLASSICO®
  Di Napoli (Tomato and Basil)
  Pasta Sauce
1 small green bell pepper, cut into
  thin strips
1 small red bell pepper, cut into thin
  strips
½ (1-pound) package CREAMETTE®
  Thin Spaghetti, uncooked
1 cup (4 ounces) shredded Provolone
  cheese

Season chicken with salt and black pepper, then coat with flour and sprinkle with paprika. In large skillet, heat 3 *tablespoons* oil. Brown chicken and garlic; drain. Stir in Classico® pasta sauce. Bring to a boil; reduce heat. Cover; simmer 20 minutes, adding green and red bell

Surprisingly Simple Chicken Cacciatore

peppers last 5 minutes. Prepare Creamette® thin spaghetti according to package directions; drain and toss with remaining *1 tablespoon* oil. Arrange on warm serving platter; top with hot chicken, sauce and cheese. Serve immediately. Refrigerate leftovers.

Makes 4 servings

Italian Country Chicken

This quick-to-prepare dish with a lively flavor is great for after work.

4 boneless, skinless chicken breast
  halves
3 tablespoons PROGRESSO® Italian
  Style Bread Crumbs
2 tablespoons PROGRESSO®
  Olive Oil
1 can (19 ounces) PROGRESSO®
  Minestrone Soup
2 tablespoons PROGRESSO® Red
  Wine Vinegar
⅛ teaspoon sugar
1 can (14 ounces) PROGRESSO®
  Artichoke Hearts, drained and
  halved
½ cup chopped fresh parsley

1. Lightly coat chicken on both sides with bread crumbs.

2. In large skillet, heat olive oil over medium heat. Add chicken; cook 15 minutes or until browned on both sides and no longer pink in center.

3. In small bowl, combine soup, vinegar and sugar. Pour over chicken; cover. Simmer 5 minutes.

4. Stir in artichoke hearts and parsley; heat thoroughly. Serve over hot pasta, if desired. *Makes 4 servings*

Prep time: 10 minutes
Cooking time: 25 minutes

Pizza Rice Casserole

1 bag SUCCESS® Rice
1 pound ground turkey or lean
    ground beef
½ cup chopped green bell pepper
½ cup chopped onion
1 jar (15½ ounces) pizza sauce
1 cup water
1 can (4 ounces) mushroom pieces,
    drained
¼ cup all-purpose flour
½ cup chopped turkey ham
½ teaspoon garlic salt
1 cup (4 ounces) shredded
    Mozzarella cheese

Prepare rice according to package
directions. Brown ground turkey with
green pepper and onion in large skillet or
saucepan, stirring occasionally to
separate turkey. Add rice, pizza sauce,
water, mushrooms, flour, ham and garlic
salt; heat thoroughly, stirring
occasionally. Sprinkle with cheese.

Makes 4 servings

Italian Vegetable Chicken

1 pound boneless skinless chicken
    breast halves
2 cloves garlic, pressed
2 teaspoons Italian herb seasoning
    Salt and black pepper to taste
1 egg white, beaten
½ cup all-purpose flour, divided
1 pound Italian sausage, cut into
    1-inch chunks
2 teaspoons olive oil (optional)
2 cups sliced mushrooms
1 large onion, chopped
1 DOLE® Red Bell Pepper, slivered
1 cup water
2 cups DOLE® Broccoli flowerets

Italian Vegetable Chicken

• Pound chicken to ¼-inch thickness with
flat side of meat mallet. Rub chicken with
garlic; sprinkle with herb seasoning, salt
and black pepper. Dip into egg white;
coat with flour. Set aside.

• In large skillet over medium-high heat,
brown sausage. Remove and pour off
drippings; set aside.

• Add chicken to same skillet, turning to
brown both sides. Remove to warm
platter. Add sausage to chicken. Keep
warm.

• Add olive oil to skillet if needed. Add
mushrooms, onion and red pepper; cook
and stir until onion is soft. Add any
remaining flour or 1 additional teaspoon
flour to skillet. Stir to blend. Continue
cooking to brown slightly. Stir in water.
Cook and stir 3 to 5 minutes until slightly
thickened. Add broccoli; heat through
until crisp-tender. Spoon over chicken.

Makes 6 servings

Prep time: 20 minutes
Cook time: 15 minutes

SEAFOOD

Grilled Fish Steaks with Tomato Basil Butter Sauce

Tomato Basil Butter Sauce
  (recipe follows)
4 fish steaks, such as halibut,
  swordfish, tuna or salmon
  (at least ¾ inch thick)
Olive oil
Salt and black pepper
Fresh basil leaves and summer
  squash slices, for garnish
Hot cooked seasoned noodles
  (optional)

Prepare Tomato Basil Butter Sauce; set aside. Rinse fish; pat dry with paper towels. Brush one side of fish lightly with oil; season with salt and pepper.

Oil hot grid to help prevent sticking. Grill fish, oil side down, on covered grill, over medium KINGSFORD® briquets, 6 to 10 minutes. Halfway through cooking time, brush top with oil and season with salt and black pepper, then turn and continue grilling until fish turns from translucent to opaque throughout. (Grilling time depends on the thickness of fish; allow 3 to 5 minutes for each ½ inch of thickness.) Serve with Tomato Basil Butter Sauce. Garnish with basil leaves and squash slices. Serve with noodles, if desired.

Makes 4 servings

Tomato Basil Butter Sauce

4 tablespoons butter or margarine,
  softened, divided
1½ cups chopped seeded peeled
  tomatoes (about 1 pound)
½ teaspoon sugar
1 clove garlic, minced
  Salt and black pepper
1½ tablespoons finely chopped fresh
  basil

Melt 1 tablespoon butter in a small skillet. Add tomato, sugar and garlic. Cook over medium-low heat, stirring frequently, until liquid evaporates and mixture thickens. Remove pan from heat; stir in remaining 3 tablespoons butter until mixture has saucelike consistency. Season to taste with salt and black pepper, then stir in basil. *Makes about 1 cup*

*Grilled Fish Steak with
Tomato Basil Butter Sauce*

Broiled Shellfish Venetian-Style

An easy way to please seafood lovers . . . shrimp and scallops, crispy coated and broiled on skewers. Serve with a squeeze of lemon.

1 cup PROGRESSO® Italian Style Bread Crumbs
⅓ cup PROGRESSO® Olive Oil
1 pound peeled and deveined uncooked shrimp
1 pound sea scallops
Lemon wedges

1. In small bowl, combine bread crumbs and olive oil.

2. In large bowl or large plastic bag, combine shrimp and scallops. Add bread crumb mixture; toss gently to coat shellfish. Cover. Refrigerate 1 hour.

3. Preheat broiler. Thread shellfish onto skewers. Place on greased rack of broiler pan.

Broiled Shellfish Venetian-Style

4. Broil, 3 inches from heat source, 5 minutes or until crisp and golden brown on both sides, turning every 2 minutes. *Do not overcook.* Serve with lemon wedges.   *Makes 6 servings*

Prep time: 15 minutes
Chilling/cooling time: 1 hour
Cooking time: 5 minutes

Variation: Thread skewers with fresh mushrooms, cherry tomatoes, onion chunks and parboiled bell pepper chunks. Broil, 3 inches from heat source, 3 minutes or until vegetables are tender, turning every minute.

Shrimp Milano

1 package (12 ounces) frozen cooked shrimp, thawed, drained
2 cups sliced mushrooms
1 cup green *or* red pepper strips
1 clove garlic, minced
¼ cup (½ stick) PARKAY® Spread Sticks
¾ pound VELVEETA® Pasteurized Process Cheese Spread, cubed
¼ cup milk
½ teaspoon dried basil leaves
⅓ cup (1½ ounces) KRAFT® 100% Grated Parmesan Cheese
8 ounces fettuccine, cooked, drained

• Cook and stir shrimp, vegetables and garlic in spread in large skillet on medium heat until vegetables are tender. Reduce heat to low.

• Add process cheese spread, milk and basil. Stir until process cheese spread is melted. Stir in Parmesan cheese.

• Add fettuccine; toss lightly.
Makes 4 servings

Prep time: 20 minutes
Cooking time: 15 minutes

Tuna & Eggplant Parmigiana

⅓ cup chopped onion
2 cloves garlic, minced
1 tablespoon olive or vegetable oil
2 large tomatoes, chopped
1 can (8 ounces) tomato sauce
⅓ cup tomato paste
2 teaspoons dried Italian seasoning, crushed
¼ teaspoon pepper
1 can (9¼ ounces) STARKIST® Tuna, drained and broken into chunks
1 eggplant, peeled (about 2 pounds)
⅔ cup grated Parmesan or Romano cheese
1 cup shredded low fat mozzarella cheese
3 tablespoons minced fresh parsley

In medium saucepan, cook and stir onion and garlic in hot oil for 3 minutes or until tender. Stir in tomatoes, tomato sauce, tomato paste, Italian seasoning and pepper. Bring to a boil; reduce heat. Simmer, uncovered, for 10 minutes, stirring occasionally. Stir tuna into sauce; remove from heat and set aside.

Preheat oven to 350°F. Cut eggplant crosswise into ¼-inch-thick slices. Bring large pot of water to a boil; add eggplant. Simmer for 20 minutes or until tender. Drain eggplant; blot dry with paper towels. In 12×8-inch casserole arrange ⅓ of eggplant; spoon ⅓ of tomato sauce mixture over top. Sprinkle ⅓ of Parmesan and mozzarella cheeses over top. Repeat layers twice.

Sprinkle parsley over top. Bake, uncovered, for 25 to 30 minutes or until hot and bubbly. *Makes 6 servings*

Prep time: 20 minutes

Nutty Pan-Fried Trout

Nutty Pan-Fried Trout

2 tablespoons vegetable oil
4 trout fillets (about 6 ounces *each*)
½ cup seasoned bread crumbs
½ cup pine nuts

Heat oil in large skillet over medium heat. Lightly coat fish with crumbs. Add to skillet. Cook 8 minutes or until fish flakes easily with fork, turning after 5 minutes. Remove fish from skillet. Place on serving platter; cover and keep warm.

Add nuts to drippings in skillet. Cook and stir 3 minutes or until nuts are lightly toasted. Sprinkle over fish. Serve immediately. *Makes 4 servings*

Squid Mediterranean

Squid Mediterranean

2 pounds cleaned whole squid
(directions on page 126)
1 tablespoon olive oil
¾ cup finely chopped onion
1 clove garlic, minced
2 cans (16 ounces *each*) Italian-style
tomatoes, drained and chopped
3 tablespoons sliced black olives
1 tablespoon drained capers
½ teaspoon dried oregano leaves,
crushed
¼ teaspoon dried marjoram leaves,
crushed
⅛ teaspoon crushed red pepper

Cut body of squid into ½-inch-thick slices; set aside. Heat olive oil in large skillet; add onion and garlic. Cook and stir until onion is tender. Add squid and remaining ingredients. Bring to a boil. Cover; reduce heat and simmer 30 minutes or until squid is tender. Serve over bed of hot cooked orzo pasta or rice, if desired. *Makes 4 servings*

Prep time: 45 minutes

Favorite recipe from **National Fisheries Institute**

Scampi Italienne

½ pound uncooked shrimp, peeled and deveined
¼ cup *plus* 1 tablespoon CRISCO® Vegetable Oil, divided
3 tablespoons dry white wine
½ teaspoon grated lemon peel
1 tablespoon lemon juice
½ teaspoon dried basil leaves
½ teaspoon dried oregano leaves
1 clove garlic, minced
¼ teaspoon salt
⅛ teaspoon pepper
2 drops hot pepper sauce
¾ cup uncooked rice
1½ cups water
2 tomatoes, cut into ½-inch pieces
¼ cup chopped fresh parsley
2 green onions with tops, sliced

1. Place shrimp in medium glass or stainless steel bowl.

2. Combine ¼ cup Crisco® Oil, wine, lemon peel, lemon juice, basil, oregano, garlic, salt, pepper and hot pepper sauce in container with tight-fitting lid. Shake well. Remove 1 tablespoon oil mixture. Reserve. Pour remaining oil mixture over shrimp. Turn to coat. Refrigerate 30 minutes, turning after 15 minutes.

3. Heat reserved 1 tablespoon marinade in medium saucepan on medium-high heat. Add rice. Stir 1 minute. Pour water over rice. Stir. Bring to a boil. Reduce heat to low. Cover. Simmer 15 to 20 minutes or until tender. Remove from heat. Fluff with fork. Stir in tomatoes. Cover.

4. Heat remaining 1 tablespoon Crisco® Oil in large skillet on high heat. Drain shrimp. Add to skillet. Stir-fry 1 minute or until shrimp turn pink.

5. Spoon rice mixture onto serving platter. Pour shrimp mixture over rice. Sprinkle with parsley and green onions. Season with additional salt and pepper, if desired.   *Makes 4 servings*

Spaghetti Squash with Tuna-Vegetable Sauce

1 spaghetti squash (about 1 pound), cut in half lengthwise
¼ cup water
1 medium zucchini, cut lengthwise into quarters and thinly sliced
1 cup chopped carrots
½ cup chopped onion
1 clove garlic, minced
1 large fresh tomato, chopped
2 cups tomato sauce
1 can (12¼ ounces) STARKIST® Tuna, drained and broken into chunks
1 teaspoon dried basil leaves, crushed
1 teaspoon dried rosemary, crushed
¼ cup grated Parmesan or Romano cheese

Microwave: Arrange squash, cut sides up, in shallow microwavable dish; add water. Cover loosely; microwave on HIGH (100% power) for 9 to 12 minutes, rotating dish once during cooking. Let stand, covered, while preparing sauce.

In large microwavable bowl, combine zucchini, carrots, onion and garlic. Microwave on HIGH for 3 to 5 minutes or until tender, stirring once. Stir in tomato, tomato sauce, tuna, basil and rosemary. Cover loosely; microwave on HIGH for 3 to 5 minutes or until sauce is heated through, stirring once. Using 2 forks, remove squash pulp by pulling it from rind. Pile onto serving platter. Spoon tuna sauce over; sprinkle with cheese. Garnish with fresh basil, if desired. Serve immediately.   *Makes 4 to 5 servings*

Prep time: 15 minutes

Snapper with Pesto Butter

½ cup butter or margarine, softened
1 cup packed fresh basil leaves,
    coarsely chopped *or* ½ cup
    chopped fresh parsley plus 2
    tablespoons dried basil leaves,
    chopped
3 tablespoons finely grated fresh
    Parmesan cheese
1 clove garlic, minced
    Olive oil
2 to 3 teaspoons lemon juice
4 to 6 red snapper, rock cod, salmon
    or other medium-firm fish fillets
    (at least ½ inch thick)
    Salt and black pepper
    Lemon wedges
    Fresh basil or parsley sprigs and
    lemon strips, for garnish

To prepare Pesto Butter, place butter, chopped basil, cheese, garlic and 1 tablespoon oil in blender or food processor; process until blended. Add lemon juice to taste. Rinse fish; pat dry with paper towels. Brush one side of fish lightly with oil; season with salt and black pepper.

Oil hot grid to help prevent sticking. Grill fillets, oil sides down, on covered grill, over medium KINGSFORD® briquets, 5 to 9 minutes. Halfway through cooking time, brush top with oil and season with salt and black pepper, then turn and continue grilling until fish turns from translucent to opaque throughout. (Grilling time depends on thickness of fish; allow 3 to 5 minutes for each ½ inch of thickness.) Serve each fillet with spoonful of Pesto Butter and wedge of lemon. Garnish with basil sprigs and lemon strips.   *Makes 4 to 6 servings*

Sole Primavera en Croûte

2 tablespoons butter or margarine
2 cups sliced mushrooms
1 cup sliced green onions
½ cup chopped red bell pepper
1½ cups bite-sized pieces king crab
    (imitation, if desired)
2 tablespoons chopped fresh parsley
1 tablespoon slivered lemon peel
1 tablespoon lemon juice
2 packages (12 ounces *each*) frozen
    puff pastry, thawed in
    refrigerator overnight
8 sole or flounder fillets (6 ounces
    each)
2 cups shredded Jarlsberg cheese
1 egg, beaten with 1 tablespoon
    water
    Sesame seeds

Heat butter in large skillet over medium-high heat until melted and bubbly. Add mushrooms and cook until browned. Add green onions and red pepper; cook and stir just until tender. Stir in crab, parsley, lemon peel and lemon juice. Remove from heat; set aside.

Preheat oven to 425°F. On lightly floured board, roll out 1 sheet pastry to 16-inch square. Cut into 4 squares. Place on ungreased baking sheet. Place 1 fillet on each. Top each fillet with ⅛ of crab filling and ¼ cup Jarlsberg cheese. Roll out second pastry sheet into 16-inch square. Cut into 4 squares. Place 1 square over each fillet. Trim and crimp edges with fork to seal. If desired, decorate top of pastry with trimmings. Brush with beaten egg. Sprinkle with sesame seeds. Repeat with remaining pastry, fish, filling and cheese. Bake 20 minutes or until pastry is golden.   *Makes 8 servings*

*Favorite recipe from **Norseland Foods, Inc.***

Snapper with Pesto Butter

Shrimp fra Diavolo
(Shrimp with Spicy Stuffing)

Everyone's favorite . . . shrimp. These are stuffed with a zesty crumb mixture and topped with marinara sauce.

1¾ pounds (about 24) shelled and deveined uncooked jumbo shrimp, with tails left on
¼ cup butter
1 jar (9 ounces) PROGRESSO® Tuscan Peppers (pepperoncini), finely chopped and drained
1 cup finely chopped green onions
1 teaspoon PROGRESSO® Garlic Puree
1 cup PROGRESSO® Italian Style Bread Crumbs
½ cup crabmeat
2 hard cooked eggs, chopped
2 tablespoons PROGRESSO® Grated Parmesan Cheese, divided
3 tablespoons PROGRESSO® Olive Oil
1 jar (14 ounces) PROGRESSO® Marinara Sauce

1. Preheat oven to 500°F.
2. Butterfly shrimp by slicing down length of underside, almost to vein.

Shrimp fra Diavolo

3. In medium saucepan, melt butter. Add Tuscan peppers, green onions and garlic; cook 3 minutes, stirring occasionally. Remove from heat. Stir in bread crumbs, crabmeat, eggs and 1 tablespoon Parmesan cheese.

4. Spread 1½ cups stuffing over bottom of 13×9-inch baking dish.

5. Lay shrimp on flat surface with split side up. Spoon remaining stuffing into crevice of each shrimp, pressing stuffing into crevice.

6. Place shrimp, stuffing sides up, in single layer over stuffing in dish; brush tops of shrimp with olive oil.

7. Bake 6 to 8 minutes or until shrimp turn pink.

8. In small pan, heat marinara sauce; drizzle over top of shrimp.

9. Sprinkle with remaining 1 tablespoon Parmesan cheese. *Makes 6 servings*

Prep time: 1 hour
Cooking time: 8 minutes

Whitefish with Red Pepper Sauce

1 pound fine-textured fish fillets (such as flounder, sole or whitefish)
2 tablespoons PARKAY® Spread Sticks
1 tablespoon dried oregano leaves, crushed
1 jar (7 ounces) roasted red peppers, undrained
¼ pound VELVEETA® Pasteurized Process Cheese Spread, cubed

• Fry fish on both sides in spread and oregano over medium-high heat until fish flakes easily with fork. Remove fish from skillet; keep warm.

• Place red peppers in blender or food processor container fitted with steel blade; cover. Process until smooth. Pour into skillet. Reduce heat to low.

• Add process cheese spread to peppers in skillet; stir until process cheese spread is melted. Serve over fish.

Makes 4 servings

Prep time: 10 minutes
Cooking time: 15 minutes

Lobster Mushroom Sauce di Riso

**1 can (10½ ounces) PROGRESSO®
  Rock Lobster Spaghetti Sauce
¼ pound lobster meat (real or
  imitation), sliced ¼ inch thick
  (about ¾ cup)
⅓ cup sliced fresh mushrooms
2 teaspoons dry sherry
¾ teaspoon seafood seasoning
2 cups rice, cooked according to
  package directions
2 tablespoons PROGRESSO® Grated
  Parmesan Cheese**

1. In medium saucepan over medium heat, combine rock lobster sauce, lobster, mushrooms, sherry and seafood seasoning; cook 5 to 8 minutes or until thoroughly heated, stirring occasionally.

2. Serve over rice. Sprinkle with cheese.

Makes 4 servings

Prep time: 10 minutes
Cooking time: 5 minutes

Rainbow Trout with Walnuts and Oregano

Rainbow Trout with Walnuts and Oregano

**2 teaspoons olive oil
2 teaspoons finely chopped shallots
4 CLEAR SPRINGS® Brand Idaho
  Rainbow Trout Fillets, butterflied
  (4 ounces *each*)
¼ cup finely chopped walnuts
¼ cup thinly sliced green onions
1 tablespoon finely chopped fresh
  oregano leaves *or* 1½ teaspoons
  dried oregano leaves, crushed**

Heat olive oil in large skillet. Add shallots; cook and stir until shallots are soft and translucent. Place trout fillets, flesh sides down, over shallots. Cook 4 minutes; turn trout over and cook 1 minute more. Remove trout to warm platter; cover and keep warm. Cook and stir walnuts, green onions and oregano in same skillet 2 minutes. Top fillets with herb-nut mixture. Serve immediately.

Makes 4 servings

Fried Calamari with Tartar Sauce

1 pound fresh or thawed frozen
  squid
1 egg
1 tablespoon milk
¾ cup fine dry plain bread crumbs
  Vegetable oil
  Tartar Sauce (recipe follows)
  Lemon wedges (optional)

To clean each squid, hold body of squid firmly in one hand. Grasp head firmly with other hand; pull head, twisting gently from side to side. (Head and contents of body should pull away in one piece.) Set aside tubular body sac. Cut tentacles off head; set aside. Discard head and contents of body. Grasp tip of pointed, thin, clear cartilage protruding from body; pull out and discard. Rinse squid under cold running water. Peel off and discard spotted outer membrane covering body sac and fins. Pull off side fins; set aside. Rinse inside of squid body thoroughly under running water. Repeat with remaining squid.

Cut each squid body crosswise into ¼-inch rings. Cut reserved fins into thin slices. (Body rings, fins and reserved tentacles are all edible parts.) Pat pieces thoroughly dry with paper towels. Beat egg with milk in medium bowl. Add squid pieces; stir to coat well. Spread bread crumbs on plate. Dip squid pieces in bread crumbs; place in shallow bowl or on waxed paper. Let stand 10 to 15 minutes before frying.

Heat 1½ inches oil in large saucepan to 350°F. (*Caution:* Squid will pop and spatter during frying; do not stand too close to pan.) Adjust heat to maintain temperature. Fry 8 to 10 pieces of squid at a time 45 to 60 seconds until light brown.

Remove with slotted spoon; drain on paper towels. Repeat with remaining squid pieces. Serve hot with Tartar Sauce and lemon wedges. Garnish as desired.

Makes 2 to 3 servings

Tartar Sauce

1 green onion with tops, thinly sliced
2 tablespoons chopped fresh parsley
1 tablespoon drained capers, minced
1 small sweet gherkin or pickle,
  minced
1⅓ cups mayonnaise

Fold green onion, parsley, capers and gherkin into mayonnaise in small bowl. Cover; refrigerate until ready to serve.

Makes about 1⅓ cups

Grilled Rainbow Trout with Italian Butter

2 tablespoons butter or margarine,
  softened
1 tablespoon finely chopped red bell
  pepper
½ teaspoon dried Italian herb
  seasoning
4 CLEAR SPRINGS® Brand Idaho
  Rainbow Trout fillets (4 ounces
  each)
2 tablespoons grated Parmesan
  cheese (optional)

Prepare grill for hot coals. Meanwhile, to prepare Italian Butter, beat butter, pepper and seasoning in small bowl until well blended; refrigerate until cold.

Place trout fillets, flesh sides down, on oiled grill over hot coals and cook about 2 minutes. Gently turn trout with spatula; cook 2 minutes more. Top each fillet with dollop of Italian Butter. Sprinkle with Parmesan cheese, if desired. Serve immediately.

Makes 4 servings

Fried Calamari with Tartar Sauce

Rainbow Trout Parmesan

Rainbow Trout Parmesan

¼ **cup seasoned bread crumbs**
¼ **cup grated Parmesan cheese**
4 **teaspoons chopped fresh parsley**
1 **tablespoon margarine, melted**
4 **CLEAR SPRINGS® Brand Idaho
Rainbow Trout fillets (4 ounces
each)**

Microwave: Combine bread crumbs, cheese, parsley and margarine in small bowl until blended. Arrange trout, skin sides down, in microwave-safe dish. Spread ¼ of bread crumb mixture evenly over each fillet; cover tightly with plastic wrap. Microwave on HIGH (100% power) 2 minutes. Rotate dish; microwave 2 to 4 minutes until fish flakes easily with fork. Garnish with tomato slices, if desired. Serve immediately.

Makes 2 to 3 servings

Fish Rolls Primavera

1 **cup shredded carrots**
1 **cup shredded zucchini**
2 **tablespoons finely chopped onion**
½ **cup fresh bread crumbs (1 slice)**
⅛ **teaspoon dried thyme leaves**
¼ **cup margarine or butter, melted**
¼ **cup REALEMON® Lemon Juice
from Concentrate**
4 **fish fillets, fresh or thawed frozen
(about 1 pound)**

Preheat oven to 375°F. In medium bowl, combine vegetables, bread crumbs and thyme. Combine margarine and ReaLemon® brand; add ¼ *cup* to vegetable mixture. Place fillets in shallow baking dish; top with equal amounts of vegetable mixture. Roll up. Pour remaining margarine mixture over fillets. Bake 15 minutes or until fish flakes easily with fork. Garnish as desired. Refrigerate leftovers. *Makes 4 servings*

Baked Halibut with Roasted Pepper Sauce

**Roasted Pepper Sauce (recipe
follows)**
1 **medium onion, thinly sliced**
1 **clove garlic, minced**
1 **halibut fillet (1½ pounds), skinned**

Preheat oven to 425°F. Grease shallow baking dish. Prepare Roasted Pepper Sauce; set aside.

Cover bottom of prepared baking dish with onion and garlic. Top with fish and sauce. Bake 20 minutes or until fish flakes easily with fork. Garnish as desired. Serve immediately.

Makes 4 to 6 servings

Roasted Pepper Sauce

1 can (7 ounces) chopped green
 chilies, drained
1 jar (7 ounces) roasted red peppers,
 drained
⅔ cup chicken broth

Combine ingredients in food processor or
blender; process until smooth.

Marinated Shrimp Italiano

⅓ cup WISH-BONE® Italian
 Dressing*
1 pound uncooked medium shrimp,
 cleaned

In large shallow nonaluminum broilerproof pan, combine Italian dressing with
shrimp. Cover and marinate in
refrigerator, turning occasionally, at least
2 hours. Broil shrimp with dressing,
turning and basting frequently, 5 minutes
or until shrimp turn pink. Serve, if
desired, over hot cooked rice and garnish
with chopped fresh cilantro or parsley.

Makes about 4 servings

Microwave: In 9-inch microwave-safe pie
plate, marinate shrimp as directed.
Arrange shrimp around outer edge of pie
plate; cover with plastic wrap, venting
small area. Microwave at HIGH (100%
Power) 2½ minutes or until shrimp turn
pink, rearranging after 2 minutes. Let
stand covered 2 minutes. Serve as
directed.

*Also terrific with WISH-BONE® Robusto
Italian or Olive Oil Vinaigrette.

Grilled Swordfish with Garlic-Basil Butter

*The fresh garlic-basil butter accentuates the
flavor of grilled fish.*

½ cup butter, softened
¼ cup chopped fresh basil
1 teaspoon LAWRY'S® Garlic Powder
 with Parsley
¾ teaspoon LAWRY'S® Seasoned
 Pepper
2 pounds (about 6) swordfish steaks
 Lemon juice

In medium bowl, combine butter, basil,
Garlic Powder with Parsley and Seasoned
Pepper. Beat until smooth with electric
mixer. Form butter mixture into special
butter molds, or spread ½ inch thick on
baking tray lined with waxed paper;
refrigerate until firm. Once firm, remove
butter from molds or cut butter into
1-inch square pats. Refrigerate until ready
to serve. Brush fish steaks with lemon
juice. Grill or broil 3 to 5 minutes on each
side or until fish flakes easily with fork
and has golden appearance. Top fish with
flavored butter. Serve immediately.

Makes 6 servings

Presentation: Garnish with lemon
wedges. Serve with a tossed green salad.

Grilled Swordfish with Garlic-Basil Butter

PIZZA & BREADS

Pesto Chicken Pizza

1 (12-inch) prepared, pre-baked pizza
   crust*
¼ cup pesto sauce**
1 can (14½ ounces) DEL MONTE®
   Pizza Style Chunky Tomatoes
2 cups shredded mozzarella cheese
1½ cups diced cooked chicken
1 small red or green pepper, thinly
   sliced
1 small zucchini, thinly sliced
5 medium mushrooms, thinly sliced

Preheat oven to 450°F. Place crust on
baking sheet. Spread pesto evenly over
crust. Top with tomatoes, cheese and
remaining ingredients. Bake 10 minutes
or until hot and bubbly. Garnish with
grated Parmesan cheese and chopped
fresh basil, if desired.

Makes 4 to 6 servings

*Substitute 4 (6-inch) prepared, pre-
baked pizza crusts. Refrigerated or frozen
pizza dough may also be used; prepare
and bake according to package directions.

**Available frozen or refrigerated at the
supermarket.

Prep time: 10 minutes
Cook time: 10 minutes

Helpful Hint: Toss vegetables in
1 tablespoon olive oil, if desired.

Italian Pizza Calzones

½ pound Italian sausage
1 (26-ounce) jar CLASSICO®
   D'Abruzzi (Beef & Pork) Pasta
   Sauce, divided
1 cup sliced fresh mushrooms
½ cup chopped green bell pepper
½ cup chopped onion
2 (8-ounce) packages refrigerated
   crescent rolls
1 egg, beaten
1 tablespoon water
1 cup (4 ounces) shredded
   mozzarella cheese

Preheat oven to 350°F. In large skillet,
brown sausage; pour off fat. Add ¾ *cup*
pasta sauce, mushrooms, green pepper
and onion; simmer uncovered 10
minutes. Meanwhile, unroll crescent roll
dough; separate into 8 rectangles. Firmly
press perforations together and flatten
slightly. In small bowl, mix egg and
water; brush on dough edges. Stir cheese
into meat mixture. Spoon equal amounts
of meat mixture on half of each rectangle
to within ½ inch of edges. Fold dough
over filling; press to seal edges. Arrange
on baking sheet; brush with egg mixture.
Bake 15 minutes or until golden brown.
Heat remaining pasta sauce; serve with
calzones. Refrigerate leftovers.

Makes 8 calzones

Pesto Chicken Pizza

Roasted Red Pepper Biscuits

Roasted red peppers and a few seasonings transform boxed biscuit mix into a colorful Italian bread. You'll be glad you tried them!

2 cups buttermilk biscuit mix
½ cup PROGRESSO® Grated Parmesan Cheese
1 teaspoon dried oregano leaves
⅛ teaspoon cayenne pepper
1 jar (7 ounces) PROGRESSO® Roasted Peppers (red), drained, patted dry on paper towel and chopped
⅔ cup milk

1. Preheat oven to 425°F.

2. In medium bowl, stir together biscuit mix, Parmesan cheese, oregano and cayenne pepper.

3. Add roasted peppers and milk to biscuit mixture; stir just until moistened.

4. Drop dough by heaping tablespoons, 2 inches apart, onto greased baking sheet.

5. Bake 12 to 14 minutes or until browned.   *Makes 1 dozen*

Prep time: 10 minutes
Cooking time: 14 minutes

Roasted Red Pepper Biscuits

Chicken Parmesan Pizza

10 ounces chicken breasts, skinned, boned and cut into 1-inch slices
¼ cup all-purpose flour
   Vegetable oil
2 cups tomato sauce, divided
1 (12-inch) BOBOLI® Brand Italian Bread Shell
¾ cup KRAFT® Natural Shredded Low-Moisture Part-Skim Mozzarella Cheese, divided
8 ripe olives, pitted and halved
1 tablespoon KRAFT® 100% Grated Parmesan Cheese
½ teaspoon dried oregano leaves, crushed

Preheat oven to 450°F. Dredge chicken in flour. Pour oil into large skillet 1 inch deep. Heat oil over medium-high heat until hot. Add chicken; fry until chicken is tender and golden brown. Remove to paper towel with slotted spoon to absorb excess oil.

Spread 1 cup tomato sauce over Boboli® Italian bread shell leaving 1-inch border. Sprinkle with ½ cup mozzarella cheese. Top with chicken, remaining 1 cup tomato sauce and olives. Sprinkle with remaining ¼ cup mozzarella cheese, Parmesan cheese and oregano. Bake on ungreased baking sheet in lower ⅓ of oven about 8 to 10 minutes or until puffed and lightly browned.

Makes 4 to 6 servings

Open-Faced Zucchini and Roasted Red Pepper Melts

½ cup HELLMANN'S® or BEST
   FOODS® Real or Light
   Mayonnaise or Reduced Fat
   Mayonnaise Dressing
1 clove garlic, minced or pressed
1 tablespoon chopped fresh basil *or*
   1 teaspoon dried basil leaves,
   crushed
1½ teaspoons chopped fresh oregano
   or ½ teaspoon dried oregano
   leaves, crushed
½ teaspoon freshly ground black
   pepper
1 loaf (14 inches) Italian bread, sliced
   lengthwise, cut crosswise in half
1 large zucchini, sliced diagonally
   into 8 slices
1 jar (7¼ ounces) roasted red
   peppers, drained, cut into
   quarters *or* 2 medium red bell
   peppers, roasted, peeled, cut into
   quarters
½ cup (2 ounces) shredded
   mozzarella cheese

Preheat broiler. In small bowl, blend
mayonnaise, garlic, basil, oregano and
black pepper. Brush cut sides of bread
with half the mayonnaise mixture. Broil
5 inches from heat 2 minutes or until
golden brown. Remove; set aside. Brush
zucchini slices with remaining
mayonnaise mixture. Broil 2 minutes,
turning once. Top each slice of bread
alternately with equal portions of
zucchini and red pepper. Sprinkle with
cheese. Broil 1 to 2 minutes or until
golden brown and cheese melts.

Makes 4 sandwiches

*Open-Faced Zucchini and
Roasted Red Pepper Melts*

Four Cheese Pizza

1 (12-inch) BOBOLI® Brand Italian
   Bread Shell *or* 4 small 6-inch
   bread shells
1 BOBOLI® Brand Pizza Sauce Pouch
   (5 ounces)
1 ounce ricotta cheese
1 ounce KRAFT® 100% Grated
   Parmesan Cheese
1 ounce KRAFT® Natural Shredded
   Cheddar Cheese
3 ounces KRAFT® Natural Shredded
   Mozzarella Cheese

Preheat oven to 450°F. Spread pizza sauce
then ricotta cheese on top of Boboli®
Italian bread shell. Sprinkle cheeses over
sauce in order above. Bake 12 to 15
minutes (5 to 8 minutes for small shells)
or until puffed and lightly browned.

Makes 4 to 6 servings

Stuffed Pizza

2 loaves (1 pound *each*) frozen bread
    dough, thawed
1¾ cups (15-ounce bottle)
    CONTADINA® Pizza Squeeze
    Pizza Sauce, divided
1 package (3 ounces) sliced
    pepperoni, quartered
1¼ cups (10-ounce package) frozen
    chopped spinach, thawed and
    squeezed dry
1 cup (4 ounces) shredded
    mozzarella cheese
1 cup (8-ounce carton) ricotta cheese
1 cup grated Parmesan cheese
1 cup (3.8-ounce can) sliced ripe
    olives, drained
1 tablespoon olive oil
1 tablespoon grated Parmesan cheese

Preheat oven to 350°F. On floured surface,
roll bread dough into two 12-inch circles.
Place one circle on greased baking sheet.
Spread with ¼ cup pizza sauce to 1 inch
from edge. In large bowl, combine
pepperoni, spinach, mozzarella, ricotta,
1 cup Parmesan cheese and olives. Spread
mixture over pizza sauce. Squeeze ¼ cup
pizza sauce evenly over filling; dampen
outside edge. Place remaining bread
dough on top and seal. Cut 8 steam vents.
Bake on lowest rack in oven for 20
minutes. Brush with olive oil; sprinkle
with 1 tablespoon Parmesan cheese. Bake
for additional 15 to 20 minutes or until
well browned. Let stand 15 minutes
before cutting. Warm remaining pizza
sauce and serve over wedges of pizza.
Makes 8 servings

Vegetable Pepperoni Pizza

*The light tang of marinated vegetables gives
special flair to this colorful pizza.*

2 (12-inch) refrigerated pizza crusts
1 can (8 ounces) PROGRESSO®
    Tomato Sauce
1 can (6 ounces) PROGRESSO®
    Tomato Paste
½ teaspoon dried oregano leaves
½ teaspoon dried basil leaves
4 ounces pepperoni slices
1 jar (7 ounces) PROGRESSO®
    Roasted Peppers (red), drained
    and sliced
1 jar (6 ounces) PROGRESSO®
    Marinated Artichoke Hearts,
    drained and coarsely chopped
1 jar (6 ounces) PROGRESSO®
    Marinated Mushrooms, drained
    and halved
2 cups (8 ounces) shredded
    mozzarella cheese
2 green onions, sliced
2 tablespoons PROGRESSO® Grated
    Parmesan Cheese

1. Preheat oven to 400°F.

2. Place crusts on two lightly greased
12-inch pizza pans. Bake 8 minutes.

3. In small bowl, combine tomato sauce,
tomato paste, oregano and basil. Spread
half of sauce mixture onto each pizza
crust.

4. Arrange pepperoni, roasted peppers,
artichoke hearts and mushrooms over
sauce mixture.

5. Top pizzas with mozzarella cheese, green onions and Parmesan cheese.

6. Bake 10 to 15 minutes or until cheese is melted and crusts are golden brown.

Makes 8 servings

Prep time: 15 minutes
Cooking time: 15 minutes

Variation: Substitute pizza crust mix for refrigerated pizza crusts. Prepare enough dough to make two pizza crusts according to package directions; press dough onto bottoms of two greased pizza pans. Bake at 400°F, 8 minutes.

Easy Calzone

"Calzone" is an Italian term for a filled turnover made with pizza dough.

1 can (10 ounces) refrigerated ready-to-use pizza dough
1 package (10 ounces) frozen chopped spinach, thawed
1 can (9¼ ounces) STARKIST® Tuna, drained and flaked
1 cup chopped tomatoes
2 cans (4 ounces *each*) sliced mushrooms, drained
1 cup shredded low fat Cheddar or mozzarella cheese
1 teaspoon Italian seasoning or dried oregano leaves, crushed
1 teaspoon dried basil leaves, crushed
¼ teaspoon garlic powder
   Vegetable oil
   Cornmeal (optional)
1 can (8 ounces) pizza sauce

Easy Calzone

Preheat oven to 425°F. Unroll pizza dough onto a lightly floured board; cut crosswise into 2 equal pieces. Roll each piece of dough into a 12-inch circle.

Squeeze all liquid from spinach; chop fine. Over the bottom half of each circle of dough, sprinkle spinach, tuna, tomatoes, mushrooms, cheese and seasonings to within 1 inch of bottom edge. Fold top half of dough over filling, leaving bottom edge uncovered. Moisten bottom edge of dough with a little water, then fold bottom edge of dough over top edge, sealing with fingers or crimping with fork. Brush top of dough lightly with oil; sprinkle with cornmeal if desired. Place 2 filled calzones on ungreased baking sheet; bake for 25 to 30 minutes or until deep golden brown. Meanwhile, in saucepan, heat pizza sauce. Cut each calzone in half crosswise to serve, passing sauce.

Makes 4 servings

Prep time: 25 minutes

Cheesy Onion Focaccia

½ cup *plus* 3 tablespoons honey, divided
2⅓ cups warm water (110° to 115°F), divided
1½ packages active dry yeast
6 tablespoons olive oil, divided
⅓ cup cornmeal
3 cups whole wheat flour
4½ teaspoons coarse salt
3 to 4 cups all-purpose flour, divided
1 large red onion, sliced
1 cup red wine vinegar
Additional cornmeal
1 cup grated Parmesan cheese
½ teaspoon onion salt
Black pepper to taste

To proof yeast, place 3 tablespoons honey in large bowl. Pour ⅓ cup water over honey. *Do not stir.* Sprinkle yeast over water. Let stand at room temperature about 15 minutes or until bubbly.*

Add remaining 2 cups water, 3 tablespoons olive oil, ⅓ cup cornmeal and whole wheat flour to yeast mixture; mix until well blended. Stir in coarse salt and 2 cups all-purpose flour. Gradually stir in enough remaining all-purpose flour until mixture clings to sides of bowl.

Turn dough out onto lightly floured surface. To knead in remaining flour, fold the dough in half toward you and press dough away from you with heels of hands. Give dough a quarter turn and continue folding, pressing and turning until the dough is smooth and satiny, about 10 minutes.

Divide dough in half. Place each half in large, lightly greased bowl; turn over to grease dough surface. Cover each with clean kitchen towel and let dough rise in warm place (85°F) until doubled in bulk.

Meanwhile, combine onion, vinegar and remaining ½ cup honey. Marinate at room temperature at least 1 hour.

Grease 2 (12-inch) pizza pans and sprinkle with additional cornmeal. Stretch dough and pat into pans; create valleys with fingertips. Cover dough with greased plastic wrap; let rise for 1 hour or until dough is doubled in size.

Preheat oven to 400°F. Drain onions and scatter them over dough. Sprinkle with remaining 3 tablespoons olive oil, Parmesan cheese and onion salt; season with black pepper. Bake 25 to 30 minutes until flatbread is crusty and golden. Cut into wedges. Serve warm.

Makes 2 breads (6 to 8 servings each)

*If yeast does not bubble, it is no longer active. Discard yeast mixture and start again. Always check the expiration date on yeast packet. Also, water that is too hot will kill yeast; it is best to use a thermometer.

Cheesy Mushroom Pizza

2 tablespoons olive oil
2 cups sliced mushrooms
½ cup pizza or tomato sauce
1 (12-inch) BOBOLI® Brand Italian Bread Shell *or* 4 small 6-inch bread shells
1 cup shredded Cheddar cheese
4 sun-dried tomatoes, cut in strips

Preheat oven to 450°F. Heat oil in skillet. Cook and stir mushrooms in oil 2 minutes. Spread sauce on bread shell; sprinkle with cheese. Top with mushrooms and tomatoes. Bake 10 minutes or until puffed and lightly browned. *Makes 4 to 6 servings*

Cheesy Onion Focaccia

Calzone

1 cup warm water (110° to 115°F)
½ teaspoon sugar
1 package (¼ ounce) active dry yeast
3 cups all-purpose flour, divided
2 tablespoons vegetable oil
½ teaspoon salt
12 ounces mozzarella cheese, diced
6 ounces creamy goat cheese
3 ounces sliced prosciutto or cooked ham, cut into strips
3 tablespoons chopped chives
1 tablespoon minced fresh garlic
2 tablespoons grated Parmesan cheese

Combine water and sugar in large bowl; sprinkle with yeast. Let stand 5 minutes to soften. Add 1½ cups flour; beat with electric mixer until smooth. Stir in oil and salt. Gradually blend in enough of remaining flour with spoon to make stiff dough. Turn out onto floured surface; knead until smooth. Return to bowl; cover and let rise in warm place until doubled.

Punch down dough; divide into 3 equal portions. Roll 1 portion on lightly floured surface into 9-inch circle. Place ⅓ of mozzarella on one side of dough; dot with ⅓ of goat cheese and top with ⅓ of prosciutto. Repeat with remaining dough, mozzarella and goat cheeses, and prosciutto. Mix chives and garlic; sprinkle over filling. Moisten edges with water and fold over to enclose, pressing firmly together. Place on lightly greased baking sheets. Let rise 30 to 45 minutes.

Preheat oven to 375°F. Cut slit in each calzone to allow steam to escape. Bake 30 to 35 minutes until browned. Remove from oven; brush tops with oil. Sprinkle each with 2 teaspoons grated Parmesan cheese.   *Makes 3 large calzones*

Favorite recipe from **Christopher Ranch of Gilroy**

Zucchini Basil Muffins

1½ cups NABISCO® 100% Bran
1¼ cups skim milk
⅓ cup FLEISCHMANN'S® Margarine, melted
¼ cup EGG BEATERS® 99% Real Egg Product
1¼ cups all-purpose flour
2 tablespoons sugar
2 teaspoons baking powder
1 teaspoon dried basil leaves
½ cup grated zucchini

Preheat oven to 400°F. Mix bran, milk, margarine and Egg Beaters®; let stand 5 minutes.

In bowl, blend flour, sugar, baking powder and basil; stir in bran mixture just until blended. Stir in zucchini. Spoon into 12 greased 2½-inch muffin-pan cups. Bake 20 to 25 minutes or until wooden pick inserted in centers comes out clean. Remove from pan. Serve warm.

Makes 12 muffins

Marinated Bell Pepper & Mushroom Pizza

Marinated Mushrooms (recipe follows)
Marinated Bell Peppers (recipe follows)
6 to 8 eggplant slices, unpeeled
Salt
Olive oil
Herb Mixture (recipe follows)
6 plum tomatoes
1 pound (1 loaf) frozen bread dough, thawed
1½ cups (6 ounces) shredded Wisconsin Whole Milk Mozzarella cheese
1 cup (4 ounces) shredded Wisconsin Provolone cheese

Prepare Marinated Mushrooms; set aside. Prepare Marinated Bell Peppers; set aside.

Place eggplant in colander over sink; rinse slices well. Salt slices; drain 1 hour. Preheat oven to 425°F. Rinse salt from eggplant; pat dry with paper towels. Lay slices on baking sheet and brush with olive oil. Bake, turning once, 30 minutes or until slightly softened. Prepare Herb Mixture. Blanch tomatoes 1 minute in boiling water; peel, seed and crush. Combine tomato mixture and Herb Mixture.

Increase oven temperature to 475°F. Roll bread dough into 14-inch circle. Press onto bottom and up sides of 12-inch deep-dish pizza pan. Layer toppings in the following order: tomato-herb mixture, eggplant slices, drained Marinated Bell Peppers, drained Marinated Mushrooms and cheeses. Bake on lower rack in oven 10 to 12 minutes until crust is golden brown.

Makes 1 (12-inch) deep-dish pizza

Marinated Bell Pepper & Mushroom Pizza

Marinated Mushrooms

4 ounces fresh mushrooms
1 tablespoon butter
1 cup olive oil
1 bay leaf
  Freshly ground black pepper to taste
1 tablespoon chopped parsley
  Dash *each* dried thyme leaves and dried marjoram leaves, crushed

Wash and quarter mushrooms. Melt butter over medium heat in medium skillet until melted and bubbly. Add mushrooms; cook and stir until browned. Cool. Combine remaining ingredients in large jar with lid; cover and shake to combine. Add cooled mushrooms and marinate at least 1 hour.

Marinated Bell Peppers

1 cup olive oil
1 clove garlic, minced
2 tablespoons balsamic vinegar
1 tablespoon red wine vinegar
½ teaspoon salt
  Freshly ground black pepper to taste
3 ounces green bell peppers, cut into strips

Combine all ingredients except green pepper strips in large jar with lid; cover and shake to combine. Add green pepper strips and marinate at least 1 hour.

Herb Mixture: Combine 1 tablespoon torn fresh basil leaves, 1 minced clove garlic, dash *each* dried marjoram leaves, rubbed sage leaves and sugar, and salt and black pepper to taste in small bowl; blend well.

Favorite recipe from **Wisconsin Milk Marketing Board** © 1994

Cheesy Turkey and Vegetable Pizza

1 can (10 ounces) refrigerated pizza crust
¼ cup *plus* 1 tablespoon olive oil, divided
1 jar (14 ounces) pizza sauce
¾ pound boneless, skinless turkey breast tenderloin, cut into 1-inch cubes
1 clove garlic, minced
1 small onion, sliced into thin rings
1 green bell pepper, sliced into thin rings
½ pound fresh mushrooms, sliced
1 can (2¼ ounces) sliced pitted ripe olives
⅓ cup freshly grated Parmesan cheese
1 teaspoon dried basil leaves, crushed
1 cup (4 ounces) shredded Monterey Jack cheese
1 cup (4 ounces) shredded Muenster cheese

Preheat oven to 425°F. Unroll dough and press into greased 12-inch pizza pan or 13×9-inch pan. Brush 1 tablespoon oil evenly over dough, then spread with

Cheesy Turkey and Vegetable Pizza

pizza sauce. Heat remaining ¼ cup oil in large skillet over medium-high heat until hot. Add turkey cubes and garlic; cook and stir 2 minutes. Add onion, green pepper and mushrooms; cook and stir 5 minutes more or until turkey is no longer pink in center. Spoon turkey mixture evenly over sauce. Top with olives. Sprinkle with Parmesan cheese and basil. Top with Monterey Jack and Muenster cheeses. Bake 20 minutes or until crust is golden brown.   *Makes 1 (12-inch) pizza*

Three-Cheese Focaccia

1 pound frozen bread dough or pizza dough, thawed according to package directions
2 tablespoons olive oil
1 small onion, thinly sliced
1 cup shredded Jarlsberg cheese
1 cup shredded Nokkelost cheese
¼ cup grated Parmesan cheese
½ to 1 teaspoon coarse salt to taste

Roll or stretch dough to fit 15×10-inch baking pan and let rise in warm place about 1 hour or until almost doubled in size.

Preheat oven to 400°F. Dimple the dough with fingertips, making deep ¼-inch indentations. Brush with olive oil. Sprinkle onion and cheeses evenly over dough. Sprinkle with salt.

Bake in lower ⅓ of oven 20 to 25 minutes until golden brown. Remove to wire rack; cool. Serve warm or at room temperature.
Makes 16 servings

*Favorite recipe from **Norseland Foods, Inc.***

Sicilian Pizza

2 onions, sliced
2 cloves garlic, minced
2 tablespoons olive oil
1 (12-inch) prepared, pre-baked pizza crust*
1 can (14½ ounces) DEL MONTE® Pizza Style Chunky Tomatoes
2 cups shredded mozzarella cheese
2 tablespoons grated Parmesan cheese

Preheat oven to 450°F. In skillet, cook onions and garlic in oil until soft. Place pizza crust on baking sheet. Spread tomatoes evenly over crust. Top with mozzarella cheese, onion mixture and Parmesan cheese. Bake 10 minutes or until hot and bubbly.

Makes 4 to 6 servings

*Substitute 4 (6-inch) prepared, pre-baked pizza crusts. Refrigerated or frozen pizza dough may also be used; prepare and bake according to package directions.

Prep time: 15 minutes
Cook time: 15 minutes

Classic Polenta

6 cups water
2 teaspoons salt
2 cups yellow cornmeal
¼ cup vegetable oil

Bring water and salt to a boil in large heavy saucepan over medium-high heat. Stirring water vigorously, add cornmeal in thin but steady stream (do not let lumps form). Reduce heat to low. Cook polenta, uncovered, 40 to 60 minutes until very thick, stirring frequently.

Classic Polenta

Polenta is ready when spoon will stand upright by itself in center of mixture. Polenta can be served at this point.*

For fried polenta, spray 11×7-inch baking pan with nonstick cooking spray. Spread polenta mixture evenly into baking pan. Cover and let stand at room temperature at least 6 hours or until cooled completely.

Unmold polenta onto cutting board. Cut polenta crosswise into 1¼-inch-wide strips. Cut strips into 2- to 3-inch-long pieces. Heat oil in large heavy skillet over medium-high heat; reduce heat to medium. Fry polenta pieces, ½ at a time, 4 to 5 minutes until golden on all sides, turning as needed. Garnish as desired.

Makes 6 to 8 servings

*Polenta is an important component of Northern Italian cooking. The basic preparation presented here can be served in two forms. Hot freshly made polenta can be mixed with ⅓ cup butter and ⅓ cup grated Parmesan cheese and served as a first course. Or, pour onto a large platter and top with a Bolognese sauce or other hearty meat sauce for a main dish. Fried polenta, as prepared here, is great as an appetizer or a side dish.

Roma Tomato Pizzas

2 loaves (2 pounds) frozen bread
    dough, thawed
⅓ cup olive oil
2 cups (2 medium) thinly sliced
    onions
2 cloves garlic, minced
12 Roma (Italian plum) tomatoes,
    sliced ⅛ inch thick
1 teaspoon dried basil leaves,
    crushed
1 teaspoon dried oregano leaves,
    crushed
    Black pepper
½ cup grated Parmesan cheese
1 can (2¼ ounces) sliced pitted ripe
    olives, drained
    Green and yellow bell pepper
    strips

Preheat oven to 450°F. Roll out each loaf on lightly floured surface into 15-inch circle; press each into greased 15-inch pizza pan or stretch into 15×10-inch baking pan. Crimp edges to form rim; prick several times with fork. Bake crusts 10 minutes. Remove from oven; set aside.

Reduce oven temperature to 400°F. Heat oil in large skillet over medium-high heat until hot. Add onions and garlic; cook and stir 6 to 8 minutes or until onions are tender. Divide onion mixture (including olive oil) between crusts. Arrange tomato slices evenly over onion mixture. Sprinkle each pizza with ½ teaspoon basil, ½ teaspoon oregano and black pepper to taste. Sprinkle each pizza with ¼ cup Parmesan cheese. Top with olives and desired amount of bell peppers. Bake 10 to 15 minutes or until toppings are heated through. *Makes 2 (15-inch) pizzas*

Carbonara Pizza

1 BOBOLI® Pizza Sauce Pouch
    (5 ounces)
2½ ounces bacon, cooked and
    crumbled
2 ounces red onions, chopped
4 teaspoons minced fresh parsley
2 tablespoons grated Parmesan
    cheese
    Black pepper to taste
1 (12-inch) BOBOLI® Brand Italian
    Bread Shell *or* 4 small 6-inch
    bread shells

Preheat oven to 450°F. Layer ingredients on Boboli® Italian bread shell in order above. Bake 12 to 15 minutes (5 to 8 minutes for small shells) or until puffed and lightly browned.

Makes 4 to 6 servings

Cheesy Tomato Bread

1 Italian bread loaf, cut in half
    lengthwise
½ cup KRAFT® Italian Dressing
12 slices tomato
½ pound VELVEETA® Pasteurized
    Process Cheese Spread, sliced
1 teaspoon dried basil leaves,
    crushed

• Heat oven to 350°F.

• Brush bread halves with dressing. Top with tomato and Velveeta®. Sprinkle with basil.

• Place bread on ungreased cookie sheet.

• Bake 6 to 8 minutes or until Velveeta® is melted. *Makes 8 servings*

Prep time: 15 minutes
Cooking time: 8 minutes

Roma Tomato Pizza

Easy Beef Pizza

Easy Beef Pizza

Quick Pizza Crust (recipe follows)
½ pound ground beef (80% lean)
1 teaspoon dried Italian seasoning
¼ teaspoon fennel seeds, crushed
¼ teaspoon crushed red pepper
1 can (8 ounces) pizza sauce
1 green bell pepper, cut into thin
   rings
1 green onion, sliced
¾ cup (6 ounces) shredded
   mozzarella cheese
¼ cup grated Parmesan cheese

Prepare Quick Pizza Crust. Preheat oven to 450°F. Heat large skillet over medium heat until hot. Crumble beef into skillet. Cook, stirring to separate meat, until no pink remains. Pour off drippings. Sprinkle Italian seasoning, fennel seeds and crushed red pepper over beef. Spread pizza sauce over baked pizza crust. Place green pepper and onion over sauce; top with beef mixture. Sprinkle with mozzarella and Parmesan cheeses. Bake 7 to 10 minutes or until cheese is melted.
Makes 4 servings

Quick Pizza Crust

1¾ to 2 cups all-purpose flour, divided
1 package (¼ ounce) fast-rising dry
   yeast
2 teaspoons sugar
½ teaspoon salt
⅔ cup warm water (110° to 115°F)
1½ teaspoons vegetable oil
   Cornmeal

Combine 1 cup flour, yeast, sugar and salt in large bowl. Stir in water and oil. Add enough remaining flour to form soft dough. Turn out onto lightly floured surface; knead 5 minutes or until smooth and elastic. Cover; let rest 10 minutes. Preheat oven to 350°F. Shape or roll dough into 12-inch circle. Sprinkle cornmeal on lightly greased 12-inch pizza pan or baking sheet. Place dough on pan, pressing gently to fit. Bake 10 minutes or until golden brown.

Favorite recipe from **National Live Stock & Meat Board**

Quick Classic Pizza

1 (12-inch) Italian bread shell or
   prepared pizza crust
1 cup (4 ounces) shredded
   mozzarella cheese
1 (14-ounce) jar CLASSICO® Pasta
   Sauce, any flavor (1½ cups)
   Pizza toppings: chopped onion,
   sliced peppers, sliced
   mushrooms, pepperoni, sliced
   olives, cooked sausage, cooked
   ground beef, cooked bacon

Preheat oven to 450°F. Top bread shell with half the cheese, pasta sauce, desired toppings and remaining cheese. Bake 10 to 12 minutes or until hot and bubbly. Let stand 5 minutes. Serve warm. Refrigerate leftovers.   *Makes 1 (12-inch) pizza*

Deli Stuffed Calzone

1¾ cups (14.5-ounce can)
    CONTADINA® Recipe Ready
    Diced Tomatoes, well drained
1¼ cups (10-ounce package) frozen
    chopped spinach, thawed and
    squeezed dry
¾ cup (3 ounces) thinly sliced
    pepperoni, chopped
¾ cup (3 ounces) thinly sliced salami,
    chopped
1 cup (4 ounces) shredded
    mozzarella cheese
1 cup ricotta cheese
½ cup chopped Spanish olives
    stuffed with pimiento
⅓ cup grated Parmesan cheese
1½ teaspoons garlic powder
1½ teaspoons dried basil leaves,
    crushed
1½ teaspoons dried oregano leaves,
    crushed
1 teaspoon seasoned pepper
2 loaves (1 pound *each*) frozen bread
    dough, thawed
2 tablespoons olive oil

Preheat oven to 350°F. In large bowl, combine tomatoes, spinach, pepperoni, salami, mozzarella cheese, ricotta cheese, olives, Parmesan cheese, garlic powder, basil, oregano and pepper; set aside filling. Cut each bread loaf in half. On lightly floured board, roll one bread dough half into 12-inch circle. Place on pizza pan. Spread 1⅓ cups of filling on half of dough circle to within ½ inch of edge. Fold dough over filling making half circle. Press edges with fork to seal. Cut 3 slits in dough to allow steam to escape. Repeat process making 3 more calzones. Bake for 20 minutes. Brush with olive oil. Bake an additional 5 to 10 minutes or until golden brown. Let stand 10 minutes before cutting. *Makes 8 servings*

Pepperoni Focaccia

1 tablespoon cornmeal
1 package (10 ounces) refrigerated
    pizza crust dough
½ cup finely chopped pepperoni
1½ teaspoons finely chopped fresh
    oregano leaves *or* ½ teaspoon
    dried oregano leaves, crushed
2 teaspoons olive oil

Preheat oven to 425°F. Grease large baking sheet, then sprinkle sheet with cornmeal; set aside.

Unroll dough onto lightly floured surface. Pat dough into 12×9-inch rectangle. Sprinkle ½ of pepperoni and ½ of oregano over one side. Fold over dough making 6×4½-inch rectangle.

Roll out dough into 12×9-inch rectangle. Place on prepared baking sheet. Prick dough with fork at 2-inch intervals, about 30 times. Brush with oil; sprinkle with remaining pepperoni and oregano.

Bake 12 to 15 minutes until golden brown. (Prick dough if dough puffs.) Cut into squares. *Makes 12 servings*

Deli Stuffed Calzone

Spicy Pepperoni Pizza

4 (6-inch) prepared, pre-baked pizza
 crusts
1 can (14½ ounces) DEL MONTE®
 Pizza Style Chunky Tomatoes
2 cups shredded mozzarella cheese
2 ounces sliced pepperoni
8 pitted ripe olives, sliced
2 tablespoons sliced green onions

Preheat oven to 450°F. Place crusts on
baking sheet. Spread tomatoes evenly
over crusts. Layer ½ of cheese, then the
pepperoni, olives and green onions. Top
with remaining cheese. Bake 6 to 8
minutes or until hot and bubbly.

Makes 4 servings

Prep time: 7 minutes
Cook time: 8 minutes

Tip: Easy recipe for kids and parents to
make together.

One Hour Pan Rolls Italiano

3½ to 4 cups all-purpose flour, divided
2 packages RED STAR® Active Dry
 Yeast or QUICK•RISE™ Yeast
2 tablespoons sugar
2 teaspoons garlic salt
1 teaspoon dried Italian herb
 seasoning
1 cup milk
½ cup water
2 tablespoons butter or margarine
1 egg
¾ cup grated Parmesan cheese,
 divided
2 tablespoons butter or margarine,
 melted

Combine 1½ cups flour, yeast, sugar,
garlic salt and seasoning in large bowl;
mix well. Heat milk, water and 2
tablespoons butter in small saucepan
until very warm (120° to 130°F); add to
flour mixture. Add egg. Blend with
electric mixer on low speed until
moistened; beat on medium speed
3 minutes. By hand, gradually stir in
½ cup cheese and enough remaining flour
to make firm dough. Knead on floured
surface 3 to 5 minutes until smooth and
elastic. Place in greased bowl, turning to
grease top. Cover with clean kitchen
towel; let rise in warm draft-free place
15 minutes.

Punch down dough. Divide dough into
4 parts. Divide each part into 4 pieces.
Shape each piece into smooth ball. Dip
tops into melted butter and roll in
remaining ¼ cup cheese. Place in well
greased 13×9-inch cake pan or two 9-inch
cake pans. Cover; let rise in warm place
about 10 minutes. Preheat oven to 375°F.
Bake 20 minutes until golden brown.
Remove from pan; cool on wire rack.

Makes 16 rolls

Dijon Garlic Bread

½ cup BLUE BONNET® 75%
 Vegetable Oil Spread, softened
¼ cup GREY POUPON® Dijon
 Mustard
1 teaspoon dried oregano leaves
1 clove garlic, crushed
1 (16-inch-long) loaf Italian bread

Preheat oven to 400°F. In small bowl,
blend spread, mustard, oregano and
garlic. Slice bread crosswise into 16 slices,
cutting ¾ of the way through. Spread
margarine mixture on each cut side of
bread. Wrap in foil. Bake 15 to 20 minutes
or until heated through.

Makes 16 servings

Grilled Pizza

A fun idea for parties, these pizzas are assembled on the grill. Because they're individual size, guests can make their own.

2 loaves (1 pound *each*) frozen bread dough, thawed
Olive oil
K.C. MASTERPIECE® Barbecue Sauce or pizza sauce
Seasonings: finely chopped garlic and fresh or dried herbs
Toppings: any combination of slivered ham, shredded barbecued chicken and grilled vegetables, such as thinly sliced mushrooms, zucchini, yellow squash, bell peppers, eggplant, pineapple chunks, tomatoes
Salt and black pepper
Cheese: any combination of shredded mozzarella, Provolone, Monterey Jack, grated Parmesan or crumbled feta

Divide each loaf of dough into 4 balls. Roll on cornmeal-coated or lightly floured surface and pat out dough to ¼-inch thickness to make small circles. Brush each circle with oil.

Arrange hot KINGSFORD® briquets on one side of grill. Oil hot grid to help prevent sticking. Vegetables, such as mushrooms, zucchini, yellow squash, bell peppers and eggplant need to be grilled until tender before using them as toppings. (See Note.)

Place 4 circles directly above medium Kingsford® briquets. (The dough will not fall through the grid.) Grill circles, on an uncovered grill, until dough starts to bubble on the top and the bottom gets lightly browned. Turn over using tongs. Continue to grill until the other side is lightly browned, then move the crusts to the cool part of the grill.

Brush each crust lightly with barbecue sauce, top with garlic and herbs, then meat or vegetables. Season with salt and black pepper, then top with cheese. Cover pizzas and grill, about 5 minutes until cheese melts, bottom of crust is crisp and pizza looks done. Repeat with remaining dough.   *Makes 8 individual pizzas*

Note: Vegetables such as mushrooms, zucchini, yellow squash, bell peppers and eggplant should be grilled before adding to pizza. If used raw, they will not have enough time to cook through. To grill, thread cut-up vegetables on skewers. Brush lightly with oil. Grill vegetables, on an uncovered grill, over hot Kingsford® briquets, until tender, turning frequently. Or place a piece of wire mesh on the grid, such as the type used for screen doors, to keep the vegetables from slipping through the grid.

Grilled Pizza

Meatza Pizza Pie

1 pound ground round
½ cup fresh bread crumbs (1 slice)
1 egg
2 teaspoons WYLER'S® or STEERO®
  Beef-Flavor Instant Bouillon
½ teaspoon Italian seasoning
½ cup CLASSICO® Di Napoli
  (Tomato & Basil) Pasta Sauce
1 (2½-ounce) jar sliced mushrooms,
  drained
2 tablespoons chopped green bell
  pepper
2 tablespoons chopped onion
1 cup (4 ounces) shredded
  mozzarella cheese

Preheat oven to 350°F. In medium bowl,
combine meat, bread crumbs, egg,
bouillon and seasoning; mix well. Press
evenly on bottom and up side to rim of 9-
inch pie plate to form crust. Bake 15
minutes; pour off fat. Spoon pasta sauce
over crust. Top with mushrooms, green
pepper, onion and cheese. Bake 10
minutes longer or until cheese melts.
Garnish as desired. Refrigerate leftovers.

Makes 1 (9-inch) pie

Plum Tomato Basil Pizza

1 can (10 ounces) refrigerated pizza
  dough
2 tablespoons cornmeal
1 cup (4 ounces) shredded
  mozzarella cheese
4 ripe seeded Italian plum tomatoes,
  sliced
½ cup fresh basil leaves
½ teaspoon TABASCO® pepper sauce
  Olive oil

*Top to bottom: Quick Classic Pizza
(page 144), Italian Pizza Calzone (page 130)
and Meatza Pizza Pie*

Preheat oven to 425°F. Prepare 12-inch
round pizza crust according to package
directions. Dust crust with cornmeal.
Distribute mozzarella cheese evenly over
crust. Layer with tomato slices and basil
leaves. Drizzle with TABASCO sauce and
olive oil. Bake 15 minutes or until the
crust is golden brown.

Makes 2 to 4 servings

Toasted Anise Biscuits

⅔ cup EGG BEATERS® 99% Real Egg
  Product
¾ cup sugar
¼ cup FLEISCHMANN'S®
  Margarine, melted
2 cups all-purpose flour
2 teaspoons baking powder
2 teaspoons anise extract
1 cup confectioner's sugar
3 to 4 teaspoons water
½ cup sliced almonds, toasted
  (optional)

Preheat oven to 350°F. Blend Egg Beaters®
and sugar; stir in margarine, flour, baking
powder and anise extract until blended.

Divide batter in half. On greased baking
sheet, spread each half into a 14×4-inch
rectangle. Bake 20 minutes or until
golden brown. Immediately cut loaves on
a diagonal into 1-inch-thick biscuits. Turn
biscuits on their side on same baking
sheet; broil 2 to 3 minutes on each side
until light golden brown. Cool on wire
rack.

Mix confectioner's sugar and enough
water for desired frosting consistency.
Spread on biscuit tops; sprinkle with
almonds if desired.   *Makes 28 biscuits*

Toasted Almond Biscuits: Substitute
2 teaspoons almond extract for anise
extract.

Vegetable Calzone

1 loaf (1 pound) frozen bread dough
1 package (10 ounces) frozen
    chopped broccoli, thawed and
    well drained
1 cup (8 ounces) SARGENTO® Light
    Ricotta Cheese
1 cup (4 ounces) SARGENTO®
    Classic Supreme® Shredded
    Mozzarella Cheese
1 clove garlic, minced
¼ teaspoon white pepper
1 egg beaten with 1 tablespoon water
1 jar (16 ounces) spaghetti sauce,
    heated (optional)
    SARGENTO® Grated Parmesan
    Cheese (optional)

Thaw bread dough and let rise according to package directions.

Preheat oven to 350°F. Combine broccoli, Ricotta and Mozzarella cheeses, garlic and pepper. Punch down bread dough and turn out onto lightly floured surface. Divide into 4 equal pieces. Roll out each piece, 1 at a time, into 8-inch circle. Place about ¾ cup cheese mixture on half the circle, leaving 1-inch border. Fold dough over to cover filling, forming semi-circle; press and crimp edges with fork tines to seal. Brush with egg mixture. Repeat with remaining dough circles.

Place on greased baking sheet. Bake 30 minutes or until brown and puffed. Transfer to rack and let cool 10 minutes. Top with hot spaghetti sauce and Parmesan cheese, if desired.

Makes 4 servings

Homemade Pizza

1½ teaspoons active dry yeast
1 teaspoon sugar, divided
½ cup warm water (110° to 115°F)
1¾ cups all-purpose flour, divided
¾ teaspoon salt, divided
2 tablespoons olive oil, divided
1 can (14½ ounces) whole peeled
    tomatoes, undrained
1 medium onion, chopped
1 clove garlic, minced
2 tablespoons tomato paste
1 teaspoon dried oregano leaves,
    crushed
½ teaspoon dried basil leaves,
    crushed
⅛ teaspoon black pepper
½ small red bell pepper, cored and
    seeded
½ small green bell pepper, cored and
    seeded
1¾ cups shredded mozzarella cheese
½ cup freshly grated Parmesan cheese
4 fresh medium mushrooms, thinly
    sliced
1 can (2 ounces) flat anchovy fillets,
    drained
⅓ cup pitted ripe olives, halved

To proof yeast, sprinkle yeast and ½ teaspoon sugar over warm water in small bowl; stir until yeast is dissolved.

Let stand 5 minutes or until mixture is bubbly.* Place 1½ cups flour and ¼ teaspoon salt in medium bowl; stir in yeast mixture and 1 tablespoon oil, stirring until a smooth, soft dough forms. Place dough on lightly floured surface; flatten slightly. To knead dough, fold dough in half toward you and press dough away from you with heels of hands. Give dough a quarter turn and continue folding, pressing and turning. Continue kneading, using as much of remaining flour as needed to form a stiff, elastic dough. Shape dough into a ball; place in large greased bowl. Turn to grease entire surface. Cover with clean kitchen towel and let dough rise in warm place 30 to 45 minutes until doubled in bulk.

For sauce, finely chop tomatoes in can with knife, reserving juice. Heat remaining 1 tablespoon oil in medium saucepan over medium heat. Add onion; cook 5 minutes or until soft. Add garlic; cook 30 seconds more. Add tomatoes with liquid, tomato paste, oregano, basil, remaining ½ teaspoon sugar, ½ teaspoon salt and black pepper. Bring to a boil over high heat; reduce heat to medium-low. Simmer, uncovered, 10 to 15 minutes until sauce thickens, stirring occasionally. Pour into small bowl; cool.

Punch dough down. Knead briefly on lightly floured surface to distribute air bubbles; let dough stand 5 minutes more. Flatten dough into circle on lightly floured surface. Roll out dough into 10-inch circle. Place circle in greased 12-inch pizza pan; stretch and pat dough out to edges of pan. Cover and let stand 15 minutes.

Preheat oven to 450°F. Cut bell peppers into ¾-inch pieces. Mix mozzarella and Parmesan cheeses in small bowl. Spread sauce evenly over pizza dough. Sprinkle with ⅔ of cheeses. Arrange bell peppers, mushrooms, anchovies and olives over cheeses. Sprinkle remaining cheeses on top of pizza. Bake 20 minutes or until crust is golden brown. To serve, cut into wedges. *Makes 4 to 6 servings*

*If yeast does not bubble, it is no longer active. Always check expiration date on yeast packet. Also, water that is too hot will kill yeast; it is best to use a thermometer.

Homemade Pizza

Supreme Style Pizza

1 (12-inch) BOBOLI® Brand Italian Bread Shell *or* 4 small 6-inch bread shells
1 BOBOLI® Pizza Sauce Pouch (5 ounces)
2 ounces Provolone cheese, shredded
2 ounces pepperoni
1 ounce Canadian bacon
1 ounce hard salami, diced
2 ounces KRAFT® Natural Shredded Mozzarella Cheese
2 ounces black olives, sliced

Preheat oven to 450°F. Layer ingredients on top of Boboli® Italian Bread Shell in order above. Bake 12 to 15 minutes (5 to 8 minutes for small shells) or until puffed and lightly browned.

Makes 4 to 6 servings

Thick 'n' Cheesy Vegetable Pizza

- 2 loaves (1 pound *each*) frozen bread dough, thawed
- 1 envelope LIPTON® Recipe Secrets™ Vegetable Soup Mix
- ¼ cup olive or vegetable oil
- 2 tablespoons chopped fresh basil leaves*
- 1 clove garlic, finely chopped
- ¼ teaspoon pepper
- 2 cups shredded mozzarella cheese
- 1 cup fresh or canned sliced mushrooms
- 1 medium tomato, coarsely chopped

Preheat oven to 425°F. Into lightly oiled 12-inch pizza pan, press dough to form crust; set aside.

In small bowl, blend vegetable soup mix, oil, basil, garlic and pepper; spread evenly on dough. Top with remaining ingredients. Bake 20 minutes or until cheese is melted and crust is golden brown. To serve, cut into wedges.

Makes about 6 servings

*Substitution: Use 2 teaspoons dried basil leaves.

Thick 'n' Cheesy Vegetable Pizza

Herbed Parmesan Muffins

- 2 cups all-purpose flour
- ¾ cup grated Parmesan cheese
- ½ cup chopped fresh basil
- 2 teaspoons sugar
- 2 teaspoons baking powder
- 2 teaspoons dried Italian herb seasoning
- ½ teaspoon baking soda
- ½ teaspoon salt
- 1¼ cups buttermilk
- ¼ cup olive or vegetable oil
- 1 egg

Preheat oven to 400°F. Grease bottoms of 12 (2½-inch) or 36 miniature muffin cups. Combine flour, cheese, basil, sugar, baking powder, herb seasoning, baking soda and salt in large bowl. Combine buttermilk, oil and egg in small bowl until blended; stir into flour mixture just until moistened. Spoon evenly into prepared muffin cups.

Bake 15 to 20 minutes (12 to 15 minutes for miniature muffins) or until golden and wooden pick inserted in centers comes out clean. Remove from pan. Serve warm.

Makes 12 regular-size or 36 miniature muffins

Chicken and Roasted Peppers Pizza

- 1 (12-inch) BOBOLI® Brand Italian Bread Shell *or* 4 small 6-inch bread shells
- 1 tablespoon olive oil
- 1 clove garlic
- ½ cup sliced onion
- ½ cup roasted red pepper strips
- ½ cup heavy cream
- 2 teaspoons tomato paste
- ¼ teaspoon crushed red pepper
  Salt and black pepper to taste
- 1 cup cooked slivered chicken

Preheat oven to 450°F. Bake Boboli® Italian bread shell on ungreased baking sheet until crisp, about 5 to 7 minutes. Heat oil in skillet. Cook and stir garlic in oil; remove garlic. Add onion to skillet; cook and stir until tender. Add pepper strips, cream, tomato paste, red pepper flakes, salt and black pepper. Cook and stir until thickened and well blended, about 2 to 3 minutes. Add chicken and heat through. Spoon into Boboli® Italian bread shell. *Makes 4 to 6 servings*

Vegetable Garden Pizza

1 (12-inch) prepared, pre-baked pizza crust*
1 can (14½ ounces) DEL MONTE® Pizza Style Chunky Tomatoes
2 cups shredded mozzarella cheese
1 small zucchini, thinly sliced
1 cup sliced mushrooms
¼ cup sliced green onions
2 tablespoons grated Parmesan cheese
¼ teaspoon dried thyme, crushed

Preheat oven to 450°F. Place pizza crust on baking sheet. Spread tomatoes evenly over crust. Top with mozzarella cheese, zucchini, mushrooms and green onions. Sprinkle with Parmesan cheese and thyme. Bake 10 minutes or until hot and bubbly. *Makes 4 to 6 servings*

*Substitute 4 (6-inch) prepared, pre-baked pizza crusts. Refrigerated or frozen pizza dough may also be used; prepare and bake according to package directions.

Prep time: 15 minutes
Cook time: 10 minutes

Focaccia Spirals

1¼ to 1½ cups all-purpose flour, divided
½ cup *plus* 1 tablespoon Regular, Quick or Instant CREAM OF WHEAT® Cereal, divided
1 envelope fast-rising yeast
2 tablespoons grated Parmesan cheese
1 teaspoon salt
1 teaspoon sugar
¾ cup hot water (125° to 130°F)
3 tablespoons olive oil, divided
2 cloves garlic, minced
1 teaspoon dried oregano leaves

In large bowl, combine 1 cup flour, ½ cup cereal, undissolved yeast, cheese, salt and sugar. Combine hot water and 1 tablespoon olive oil; stir into flour mixture until smooth. Stir in enough remaining flour to make a soft dough. Knead on floured surface for 6 to 8 minutes or until dough is smooth and elastic. Cover; let rise for 20 minutes.

Divide dough into 6 equal pieces; shape each into 16-inch rope. Coil 1 rope to form each roll; place on greased baking sheet which has been sprinkled with remaining 1 tablespoon cereal. Cover; let rise in warm draft-free place until doubled in size, about 30 minutes.

Preheat oven to 400°F. In small skillet, brown garlic in remaining 2 tablespoons oil. Brush dough with 1 tablespoon oil mixture; sprinkle with oregano. Bake 18 to 20 minutes or until golden brown. Brush tops of baked rolls with remaining oil mixture and serve warm.
Makes 6 rolls

Bread Stick Variation: Divide dough into 12 equal pieces. Shape each piece into 8-inch rope. Repeat procedure as above for rising and baking times.

SALADS & SIDE DISHES

Marinated Three Bean Salad

1 can (10½ ounces) PROGRESSO® Red Kidney Beans, drained
1 can (10½ ounces) PROGRESSO® Cannellini Beans, drained
1 can (10½ ounces) PROGRESSO® Chick Peas, drained
1 medium green bell pepper, cut into matchstick strips
1 small onion, thinly sliced and separated into rings
½ cup sliced celery
⅓ cup halved carrot slices
¼ cup PROGRESSO® Olive Oil
¼ cup PROGRESSO® Red Wine Vinegar
2 tablespoons PROGRESSO® Grated Parmesan Cheese
¾ teaspoon Italian seasoning
¼ teaspoon sugar

1. In large bowl, combine beans, chick peas and vegetables.
2. In small bowl, whisk together remaining ingredients; pour over bean mixture.
3. Refrigerate several hours or overnight.
Makes 8 servings

Prep time: 25 minutes
Chilling time: 3 hours

Garden Salad with Basil

2 medium tomatoes, halved and thinly sliced
1 small white onion, halved and thinly sliced
1 small cucumber, peeled, halved and thinly sliced
3 stalks fennel or celery, thinly sliced
½ cup olive or vegetable oil
⅓ cup herb vinegar
1½ teaspoons LAWRY'S® Seasoned Pepper
½ teaspoon LAWRY'S® Seasoned Salt
¾ teaspoon LAWRY'S® Garlic Powder with Parsley
4 cups torn romaine lettuce greens
1 bunch fresh basil (8 large leaves), coarsely chopped
Croutons

In large salad bowl, combine tomatoes, onion, cucumber and fennel. In small bowl, combine oil, vinegar, Seasoned Pepper, Seasoned Salt and Garlic Powder with Parsley; blend well. Add to onion mixture; toss gently. Add romaine, basil and croutons; toss.   *Makes 6 servings*

Presentation: Serve on chilled salad plates.

Marinated Three Bean Salad

Pasta Salad in Artichoke Cup

Pasta Salad in Artichoke Cups

5 cloves garlic, peeled
½ cup white wine
6 medium whole artichokes
1 lemon, cut in half
6 cups chicken broth
1 tablespoon *plus* 1 teaspoon olive
  oil, divided
1 package (2 ounces) artichoke hearts
8 ounces corkscrew pasta or pasta
  twists
½ teaspoon dried basil leaves,
  crushed
  Basil Vinaigrette Dressing
  (recipe follows)

Place garlic and wine in 1-quart saucepan. Bring to a boil over high heat; reduce heat to low. Simmer 10 minutes.

Meanwhile, cut bottoms from whole artichokes so that they will sit flat. Remove outer leaves. Cut 1 inch off tops of artichokes. Snip tips from remaining leaves with scissors. To help prevent discoloration, rub ends with lemon.

Place chicken broth in 6-quart Dutch oven. Bring to a boil over high heat. Add artichokes, wine mixture and 1 tablespoon oil. Reduce heat to low. Cover; simmer 25 to 30 minutes or until artichoke leaves pull easily from base. Drain.

Cook artichoke hearts according to package directions. Drain well. Cut into slices to make 2 cups. Set aside.

Cook pasta according to package directions. Drain in colander. Place pasta in large bowl. Sprinkle with remaining 1 teaspoon oil and basil. Add artichoke hearts and 1 cup Basil Vinaigrette Dressing to pasta; toss gently to coat.

Carefully spread outer leaves of whole artichokes. Remove the small heart leaves by grasping with fingers, then pulling and twisting. Scoop out the fuzzy choke with spoon. Fill with pasta mixture. Cover; refrigerate until serving time. Serve with remaining dressing. Garnish as desired.   *Makes 6 servings*

Basil Vinaigrette Dressing

⅓ cup white wine vinegar
2 tablespoons Dijon-style mustard
3 cloves garlic, peeled
¾ cup coarsely chopped fresh basil
  leaves
1 cup olive oil
  Salt and black pepper to taste

Place vinegar, mustard and garlic in blender or food processor. Cover; process until garlic is well mixed. Add basil; process until mixture is blended. With motor running, slowly pour olive oil through feed tube until well blended. Season with salt and black pepper.
          Makes about 1½ cups

Homestyle Zucchini & Tomatoes

2 tablespoons vegetable oil
3 medium zucchini, thinly sliced
    (about 4½ cups)
1 medium clove garlic, finely
    chopped*
1 can (14½ ounces) whole peeled
    tomatoes, drained and chopped
    (reserve liquid)
1 envelope LIPTON® Recipe
    Secrets™ Golden Onion
    Soup Mix**
½ teaspoon dried basil leaves

In large skillet, heat oil over medium-high heat. Add zucchini and garlic; cook, stirring occasionally, 3 minutes. Stir in tomatoes, then golden onion soup mix thoroughly blended with reserved liquid and basil. Bring to a boil, then simmer, stirring occasionally, 10 minutes or until zucchini is tender and sauce is slightly thickened. *Makes about 4 servings*

*Substitution: Use ¼ teaspoon LAWRY'S® Garlic Powder with Parsley.

****Also terrific with Lipton® Recipe Secrets™ Onion Soup Mix.

Microwave: In 2-quart microwave-safe casserole, combine zucchini with tomatoes. Stir in golden onion soup mix thoroughly blended with reserved liquid, garlic and basil. Microwave, covered, at HIGH (100% power) 5 minutes, stirring once. Uncover and microwave at HIGH 4 minutes or until zucchini is tender, stirring once. Let stand covered 2 minutes.

Quick Risotto

3 tablespoons butter or margarine
1 teaspoon finely chopped garlic
1 cup sliced zucchini
1 package LIPTON® Rice & Sauce–
    Chicken Flavor
2 cups water
2 tablespoons grated Parmesan
    cheese

In large skillet, melt butter and cook garlic with zucchini over medium heat, stirring occasionally, 1 minute or until almost tender. Stir in rice & chicken flavor sauce and cook over medium heat, stirring constantly, 1 minute or until golden brown. Add water and bring to a boil. Reduce heat and simmer, stirring occasionally, 10 minutes or until rice is tender. Stir in cheese. Serve, if desired, with additional cheese, chopped parsley and pepper. *Makes about 4 servings*

Homestyle Zucchini & Tomatoes

Marinated Vegetable Spinach Salad

Mustard Tarragon Marinade
  (recipe follows)
8 ounces fresh mushrooms,
  quartered
2 slices purple onion, separated into
  rings
16 cherry tomatoes, halved
4 cups fresh spinach leaves, washed
  and stems removed
3 slices (3 ounces) SARGENTO®
  Preferred Light® Sliced
  Mozzarella Cheese, cut into
  julienned strips
Fresh ground black pepper
  (optional)

Prepare marinade. Place mushrooms, onion and tomatoes in bowl. Toss with marinade and let stand 15 minutes. Meanwhile, dry spinach leaves. Arrange on 4 individual serving plates. Divide marinated vegetables between plates and top each salad with ¼ of the cheese. Serve with pepper, if desired.

Makes 4 servings

Mustard Tarragon Marinade

3 tablespoons red wine vinegar
1 tablespoon Dijon-style mustard
½ tablespoon dried tarragon leaves
2 tablespoons olive oil

Combine vinegar, mustard and tarragon in small bowl. Slowly whisk in oil until slightly thickened.

Risotto with Shellfish Genoa Style
(Risotto con Frutti di Mare alla Genovese)

2 teaspoons instant minced garlic
¼ cup instant minced onion
  Water
2 pounds mussels, scrubbed with
  beards removed
1 dozen littleneck clams, scrubbed
6 tablespoons olive oil, divided
3 cups coarsely chopped fresh
  tomatoes
1 tablespoon dried basil leaves,
  crushed
1 teaspoon dried tarragon leaves,
  crushed
1 teaspoon salt
¼ teaspoon black pepper, divided
4 bottles (8 ounces *each*) clam juice
2 cups Arborio rice*
½ cup dry white wine
2 tablespoons butter
1 teaspoon dried oregano leaves,
  crushed
1 pound large shrimp, shelled and
  deveined

Combine garlic, onion and ⅓ cup water in cup; set aside to soften, about 10 minutes. Place mussels, clams and 1 cup water in large skillet with tight fitting lid. Cover and cook 3 to 5 minutes removing shells as they open. Discard any unopened shells. Cool slightly; remove meat from shells (makes about 1½ cups); set aside. Strain cooking liquid into 2-cup measure, adding water to make 2 cups liquid; set aside. Heat 2 tablespoons oil in

*A short-grain rice available at specialty stores and some supermarkets.

large skillet until hot. Add onion mixture; cook and stir about 4 minutes or until pale gold. Add tomatoes, basil, tarragon, salt and ⅛ teaspoon black pepper; cook, stirring occasionally, about 10 minutes or until sauce forms; set aside.

Combine clam juice and reserved 2 cups cooking liquid in medium saucepan; bring to a boil. Meanwhile, heat remaining 4 tablespoons oil in large saucepan until hot. Add rice; cook and stir about 1 minute or until coated with oil. Stir in wine and remaining ⅛ teaspoon black pepper; cook, stirring constantly, until all liquid is absorbed.

Gradually add clam juice mixture, a little at a time, stirring constantly, allowing the liquid to be absorbed before adding more. Cook about 20 minutes or until rice is tender but firm. Stir in butter and oregano.

To serve, about 5 minutes before risotto is done reheat reserved tomato sauce. Add shrimp; cook until barely pink. Stir in reserved mussels and clams; cook 1 minute more. Place mound of rice on each plate; top with shellfish and tomato sauce. *Makes 8 servings*

Favorite recipe from **American Spice Trade Association**

Risotto with Shellfish Genoa Style

Fennel, Olive and Radicchio Salad

11 Italian- or Greek-style black olives, divided
¼ cup olive oil
1 tablespoon lemon juice
1 flat anchovy fillet *or* ½ teaspoon anchovy paste
¼ teaspoon salt
   Generous dash black pepper
   Generous dash sugar
1 fresh fennel bulb
1 head radicchio*
   Fennel greenery for garnish

For dressing, cut 3 olives in half; remove and discard pits. Place pitted olives, oil, lemon juice and anchovy in food processor or blender; process 5 seconds. Add salt, black pepper and sugar; process until olives are finely chopped, about 5 seconds more. Set aside.

Cut off and discard fennel stalks. Cut off and discard root end at base of fennel bulb and any discolored parts of bulb. Cut fennel bulb lengthwise into 8 wedges; separate each wedge into segments. Separate radicchio leaves; rinse thoroughly under running water. Drain well. Arrange radicchio leaves, fennel and remaining olives on serving plate. Spoon dressing over salad. Garnish, if desired. Serve immediately.

Makes 4 servings

*Radicchio, a tart red chicory, is available in large supermarkets and specialty food shops. If not available, 2 heads of Belgian endive can be used; although it does not provide the dramatic red color, it will give a similar texture and its slightly bitter flavor will go well with the robust dressing and the sweet anise flavor of fennel.

Green Beans with Pine Nuts

1 pound green beans, stem ends removed
2 tablespoons butter or margarine
2 tablespoons pine nuts
   Salt and black pepper to taste

Cook beans in 1 inch water in covered 3-quart saucepan 4 to 8 minutes or until crisp-tender; drain. Melt butter in large skillet over medium heat. Add pine nuts; cook, stirring frequently, until golden. Add beans; stir gently to coat beans with butter. Season with salt and black pepper.

Makes 4 servings

Ratatouille

2 tablespoons WESSON® Oil
2 medium zucchini, diced
1 small eggplant, peeled and diced
1 cup chopped onion
½ teaspoon minced garlic
1 (15-ounce) can HUNT'S® Ready Tomato Sauces Original Italian
1 teaspoon sugar
¾ teaspoon dried basil leaves, crushed

In medium saucepan, in hot oil, cook and stir zucchini, eggplant, onion and garlic about 5 minutes. Stir in *remaining* ingredients. Simmer, covered, stirring occasionally, 15 to 20 minutes or until vegetables are very tender. Serve immediately. *Makes 6 to 8 servings*

Fennel, Olive and Radicchio Salad

Rice Napoli

2 bags SUCCESS® Brown Rice
1 tablespoon reduced-calorie
    margarine
1 large green bell pepper, chopped
1 garlic clove, minced
1 can (14½ ounces) Italian-style
    tomatoes, drained
1 envelope (.7 ounce) Italian
    dressing mix
1 cup (4 ounces) shredded
    mozzarella cheese
½ cup sliced pitted ripe olives
    (optional)

Prepare rice according to package directions.

Melt margarine in large skillet over medium-high heat. Add green pepper and garlic; cook and stir until pepper is crisp-tender. Add tomatoes and dressing. Bring to a boil. Reduce heat to low; simmer 10 minutes, stirring occasionally. Stir in rice. Top with cheese. Sprinkle with olives, if desired.

Makes 8 servings

Rice Napoli

Risotto Primavera

1 cup sliced fresh mushrooms
1 cup diced red bell pepper
1 cup sliced zucchini*
¼ cup butter or margarine, divided
½ cup chopped onion
1 cup uncooked rice
⅓ cup dry white wine
2 cups chicken broth
3 cups water
¼ cup grated Parmesan cheese
    Salt and ground white pepper to
    taste
½ cup heavy cream

Cook mushrooms, red pepper and zucchini until crisp-tender in 2 tablespoons butter in large skillet over medium heat. Remove vegetables; set aside. Cook onion in remaining 2 tablespoons butter until soft. Add rice and stir 2 to 3 minutes. Add wine; stir until absorbed. Increase heat to medium-high; stir in 1 cup broth. Cook, uncovered, stirring frequently, until broth is absorbed. Continue stirring and adding remaining 1 cup broth and water, allowing each cup to be absorbed before adding another, until rice is tender and mixture has a creamy consistency, 25 to 30 minutes. Stir in cheese, salt, pepper, cream and reserved vegetables. Stir until mixture is creamy, about 2 to 3 minutes. Serve immediately.   *Makes 6 servings*

*Any type of fresh vegetable may be substituted.

*Favorite recipe from **USA Rice Council***

Herb Stuffed Artichokes

¼ cup plain bread crumbs
½ cup EGG BEATERS® 99% Real Egg Product
¼ cup grated Parmesan cheese
2 tablespoons FLEISCHMANN'S® Margarine, melted
2 tablespoons lemon juice
1 teaspoon Italian seasoning
1 clove garlic, crushed
6 large artichokes, prepared for stuffing and par boiled

Preheat oven to 350°F. In medium bowl, blend bread crumbs, egg product, Parmesan cheese, margarine, lemon juice, Italian seasoning and garlic. Stuff artichokes with bread crumb mixture. Place stuffed artichokes into 13×9×2-inch baking dish. Fill dish with 1 inch hot water. Cover with foil and bake until artichokes are tender and stuffing is hot, about 20 to 30 minutes.

Makes 6 servings

Valley Eggplant Parmigiano

2 eggplants (about 1 pound *each*)
⅓ cup olive or vegetable oil
1 container (15 ounces) ricotta cheese
2 packages (1 ounce *each*) HIDDEN VALLEY RANCH® Milk Recipe Original Ranch® Salad Dressing Mix
2 eggs
2 teaspoons dry bread crumbs
1 cup tomato sauce
½ cup shredded mozzarella cheese
1 tablespoon grated Parmesan cheese
Chopped fresh parsley

Valley Eggplant Parmigiano

Preheat oven to 350°F. Cut eggplants into ½-inch slices. Brush some of the oil onto two large baking sheets. Arrange eggplant slices in single layer on sheets and brush tops with additional oil. Bake about 20 minutes or until eggplant is fork-tender.

In large bowl, whisk together ricotta cheese and salad dressing mix; whisk in eggs. In 13×9-inch baking dish, layer half the eggplant. Sprinkle 1 teaspoon bread crumbs over eggplant; spread all the ricotta mixture on top. Arrange remaining eggplant in another layer. Sprinkle with remaining 1 teaspoon bread crumbs; top with tomato sauce. Sprinkle cheeses on top. Bake about 30 minutes or until cheeses begin to brown. Sprinkle with parsley.   *Makes 6 to 8 servings*

Beef, Tomato and Basil Salad

Beef, Tomato and Basil Salad

12 fresh basil leaves
1 large tomato, cut into 6 slices
6 thin slices cooked beef eye round roast (about 6 ounces)
4 teaspoons *each* olive oil and red wine vinegar
1 small clove garlic, minced
⅛ teaspoon salt
Freshly ground black pepper

Place 2 basil leaves on each tomato slice. Arrange alternating slices of tomato/basil and cooked beef eye round roast on each of 2 dinner plates. Combine oil, vinegar, garlic and salt in small bowl until well blended; drizzle over salad. Season with black pepper. *Makes 2 servings*

Prep time: 8 to 10 minutes

Note: To prepare roast, place 2-pound beef eye round roast on rack in open roasting pan in 325°F (slow) oven. Do not add water. Do not cover. Roast to 135°F. Allow approximately 20 to 22 minutes per pound. Let roast stand until temperature rises to 140°F for rare before carving. A beef eye roast will yield four 3-ounce cooked servings per pound.

*Favorite recipe from **National Live Stock & Meat Board***

Potato Salad Italian-Style

1½ cups HELLMANN'S® or BEST FOODS® Real or Light Mayonnaise or Reduced Fat Mayonnaise Dressing
¼ cup MAZOLA® Corn Oil
2 tablespoons wine vinegar
1 tablespoon chopped fresh basil *or* 1 teaspoon dried basil leaves
1½ teaspoons chopped fresh oregano *or* ½ teaspoon dried oregano leaves
1 clove garlic, minced
½ teaspoon freshly ground black pepper
3 pounds small red potatoes, cooked and quartered
1 jar (7¼ ounces) roasted red peppers, drained and cut into ½-inch strips
1 jar (6 ounces) marinated artichoke hearts, drained and quartered
1 can (6 ounces) pitted ripe olives, drained and cut in half
1 cup thinly sliced pepperoni
Salt to taste

In large bowl, combine mayonnaise, corn oil, vinegar, basil, oregano, garlic and black pepper. Add potatoes, roasted red peppers, artichoke hearts, olives, pepperoni and salt; toss to coat well. Serve at room temperature or cover and refrigerate until chilled.

Makes 8 servings

Italian Pasta Salad

8 ounces uncooked mostaccioli or
 ziti macaroni
2 large tomatoes, coarsely chopped
1½ cups broccoli flowerets, cooked
1 medium green bell pepper,
 chopped
1 cup (8 ounces) WISH-BONE®
 Robusto Italian Dressing
1 tablespoon chopped fresh basil
 leaves*
1 package (8 ounces) mozzarella
 cheese, diced
¼ cup grated Parmesan cheese

Cook macaroni according to package
directions; drain and rinse with cold
water until completely cool.

In large salad bowl, combine tomatoes,
broccoli, green pepper, robusto Italian
dressing and basil. Add cheeses and
macaroni, then toss lightly; cover and
refrigerate until chilled.

Makes about 10 side-dish servings

Substitution: Use 1 teaspoon dried basil
leaves.

Grilled Vegetables with Balsamic Vinaigrette

1 medium eggplant (about
 1¼ pounds)
2 medium zucchini
2 to 3 medium yellow squash
2 medium red bell peppers
¾ cup olive oil
¼ cup balsamic vinegar
1 teaspoon salt
¼ teaspoon black pepper
1 clove garlic, minced
2 to 3 tablespoons finely chopped
 mixed fresh herbs

Trim, then slice eggplant, zucchini and
yellow squash lengthwise into ¼- to
½-inch-thick slices. Core, seed and cut red
peppers into 1-inch-wide strips. Place
vegetables in a deep serving platter or
wide shallow casserole. Combine oil,
vinegar, salt, black pepper, garlic and
chopped herbs in small bowl. Pour
vinaigrette over vegetables; turn to coat.
Let stand 30 minutes or longer. Remove
vegetables, reserving vinaigrette.

Oil hot grid to help prevent sticking. Grill
vegetables, on a covered grill, over
medium KINGSFORD® briquets, 8 to 16
minutes until fork-tender, turning once or
twice. (Time will depend on the
vegetable; eggplant takes the longest.)
As vegetables are done, return to platter,
then turn to coat with reserved
vinaigrette. (Or, cut eggplant, zucchini
and yellow squash into cubes, then toss
with red peppers and vinaigrette. Serve
warm or at room temperature.)

Makes 6 servings

Grilled Vegetables with Balsamic Vinaigrette

Risotto with Peas and Mushrooms

1 cup frozen peas
1 cup sliced fresh mushrooms
2 tablespoons butter or margarine, divided
½ cup chopped onion
1 cup uncooked rice
⅓ cup dry white wine
2 cups chicken broth
3 cups water
¼ cup grated Parmesan cheese
    Salt and ground white pepper to taste
½ cup heavy cream

Cook peas and mushrooms in 1 tablespoon butter in large skillet over medium heat several minutes. Remove vegetables; set aside. Cook onion in remaining 1 tablespoon butter until soft. Add rice and stir 2 to 3 minutes. Add wine; stir until absorbed. Increase heat to medium high; stir in 1 cup broth. Cook, uncovered, stirring frequently, until broth is absorbed. Continue stirring and adding remaining 1 cup broth and water, allowing each cup to be absorbed before adding another, until rice is tender and mixture has a creamy consistency, 25 to 30 minutes. Stir in cheese, seasonings, cream and reserved vegetables. Stir until mixture is creamy, about 2 to 3 minutes. Serve immediately.   *Makes 6 servings*

Favorite recipe from **USA Rice Council**

Skinny Eggplant Parmigiana

1¾ teaspoons olive oil
1½ cups finely chopped onions
2 cloves garlic, minced
2 cups canned whole tomatoes
½ teaspoon dried oregano leaves, crushed
⅛ teaspoon black pepper
1 bay leaf
¾ pound eggplant, unpeeled and cut into ½-inch-thick slices
1 egg white, lightly beaten
½ cup seasoned fine bread crumbs
¾ cup California ripe olives, sliced
¼ cup grated Parmesan cheese
¼ cup shredded part-skim mozzarella cheese

Coat large skillet with nonstick cooking spray and add oil. Heat over medium-high heat; add onions and garlic. Cook and stir until tender. Add tomatoes, oregano, black pepper and bay leaf. Cover and simmer 15 minutes. Remove from heat. Remove and discard bay leaf. Place tomato mixture in blender or food processor; process until smooth. Place half the tomato mixture in 13×9-inch baking dish coated with cooking spray; set aside.

Preheat oven 375°F. Dip eggplant slices in beaten egg white and dredge in bread crumbs. Arrange eggplant slices on top of tomato mixture in pan. Pour remaining tomato mixture on eggplant slices. Sprinkle with olives and cheeses. Bake 35 minutes or until sauce is bubbly.
Makes 6 servings

Favorite recipe from **California Olive Industry**

Risotto with Peas and Mushrooms

Grilled Pasta Salad

Grilled Pasta Salad

4 medium zucchini and/or yellow
   squash, sliced
1 medium Spanish onion, halved
   and cut into large chunks
1 envelope LIPTON® Recipe
   Secrets™ Savory Herb with Garlic
   Soup Mix*
¼ cup olive or vegetable oil
8 ounces uncooked penne, rotini or
   ziti pasta, cooked according to
   package directions and drained
¾ cup diced roasted red peppers
¼ cup red wine vinegar, apple cider
   vinegar or white vinegar

On broiler pan or heavy-duty aluminum foil, arrange zucchini and onion. Brush with savory herb with garlic soup mix blended with oil. Grill or broil 5 minutes or until golden brown and crisp-tender.

In large bowl, toss cooked pasta, vegetables, roasted peppers and vinegar. Serve warm or at room temperature.

*Makes about 4 main-dish or
8 side-dish servings*

*Also terrific with Lipton® Recipe Secrets™ Italian Herb with Tomato or Golden Onion Soup Mix.

Caesar Dressing

1 cup HELLMANN'S® or BEST
 FOODS® Real or Light
 Mayonnaise or Reduced Fat
 Mayonnaise Dressing
3 tablespoons milk
2 tablespoons cider vinegar
2 tablespoons grated Parmesan
 cheese
½ teaspoon sugar
⅛ teaspoon garlic powder

In small bowl, combine mayonnaise,
milk, vinegar, Parmesan, sugar and garlic
powder until well blended. Cover;
refrigerate. *Makes about 1¼ cups*

Italian Garden Medley

*Three of Italy's most popular vegetables are
combined into an easy casserole and topped
with crisp seasoned bread crumbs.*

2 tablespoons PROGRESSO®
 Olive Oil
4 cups thinly sliced zucchini, cut on
 diagonal (about 3 medium
 zucchini)
1 medium onion, sliced and
 separated into rings
3 medium tomatoes, coarsely
 chopped
1 cup (4 ounces) shredded
 mozzarella cheese
1 cup vegetable juice
1 teaspoon cornstarch
½ teaspoon salt
½ teaspoon garlic powder
¼ teaspoon ground black pepper
¼ cup PROGRESSO® Italian Style
 Bread Crumbs

1. Preheat oven to 350°F.

2. In large skillet, heat olive oil. Add
zucchini and onion; cook 4 minutes or
until zucchini is crisp-tender, stirring
occasionally.

3. In 2-quart casserole, combine zucchini
mixture, tomatoes, cheese, juice,
cornstarch, salt, garlic powder and
pepper. Top with bread crumbs.

4. Bake 30 minutes or until thoroughly
heated. Broil 2 to 3 minutes or until top is
golden brown. *Makes 6 servings*

Prep time: 20 minutes
Cooking time: 32 minutes

Stuffed Tomatoes

1 bag SUCCESS® Rice
½ pound fresh mushrooms, sliced
½ cup sliced zucchini
½ cup thinly sliced carrots
½ cup sliced green onions
4 medium tomatoes

Dressing

⅓ cup fat-free mayonnaise
⅓ cup fat-free sour cream
1½ tablespoons tarragon vinegar
1 tablespoon Dijon-style mustard
1 teaspoon salt
1 teaspoon dried dill weed

Prepare rice according to package
directions. Cool.

Place rice in large bowl. Add mushrooms,
zucchini, carrots and green onions; mix
lightly. Cut tops off tomatoes; scoop out
pulp. Invert tomatoes onto paper towels
to drain while preparing dressing.

Combine dressing ingredients in small
bowl; blend well. Pour over rice mixture;
toss gently to coat. Spoon into tomato
shells. *Makes 4 servings*

Two-Squash Risotto

1 can (about 14 ounces) chicken
   broth
3 tablespoons butter or margarine
1 cup UNCLE BEN'S®
   CONVERTED® Brand Rice
1 cup coarsely chopped onion
2 cloves garlic, minced
1 cup thin zucchini strips
1 cup thin yellow squash strips
½ cup shredded mozzarella cheese
   Black pepper
4 slices crisply cooked bacon,
   crumbled (optional)

Add water to broth to make 2¼ cups
liquid; set aside. Melt butter in large
saucepan. Add rice, onion and garlic.
Cook over medium heat 3 to 4 minutes,
stirring constantly. Add liquid. Bring to a
boil. Reduce heat. Cover tightly and
simmer 20 minutes. Stir in zucchini and
yellow squash. Let stand, covered, about
5 minutes or until all liquid is absorbed.
Stir in cheese. Sprinkle with black pepper
and bacon, if desired.   *Makes 6 servings*

Two-Squash Risotto

Polenta with Ratatouille Sauce

 3 cups water
¾ cup Regular, Quick or Instant
   CREAM OF WHEAT® Cereal
 2 cloves garlic, minced, divided
¼ cup grated Parmesan cheese,
   divided
½ teaspoon dried basil leaves,
   divided
 3 tablespoons olive oil, divided
 1 small eggplant, chopped (about
   2½ cups)
⅓ cup sliced onion
⅓ cup chopped green bell pepper
 1 tablespoon lemon juice
 1 cup chopped tomato
¾ cup tomato juice

In large saucepan, over high heat, bring
water to a boil; slowly sprinkle in cereal
and half the garlic. Cook and stir cereal
until thickened, about 1 to 3 minutes;
remove from heat. Spread mixture in
greased and foil-lined 8×8×2-inch
baking pan. Sprinkle top with
2 tablespoons Parmesan cheese and
¼ teaspoon basil leaves. Cover;
refrigerate until firm, about 30 minutes.
Cut into 4 (4-inch) squares; then cut
squares diagonally in half to form
triangles.

In large skillet, over medium-high heat,
cook half the triangles in 2 teaspoons oil
until crisp and golden on each side, about
5 minutes; remove from skillet and keep
warm. Repeat with remaining triangles
and 2 teaspoons oil.

Meanwhile, for sauce, in large skillet over
medium heat, cook eggplant, onion,
pepper and remaining garlic in remaining

oil and lemon juice until slightly tender, about 5 minutes. Stir in tomato, tomato juice and remaining ¼ teaspoon basil leaves; bring to a boil. Reduce heat to low; simmer 2 to 3 minutes or until tender. Serve warm over polenta topped with remaining 2 tablespoons Parmesan cheese. *Makes 8 servings*

Peppers Piemontese

4 red bell peppers
1 clove fresh garlic, minced
1 tablespoon olive oil
  Salt and black pepper to taste
1 tablespoon drained capers
3 anchovies
1 tablespoon red wine vinegar
   (optional)

Place bell peppers under broiler and broil, turning occasionally, until skins are well blistered and charred all over. Place peppers in small paper bag and close. Let steam 5 minutes. Peel off skins working under cold running water. Cut peppers in half; remove seeds and cores.

Cook and stir garlic lightly in hot oil. Add bell peppers; cook and stir over low heat 3 to 4 minutes, turning with spatula, until peppers are hot and tender. Add salt and black pepper; sprinkle with capers. Top with anchovies. Serve warm *or* sprinkle with wine vinegar and refrigerate until chilled. Garnish with lemon wedges and chopped fresh parsley, if desired. *Makes 4 servings*

Favorite recipe from **Christopher Ranch of Gilroy**

Zucchini Italiano

Zucchini Italiano

3 tablespoons olive or vegetable oil
4 medium zucchini, cut into 1½-inch
   julienned pieces
¼ cup minced onion
¼ cup minced green bell pepper
1 medium tomato, finely chopped
¾ teaspoon LAWRY'S® Garlic Powder
   with Parsley
¼ teaspoon LAWRY'S® Seasoned Salt
¼ teaspoon dried marjoram leaves,
   crushed

In medium skillet, heat oil; add remaining ingredients and lightly cook and stir about 10 minutes or until vegetables are crisp-tender.

Makes 4 servings

Presentation: Sprinkle vegetables with grated Parmesan cheese just before serving.

Antipasto Rice

1½ cups water
½ cup tomato juice
1 cup uncooked rice
1 teaspoon dried basil leaves
1 teaspoon dried oregano leaves
½ teaspoon salt (optional)
1 can (14 ounces) artichoke hearts, drained and quartered
1 jar (7 ounces) roasted red peppers, drained and chopped
1 can (2¼ ounces) sliced ripe olives, drained
2 tablespoons chopped fresh parsley
2 tablespoons lemon juice
½ teaspoon black pepper
2 tablespoons grated Parmesan cheese

Combine water, tomato juice, rice, basil, oregano and salt in 2- to 3-quart saucepan. Bring to a boil; stir once or twice. Reduce heat; cover and simmer 15 minutes or until rice is tender and liquid is absorbed. Stir in artichokes, red peppers, olives, parsley, lemon juice and black pepper. Cook 5 minutes longer or until thoroughly heated. Sprinkle with cheese. *Makes 8 servings*

Microwave: Combine water, tomato juice, rice, basil, oregano and salt in deep 2- to 3-quart microproof baking dish. Cover and cook on HIGH (100% power) 5 minutes. Reduce setting to MEDIUM (50% power) and cook 15 minutes or until rice is tender and liquid is absorbed. Add artichokes, red peppers, olives, parsley, lemon juice and black pepper. Cook on HIGH 2 to 3 minutes or until mixture is thoroughly heated. Sprinkle with cheese.

*Favorite recipe from **USA Rice Council***

Eggplant Northern Italian Style

4 baby eggplants*
1 tablespoon olive oil
1 large clove fresh garlic, minced
1¼ cups diced mozzarella cheese
1 small tomato, peeled and diced
1 tablespoon chopped fresh parsley
⅛ teaspoon dried oregano leaves, crushed
1 can (7¾ ounces) marinara sauce
Salt and black pepper to taste

Preheat oven to 375°F. Cut eggplants in half lengthwise. Cut "X" in meaty parts of halves with sharp knife. Place in large skillet; add water to ½ inch deep and bring to a boil over medium-high heat. Cover and simmer 10 to 15 minutes until eggplant is tender when pierced with fork. Remove from pan and drain well. Heat oil in same skillet. Add garlic; cook and stir until golden. Combine cheese, tomato, garlic, parsley and oregano in medium bowl. Measure about 3 to 4 tablespoons marinara sauce for each serving into large baking dish or into 4 individual dishes. Sprinkle eggplant lightly with salt and black pepper; place, skin sides down, in sauce. Top with tomato-cheese mixture. Bake about 25 minutes or until heated through.
Makes 4 servings (2 halves each)

*One small regular eggplant, about 14 to 16 ounces may be substituted. Quarter eggplant lengthwise and proceed as directed. Allow one quarter per serving.

*Favorite recipe from **Christopher Ranch of Gilroy***

Antipasto Rice

Artichoke Spinach Salad

Artichoke Spinach Salad

½ cup PROGRESSO® Olive Oil
¼ cup PROGRESSO® Red Wine
    Vinegar
1 tablespoon lemon juice
1 tablespoon Dijon-style mustard
½ teaspoon sugar
½ teaspoon salt
½ teaspoon dried dill weed
¼ teaspoon ground black pepper
6 ounces (about 6 cups) fresh
    spinach, washed, trimmed and
    torn into bite-size pieces
1 cup shredded red cabbage
1 can (14 ounces) PROGRESSO®
    Artichoke Hearts, drained and
    quartered
4 ounces cooked ham, cut into thin
    strips
4 ounces Muenster or provolone
    cheese, cut into thin strips

1. For dressing, whisk together olive oil,
vinegar, lemon juice, mustard, sugar, salt,
dill and pepper.

2. In large bowl, combine spinach,
cabbage, artichoke hearts, ham and
cheese.

3. Pour dressing over salad; toss gently.
Makes 4 main-dish servings

Prep time: 20 minutes

Risotto Milanese

1½ cups sliced fresh mushrooms
2 tablespoons butter or margarine,
    divided
½ cup chopped onion
1 cup uncooked rice
1/16 teaspoon saffron*
⅓ cup dry white wine
2 cups chicken broth, divided
3 cups water
¼ cup grated Parmesan cheese
¼ cup milk

Cook mushrooms in 1 tablespoon butter
in large nonstick skillet over medium
heat. Remove mushrooms; set aside.
Cook onion in remaining 1 tablespoon
butter until soft. Add rice and saffron; stir
2 to 3 minutes. Add wine; stir until
absorbed. Increase heat to medium-high;
stir in 1 cup broth. Cook, uncovered,
stirring frequently, until broth is
absorbed. Continue stirring and adding
remaining 1 cup broth and water,
allowing each cup to be absorbed before
adding another, until rice is tender and
mixture has a creamy consistency, 25 to
30 minutes. Stir in cheese, milk and
reserved mushrooms; serve immediately.
Makes 6 servings

*Substitute ground turmeric for the
saffron, if desired.

Favorite recipe from **USA Rice Council**

Garlic Mushrooms

32 large fresh mushrooms
½ cup olive or vegetable oil
2 cloves garlic, minced

Remove stems from mushrooms; discard. Combine oil and garlic in medium bowl. Add mushroom caps; toss lightly to coat. Remove mushrooms with slotted spoon; place on piece of heavy-duty foil. Close foil over mushrooms; seal edges tightly. Grill at edge of grid, over medium-hot KINGSFORD® briquets, 10 to 15 minutes or until tender. *Makes 8 servings*

Italian Scallop Marinade

2 cups broccoli flowerets
2 small red, green *or* yellow peppers, cut into strips
4 ounces KRAFT® Natural Swiss Cheese Slices, cut into 2-inch strips
1 cup sliced mushrooms
1 bottle (8 ounces) KRAFT® House Italian Dressing
1 pound sea scallops
1 tablespoon PARKAY® Spread Sticks
8 cups torn mixed salad greens

• Toss broccoli, peppers, cheese and mushrooms with dressing in large bowl; cover. Refrigerate at least 30 minutes to marinate.

• Cook and stir scallops in spread in large skillet on medium heat 6 to 8 minutes or until opaque; drain.

• Spoon vegetable mixture over salad greens on dinner plates; top with scallops. *Makes 4 servings*

Prep time: 15 minutes plus refrigerating
Cooking time: 8 minutes

Vegetables Italiano

1 cup Italian seasoned bread crumbs
⅓ cup grated Parmesan cheese
⅔ cup HELLMANN'S® or BEST FOODS® Light Mayonnaise
6 cups assorted vegetables: broccoli florets, carrot slices, cauliflower florets, small mushrooms, green and/or red bell pepper strips, yellow squash slices and/or zucchini strips

Preheat oven to 425°F. In large plastic food storage bag, combine crumbs and Parmesan; shake to blend well. In another large plastic food storage bag, combine mayonnaise and vegetables; shake to coat well. Add mayonnaise-coated vegetables, half at a time, to crumb mixture; shake to coat well. Arrange in single layer on ungreased baking sheet so that pieces do not touch. Bake 10 minutes or until golden. *Makes 8 servings*

Vegetables Italiano

Insalata di Riso con Basilico
(Italian Rice Salad with Basil)

1 cup Arborio or short-grain rice
2 tablespoons olive oil
1 cup diced eggplant
1½ cups diced zucchini
1 cup diced red bell pepper
3 tablespoons olive oil
2 tablespoons lemon juice
2½ teaspoons dried basil leaves, crushed
1 teaspoon salt
½ teaspoon garlic powder
¼ teaspoon black pepper

Bring 3 quarts water to a boil in 4-quart saucepan. Add rice; cover and cook 14 to 16 minutes until tender. Meanwhile, heat 2 tablespoons oil in large skillet over medium-high heat until hot. Add eggplant, zucchini and red pepper; cook and stir about 5 minutes or until crisp-tender. Set aside. To prepare dressing, combine 3 tablespoons oil, lemon juice, basil, salt, garlic powder and black pepper in small bowl until well blended; set aside. Drain rice; rinse with cold water. Drain well. Combine rice, reserved vegetables and dressing in large bowl; toss to coat well. Serve at room temperature over lettuce leaves.

Makes 4 servings (4 cups)

Favorite recipe from **American Spice Trade Association**

Insalata di Riso con Basilico

Herbed Fennel with Tomatoes

2 medium fennel bulbs with 2-inch
    stalks (about 1¼ pounds)
5 tablespoons olive oil, divided
1 clove garlic, minced
3 large plum tomatoes, sliced
    crosswise
¼ cup sliced pitted ripe olives
¼ cup red wine
1 tablespoon chopped fresh basil
    leaves *or* 1 teaspoon dried basil
    leaves, crushed
  Salt and black pepper to taste
¼ cup freshly grated Parmesan cheese
  Fennel greenery, for garnish

Preheat oven to 400°F. To prepare fennel, trim off feathery fennel leaves; set aside. Cut off and discard any green stems; trim thin slice from base. Halve bulbs; remove tough core wedge from each half, leaving enough root base to hold fennel together. Thinly slice bulbs lengthwise.

Heat 4 tablespoons oil in large skillet over medium heat. Cook and stir fennel and garlic in hot oil 5 minutes or until fennel is tender. Grease 13×9-inch baking dish with remaining 1 tablespoon oil. Make alternating rows of fennel and tomatoes, overlapping slices slightly.

Sprinkle olives over vegetables. Pour wine over vegetables and sprinkle with basil; season with salt and black pepper. Sprinkle cheese over top. Bake 15 to 20 minutes until cheese melts and wine has almost evaporated. Chop enough reserved fennel leaves to make 1 tablespoon. Sprinkle over top. Garnish, if desired. Serve immediately.

Makes 4 servings

Risotto with Sausage and Shrimp

½ pound sweet Italian sausage,
    crumbled
½ pound medium shrimp, peeled and
    deveined
3 tablespoons butter or margarine,
    divided
½ cup chopped onion
1 cup uncooked rice
⅓ cup dry white wine
2 cups chicken broth
¼ cup grated Parmesan cheese
  Ground white pepper to taste
½ cup heavy cream

Cook sausage in large skillet over medium heat. Remove from skillet; drain on paper towels. Set aside. Cook shrimp in 2 tablespoons butter until it turns pink. Remove from skillet; set aside. Cook onion until soft in remaining 1 tablespoon butter. Add rice and stir 2 to 3 minutes. Add wine; stir until absorbed. Increase heat to medium-high; stir in 1 cup broth. Cook, uncovered, stirring frequently, until broth is absorbed. Continue stirring and adding remaining 1 cup broth and 3 cups water, allowing each cup to be absorbed before adding another, until rice is tender and mixture has a creamy consistency, 25 to 30 minutes. Stir in cheese, pepper, cream, and reserved sausage and shrimp. Stir until mixture is creamy, about 2 to 3 minutes. Serve immediately.

Makes 6 servings

Favorite recipe from **USA Rice Council**

Tomato, Mozzarella & Basil Salad

2 tablespoons red wine vinegar
1 clove garlic, minced
½ teaspoon salt
¼ teaspoon dry mustard
   Generous dash black pepper
⅓ cup olive or vegetable oil
4 Italian plum tomatoes
6 ounces mozzarella cheese
8 to 10 fresh basil leaves

For dressing, combine vinegar, garlic, salt, mustard and black pepper in small bowl. Whisk in oil until thoroughly blended. Slice tomatoes and cheese into ¼-inch-thick slices. Trim cheese slices to size of tomato slices. Place tomato and cheese slices in large, shallow bowl or glass baking dish. Pour dressing over slices. Marinate, covered, in refrigerator for at least 30 minutes or up to 3 hours, turning slices occasionally.

Layer basil leaves with largest leaf on bottom, then roll up jelly-roll fashion. Slice basil roll into ¼-inch-thick slices; separate into strips. Arrange tomato and cheese slices alternately on serving plate or 4 individual salad plates. Sprinkle with basil strips; drizzle with remaining dressing. *Makes 4 servings*

Colorful Grape, Pepper and Pasta Salad

8 ounces thin spaghetti, cooked
   according to package directions
   Mustard Walnut Vinaigrette,
   divided (recipe follows)
1 cup California seedless grapes
½ cup thinly sliced red or yellow bell
   pepper
2 tablespoons *each* minced celery
   and green onion
1 tablespoon chopped fresh tarragon
   or ½ teaspoon dried tarragon
   leaves, crushed
   Salt and black pepper to taste
¼ cup walnuts,* quartered

Combine hot spaghetti and 3 tablespoons Mustard Walnut Vinaigrette in large bowl; toss to coat. Cool. Add remaining ingredients including remaining vinaigrette; mix well. Serve in lettuce-lined bowl; garnish with tarragon sprigs, if desired. *Makes 4 servings*

Mustard Walnut Vinaigrette: Whisk together 3 tablespoons white wine vinegar, 2 tablespoons olive oil, 2 tablespoons Dijon-style mustard, 1 minced clove garlic, ½ teaspoon sugar and ⅛ teaspoon black pepper until well blended. Makes about ⅓ cup.

*Walnuts may be omitted; substitute 1 tablespoon walnut oil for 1 tablespoon olive oil in vinaigrette.

Favorite recipe from **California Table Grape Commission**

Tomato, Mozzarella & Basil Salad

Antipasto Salad

Antipasto Salad

1¼ cups HELLMANN'S® or BEST
    FOODS® Real or Light
    Mayonnaise or Reduced Fat
    Mayonnaise Dressing
⅓ cup grated Parmesan cheese
⅓ cup chopped fresh parsley
¼ teaspoon dried oregano
¼ teaspoon dried basil
⅛ teaspoon freshly ground black
    pepper
1 clove garlic, minced or pressed
4 ounces thin spaghetti, cooked
    according to package directions
    and drained
4 ounces salami, cut into matchsticks
1 can (14 ounces) artichoke hearts,
    drained and quartered
1 cup sliced fresh mushrooms
1 small zucchini, cut into
    matchsticks

In large bowl, combine mayonnaise,
Parmesan, parsley, oregano, basil, pepper
and garlic. Stir in spaghetti, salami,
artichoke hearts, mushrooms and
zucchini. Cover; refrigerate until chilled.
Garnish as desired.

Makes about 6 servings

Pasta Salad with Pesto and Almonds

1 cup BLUE DIAMOND® Chopped
    Natural Almonds
1 tablespoon butter or margarine
16 ounces uncooked corkscrew pasta
1 cup prepared pesto
½ cup freshly grated Parmesan cheese
¼ cup white wine vinegar
¼ cup olive oil
½ teaspoon salt
¼ teaspoon white pepper
1 cup frozen green peas, thawed
4 green onions, sliced
4 ounces cooked ham, julienned
1 red bell pepper, diced

Cook and stir almonds in butter in small
skillet over medium-high heat until crisp;
set aside. Cook pasta according to
package directions; drain. Meanwhile,
combine pesto, cheese, vinegar, oil, salt
and white pepper in small bowl until
well blended. Toss hot pasta with peas
and pesto dressing in large bowl. Fold in
onions, ham, bell pepper and reserved
almonds. Serve immediately.

Makes 4 to 6 servings

Italian Herb Dressing

⅔ **cup vegetable oil**
⅓ **cup HEINZ® Gourmet Wine**
    Vinegar
1 **clove garlic, split**
1 **teaspoon dry mustard**
½ **teaspoon salt**
½ **teaspoon dried basil leaves,**
    crushed
½ **teaspoon dried oregano leaves,**
    crushed
¼ **teaspoon crushed red pepper**

In jar, combine all ingredients; cover and shake vigorously. Refrigerate until chilled to allow flavors to blend. Remove garlic; shake again before serving over tossed green salads. *Makes 1 cup*

Spinach Gnocchi

2 **packages (10 ounces *each*) frozen**
    chopped spinach
1 **cup ricotta cheese**
2 **eggs**
⅔ **cup freshly grated Parmesan cheese**
    (about 2 ounces), divided
1 **cup *plus* 3 tablespoons all-purpose**
    flour, divided
½ **teaspoon salt**
⅛ **teaspoon black pepper**
⅛ **teaspoon ground nutmeg**
3 **tablespoons butter or margarine,**
    melted

Cook spinach according to package directions. Drain well; let cool. Squeeze spinach dry; place in medium bowl. Stir in ricotta cheese. Add eggs; mix well. Add ⅓ cup Parmesan cheese, 3 tablespoons flour, salt, black pepper and nutmeg; mix well. Cover and refrigerate 1 hour.

Spread remaining 1 cup flour in shallow baking pan. Press heaping tablespoonful of spinach mixture between spoon and your hand to form oval gnocchi; place on flour. Repeat with remaining spinach mixture. Roll gnocchi lightly in flour to coat evenly; discard excess flour. Drop 8 to 12 gnocchi into large pot of boiling salted water; reduce heat to medium. Cook, uncovered, 5 minutes or until gnocchi are slightly puffed and slightly firm to the touch. Remove gnocchi with slotted spoon; drain on paper towels. Immediately transfer to greased broilerproof shallow baking dish. Reheat water to boiling. Repeat with remaining gnocchi in batches of 8 to 12. Arrange in single layer in baking dish.

Preheat broiler. Spoon butter over gnocchi; sprinkle with remaining ⅓ cup cheese. Broil gnocchi 5 inches from heat source 2 to 3 minutes until cheese melts and browns lightly. Serve immediately. Garnish as desired.
    Makes 4 to 6 servings (about 24 gnocchi)

Spinach Gnocchi

Tomato Risotto Pronto

1 can (14½ ounces) DEL MONTE®
    Italian Recipe Stewed Tomatoes
2 large mushrooms, sliced
1 tablespoon olive oil
1 cup uncooked long grain white rice
1 clove garlic, minced
⅛ to ¼ teaspoon pepper
1¼ cups chicken broth
¼ cup grated Parmesan cheese

Drain tomatoes reserving liquid; pour liquid into measuring cup. Add water to measure 1⅔ cups. In large saucepan, brown mushrooms in oil. Add rice, garlic and pepper; cook 2 minutes. Add reserved liquid and tomatoes; bring to boil. Cover and cook over low heat 18 minutes. Remove cover; increase heat to medium. Gradually stir in ½ cup broth. When liquid is gone, gradually add another ½ cup broth, adding remaining ¼ cup broth when liquid is gone. Add cheese. Rice should be tender-firm but creamy. Serve immediately.

Makes 4 to 6 servings

Prep time: 8 minutes
Cook time: 32 minutes

Parmesan Potato Slices

½ cup grated Parmesan cheese
¼ cup all-purpose flour
2 tablespoons chopped fresh basil
    leaves *or* 2 teaspoons dried basil
    leaves, crushed
1 tablespoon dried parsley flakes
¾ teaspoon salt
¼ teaspoon paprika
⅛ teaspoon black pepper
⅓ cup margarine
6 medium potatoes, cut into 1-inch
    slices

Preheat oven to 375°F. In plastic bag, combine cheese, flour, basil, parsley, salt, paprika and black pepper. Melt margarine in large shallow baking dish. Drop potatoes, a few at a time, into flour mixture; shake to coat. Place potatoes in single layer in margarine. Bake, uncovered, 45 to 50 minutes, turning potatoes once after 20 minutes.

Makes 6 to 8 servings

*Favorite recipe from **Hudson Foods, Inc.***

Glorious Garbanzo Salad

5 cups cooked low-sodium garbanzo
    beans, well drained
⅓ cup chopped toasted* California
    walnuts
3 medium tomatoes, diced
¼ cup chopped fresh parsley
¼ cup chopped green onion
½ cup nonfat cottage cheese
1 tablespoon olive oil
3 tablespoons wine vinegar
1 clove garlic, minced
1 teaspoon salt
½ teaspoon black pepper

Rinse beans under running water, then drain well again. Place in medium bowl. Add walnuts, tomatoes, parsley and green onion; set aside.

Whisk together cottage cheese, oil, vinegar, garlic, salt and black pepper in small bowl. Pour over salad ingredients and toss to combine. Refrigerate until chilled, tossing occasionally. Season with additional black pepper and vinegar to taste, if desired. *Makes 8 servings*

*Toasting is optional.

*Favorite recipe from **Walnut Marketing Board***

Italian Vegetable Salad

Italian Vegetable Salad

1 can (16 ounces) VEG-ALL® Mixed
  Vegetables, drained
1 can (16 ounces) garbanzo beans,
  drained
¼ cup chopped green onion
½ cup chopped celery
¼ cup olive oil
3 tablespoons vinegar
1 teaspoon sugar
1 teaspoon dried basil leaves
1 clove garlic, minced
½ cup ripe olives, sliced
1 cup cherry tomatoes, quartered
2 tablespoons chopped fresh parsley

Combine Veg-All® mixed vegetables,
beans, onion and celery in medium glass
bowl.

Whisk together oil, vinegar, sugar, basil
and garlic; blend well and pour over
vegetable-bean mixture. Let stand several
hours or overnight to marinate. Add
olives, tomatoes and parsley before
serving; toss to coat. Serve over lettuce
leaves, if desired.

Makes 4 to 6 servings

Risotto alla Milanese

¼ teaspoon saffron threads
3½ to 4 cups chicken broth, divided
7 tablespoons butter or margarine, divided
1 large onion, chopped
1½ cups uncooked Arborio or other short-grain white rice
½ cup dry white wine
½ teaspoon salt
Dash black pepper
¼ cup freshly grated Parmesan cheese
Chopped fresh parsley

Crush saffron in mortar with pestle to a powder. Bring broth to a boil in small saucepan over medium heat; reduce heat. Stir ½ cup broth into saffron to dissolve; set aside. Keep remaining broth hot.

Heat 6 tablespoons butter in large heavy skillet or 2½-quart saucepan over medium heat until melted and bubbly. Add onion; cook and stir 5 minutes or until onion is soft. Stir in rice; cook and stir 2 minutes. Stir in wine, salt and black pepper. Cook, uncovered, over medium-high heat 3 to 5 minutes until wine has evaporated, stirring occasionally. Measure ½ cup hot broth; stir into rice. Reduce heat to medium-low, maintaining a simmer. Cook and stir until broth has absorbed. Repeat, adding ½ cup broth 3 more times, cooking and stirring until broth has absorbed. Add saffron-flavored broth to rice and cook until absorbed. Continue adding remaining broth, ½ cup at a time, and cooking until rice is tender but firm and mixture has slightly creamy consistency. (Not all the broth may be necessary. Total cooking time of rice will be about 20 minutes.)

Remove risotto from heat. Stir in remaining 1 tablespoon butter and cheese. Sprinkle with parsley. Garnish as desired. *Makes 6 to 8 servings*

Risotto alla Milanese

Ranch Italian Pasta Salad

1 pound fusilli or other spiral or shell-shaped pasta, cooked according to package directions and drained
2 cups sliced fresh mushrooms
1½ cups cooked broccoli flowerets
1 cup prepared HIDDEN VALLEY RANCH® Ranch Italian salad dressing
4 ounces salami, cut into julienned strips
1 red bell pepper, minced
¼ cup grated Parmesan cheese
2 tablespoons chopped fresh parsley

In large bowl, combine all ingredients, tossing thoroughly with salad dressing. Cover and refrigerate at least 1 hour before serving. *Makes 4 to 6 servings*

Veg-All® Pasta & Tuna Salad Italienne

6 ounces uncooked fettuccine
1 can (16 ounces) VEG-ALL® Mixed Vegetables, drained
1 can (6½ ounces) water-packed tuna, drained and flaked
½ cup chopped tomato
½ cup prepared Italian oil & vinegar dressing
½ cup chopped onion
¼ cup chopped fresh parsley
2 tablespoons grated Parmesan cheese
¼ teaspoon black pepper

Cook fettuccine according to package directions; drain. Combine all ingredients in large bowl; toss well. Refrigerate several hours or until chilled. Garnish with fresh herbs, if desired.

Makes 6 to 8 servings

Savory Orzo-Zucchini Boats

Savory Orzo-Zucchini Boats

    3 large zucchini
 ⅓ cup HELLMANN'S® or BEST
    FOODS® Real or Light
    Mayonnaise or Reduced Fat
    Mayonnaise Dressing
 ¼ cup milk
 1 tablespoon Dijon-style mustard
 1 tablespoon lemon juice
 ¼ teaspoon salt
 ¼ teaspoon freshly ground black
    pepper
 ¼ teaspoon ground ginger
 8 ounces cooked ham, cut into
    matchsticks
 4 ounces Jarlsberg cheese, cut into
    matchsticks
 2 cups coarsely chopped spinach
    leaves
 ⅔ cup orzo macaroni, cooked
    according to package directions
    and drained
 ¼ cup minced green onions

Cut zucchini lengthwise in half. Scoop out pulp, leaving ¼-inch-thick shells; discard pulp. Cook shells in boiling water until tender-crisp. Rinse with cold water; drain well. In large bowl, combine mayonnaise, milk, mustard, lemon juice, salt, pepper and ginger. Stir in ham, cheese, spinach, macaroni and green onions. Spoon into zucchini halves.

Makes 6 servings

Sicilian Pepper and Potato Gratin

 2 tablespoons olive or vegetable oil
 ½ teaspoon LAWRY'S® Garlic Powder
    with Parsley
 ¾ pound red potatoes, thinly sliced
 1 red bell pepper, sliced into thin
    rings
 3 small zucchini, sliced
 1 teaspoon LAWRY'S® Seasoned Salt
 ½ teaspoon dried thyme, crushed
 ½ cup (4 ounces) grated Swiss cheese
 ½ cup (4 ounces) grated mozzarella
    cheese

Preheat oven to 375°F. In small bowl, combine oil and Garlic Powder with Parsley. Brush bottom of 1½-quart casserole with ½ of mixture. Layer ½ of potatoes, ½ of red pepper and ½ of zucchini in casserole. Sprinkle with ½ teaspoon Seasoned Salt, ¼ teaspoon thyme and ½ of cheeses. Repeat layers. Cover and bake 25 to 30 minutes or until potatoes are soft and cheeses are melted.

Makes 6 servings

Presentation: Serve with grilled chicken or fish steaks.

Hint: To prevent potatoes from discoloring, place in cold water after slicing. Drain and pat dry with paper towel before assembling.

Baked Polenta Jarlsberg

Polenta

    1½ cups yellow corn meal
    1 cup diced baked ham
    ½ cup butter or margarine, divided
    ½ cup sliced green onions
    ½ cup chopped fresh parsley
    1 cup shredded Jarlsberg cheese
    ½ cup freshly grated Parmesan cheese
    2 eggs, beaten

Sauce

    2 tablespoons olive oil
    2 pounds plum tomatoes, coarsely
        chopped
    1 can (16 ounces) tomato sauce
    1 package (10 ounces) frozen peas,
        thawed
    ¼ cup chopped fresh basil *or*
        1 tablespoon dried basil leaves,
        crushed
    ¼ teaspoon crushed red pepper

Gradually stir corn meal into 1 quart boiling salted water in large heavy saucepan. Simmer 20 minutes, stirring occasionally.

Preheat oven to 350°F. Meanwhile, cook and stir ham in ¼ cup butter in 10-inch ovenproof skillet until heated through. Stir green onions, parsley, cheeses and eggs into corn meal. Stir in ham. Melt 2 tablespoons butter in same skillet. Spread polenta mixture evenly into skillet. Dot with remaining 2 tablespoons butter. Bake 1 hour or until golden-brown and set. Let stand at room temperature for 30 minutes.

Meanwhile, heat olive oil in medium saucepan over medium heat. Add tomatoes; cook until soft. Add remaining ingredients. Bring to a boil; reduce heat to low. Simmer 10 minutes. Serve over polenta. *Makes 6 to 8 servings*

*Favorite recipe from **Norseland Foods, Inc.***

Asparagus with Roasted Peppers

This colorful salad—made easy with prepared roasted peppers—tastes as good as it looks.

    16 asparagus spears
    1 jar (7 ounces) PROGRESSO®
        Roasted Peppers (red), drained
        and cut into strips
    ¼ cup PROGRESSO® Olive Oil
    4 teaspoons raspberry vinegar
    ⅛ teaspoon salt
    Ground black pepper, to taste

1. Steam asparagus just until tender. Combine with roasted peppers; refrigerate until chilled.

2. For dressing, whisk together remaining ingredients; chill.

3. When ready to serve, place asparagus on serving platter; top with roasted peppers, arranging in decorative design, if desired. Serve with dressing.
Makes 4 servings

Prep time: 10 minutes
Cooking time: 10 minutes
Chilling/cooling time: 2 hours

Microwave: In 1½-quart microwave-safe casserole, place asparagus and ¼ cup water; cover. Microwave on HIGH (100% power) 3 minutes or just until tender; drain. Add roasted peppers; chill. Continue as directed in Steps 2 through 3.

Asparagus with Roasted Peppers

Creamy Italian Pasta Salad

1 cup HELLMANN'S® or BEST
  FOODS® Real or Light
  Mayonnaise or Reduced Fat
  Mayonnaise Dressing
2 tablespoons red wine vinegar
1 clove garlic, minced
1 tablespoon chopped fresh basil *or*
  1 teaspoon dried basil leaves
1 teaspoon salt
¼ teaspoon freshly ground black
  pepper
1½ cups twist or spiral pasta, cooked
  according to package directions,
  rinsed with cold water and
  drained
1 cup quartered cherry tomatoes
½ cup coarsely chopped green bell
  pepper
½ cup slivered pitted ripe olives

In large bowl, combine mayonnaise,
vinegar, garlic, basil, salt and black
pepper. Stir in pasta, cherry tomatoes,
green pepper and olives. Cover;
refrigerate until chilled.

Makes about 6 servings

*Top to bottom: Easy Macaroni Salad and
Creamy Italian Pasta Salad*

Easy Macaroni Salad

1 cup HELLMANN'S® or BEST
  FOODS® Real or Light
  Mayonnaise or Reduced Fat
  Mayonnaise Dressing
2 tablespoons vinegar
1 tablespoon prepared yellow
  mustard
1 teaspoon sugar
1 teaspoon salt
¼ teaspoon freshly ground black
  pepper
8 ounces elbow macaroni, cooked
  according to package directions,
  rinsed with cold water and
  drained
1 cup sliced celery
1 cup chopped green or red bell
  pepper
¼ cup chopped onion

In large bowl, combine mayonnaise,
vinegar, mustard, sugar, salt and black
pepper. Add macaroni, celery, green
pepper and onion; toss to coat well.
Cover; refrigerate until chilled. Garnish
as desired.   *Makes about 8 servings*

Elsie's Eggplant Supreme

2 eggplants, cut into ½-inch-thick
  slices
  Salt
10 large cloves fresh garlic, divided
½ cup all-purpose flour
½ cup biscuit mix
1 teaspoon dried oregano leaves,
  crushed
½ teaspoon black pepper
1 egg
1 to 2 tablespoons water
  Olive oil
  Vegetable oil

Place eggplant slices on paper towels in single layer and sprinkle both sides with salt. Set aside for 30 minutes.

Press 6 cloves garlic through garlic press into medium bowl. Stir in flour, biscuit mix, oregano, black pepper, egg and enough water to make the consistency of pancake batter. Add oil ¼ inch deep to large skillet using half olive oil and half vegetable oil. Heat oil over medium heat. Crush remaining 4 cloves of garlic with flat edge of knife and add to oil until lightly brown. Before removing cloves, press them against the skillet using fork to release oils from garlic into cooking oil. Discard cloves. Coat each eggplant slice with batter. Add to oil and fry, being careful not to brown too fast. Serve immediately. *Makes 8 servings*

Favorite recipe from **Christopher Ranch of Gilroy**

Fresh Seafood and Linguine Salad

Fresh Seafood and Linguine Salad

1½ pounds small squid, cleaned (directions on page 126)
4 pounds mussels, scrubbed and beards removed
1½ to 3 dozen clams, scrubbed
8 ounces uncooked linguine, cooked according to package directions, rinsed and drained
Olive oil
¼ cup fresh squeezed lemon juice
2 cloves garlic, minced
½ teaspoon salt
¼ teaspoon black pepper
1 red onion, thinly sliced and separated into rings (optional)
⅓ cup finely chopped fresh Italian parsley (optional)

Rinse squid thoroughly. Cut squid bodies into ¼-inch rings; finely chop tentacles and fins. Steam mussels and clams until they open; do not remove from shells. Discard any unopened shells. Toss linguine with 2 tablespoons olive oil.

Add just enough olive oil to large saucepan to cover bottom. Heat over medium heat; add squid. Cook, stirring constantly, 2 minutes. Place squid in large glass bowl. Add linguine, mussels and clams.

Combine ½ cup olive oil, lemon juice, garlic, salt and black pepper in small bowl; blend well. Pour over salad; toss gently to coat. Cover; refrigerate at least 3 hours. Adjust seasonings with additional lemon juice, salt and black pepper, if necessary. Garnish with onion rings and parsley. *Makes 6 servings*

Favorite recipe from **New Jersey Department of Agriculture**

Fried Eggplant

1 medium eggplant (about 1 pound)
1 teaspoon salt
½ teaspoon active dry yeast
1½ cups warm water (110° to 115°F)
2 cups all-purpose flour, divided
⅛ teaspoon black pepper
6 ounces mozzarella cheese
4½ tablespoons olive oil, divided
2 tablespoons minced fresh basil
   leaves *or* ½ teaspoon dried basil
   leaves, crushed
Vegetable oil
1 egg white
Lemon slices (optional)
Fresh basil leaf, for garnish

Rinse eggplant; cut crosswise into ¼-inch-thick slices. Place in large colander over bowl; sprinkle with salt. Drain 1 hour.

Sprinkle yeast over warm water in medium bowl; stir until dissolved. Whisk in 1½ cups flour and black pepper until smooth. Let batter stand at room temperature 30 minutes.

Cut cheese into ⅛-inch-thick slices. Trim cheese slices to size of eggplant slices; set aside.

Rinse eggplant and drain well; pat slices dry between paper towels. Heat 1½ tablespoons olive oil in large skillet over medium-high heat; add as many eggplant slices in single layer without crowding to hot oil. Cook 2 minutes per side until slices are light brown. Remove with slotted spatula; drain on paper towels. Repeat with remaining olive oil and eggplant slices. Sprinkle cheese slices with basil. Place each cheese slice between 2 eggplant slices; press firmly together. Spread remaining ½ cup flour on plate. Dip eggplant stacks in flour to coat lightly.

Heat 1½ inches vegetable oil in large saucepan to 350°F. Adjust heat to maintain temperature. Beat egg white in small bowl with electric mixer at high speed until stiff peaks form; fold into yeast batter. Dip eggplant stacks, 1 at a time, into batter; gently shake off excess. Fry stacks in oil, 3 at a time, 2 minutes per side until browned. Remove with slotted spatula; drain on paper towels. Serve hot with lemon slices. Garnish, if desired.

Makes 4 to 6 servings

Rice and Cabbage Italiano

6 slices bacon, diced
1 cup chopped onion
2 cloves garlic, minced
1 can (8 ounces) tomato sauce
1 cup chicken broth
½ small cabbage, shredded (about
   1 quart)
½ teaspoon dried oregano leaves,
   crushed
¼ teaspoon ground black pepper
¼ teaspoon crushed red pepper
3 cups cooked rice
Grated Romano or Parmesan
   cheese

Cook and stir bacon, onion and garlic in large skillet until bacon is crisp. Pour off fat, returning 2 tablespoons to skillet. Add tomato sauce, broth, cabbage, oregano, black pepper and red pepper to skillet. Cover and simmer about 5 minutes or until cabbage is crisp-tender. Stir in rice and cook 5 minutes longer. Sprinkle with cheese before serving.

Makes 6 servings

Favorite recipe from **USA Rice Council**

Fried Eggplant

DESSERTS

Kahlúa® Tiramisu for Two

12 small packaged ladyfingers
2 egg yolks
½ cup powdered sugar
4 ounces softened cream cheese,
    beaten until fluffy
⅓ cup whipping cream, whipped
¼ cup KAHLÚA®
½ teaspoon instant espresso powder,
    dissolved in 1 tablespoon water
1 ounce semisweet chocolate,
    chopped fine
2 teaspoons unsweetened cocoa
    powder

Preheat oven to 325°F. Arrange ladyfingers in single layer on baking sheet. Toast in oven 10 minutes. Set aside. Whisk yolks with sugar until smooth and thick in medium bowl. Whisk in cream cheese. Fold in whipped cream.

Stir Kahlúa® into espresso mixture. Combine chopped chocolate and cocoa in another small bowl.

Place 2 tablespoons cream cheese mixture in bottom of each of two (12-ounce) wine goblets or dessert dishes. Top each with 3 ladyfingers, 3 to 4 teaspoons Kahlúa® mixture and ⅓ cup cream cheese mixture. Cover each with ¼ of chocolate mixture, 3 ladyfingers and 3 to 4 teaspoons Kahlúa®

mixture. Top each dessert with ½ of the remaining cream cheese mixture; smooth top. Sprinkle with remaining chocolate mixture. Cover; refrigerate several hours before serving. *Makes 2 servings*

Chocolate Amaretto Pie

1 (9-inch) unbaked pastry shell
1 (3-ounce) package cream cheese,
    softened
2 (1-ounce) bars unsweetened baking
    chocolate, melted
⅛ teaspoon salt
1 (14-ounce) can EAGLE® Brand
    Sweetened Condensed Milk
    (NOT evaporated milk)
2 eggs
¼ to ⅓ cup amaretto liqueur
1 cup sliced almonds, toasted if
    desired

Preheat oven to 350°F. In large bowl, beat cheese, chocolate and salt until well blended. Gradually beat in sweetened condensed milk until smooth. Add eggs; mix well. Stir in liqueur and almonds. Pour into pastry shell. Bake 30 to 35 minutes or until center is set. Cool. Serve warm or chilled. Garnish as desired. Refrigerate leftovers.

Makes 1 (9-inch) pie

Kahlúa® Tiramisu for Two

192

Simple Spumoni

Simple Spumoni

2 cups whipping cream
⅔ cup sweetened condensed milk
½ teaspoon rum flavoring
1 can (21 ounces) cherry pie filling
½ cup chopped almonds
½ cup miniature chocolate chips

Combine cream, sweetened condensed milk and rum flavoring in large bowl; refrigerate 30 minutes. Beat just until soft peaks form. *Do not overbeat.* Fold in remaining ingredients. Pour into 8×8-inch pan. Cover; freeze about 4 hours or until firm. Scoop out to serve. Garnish as desired.   *Makes about 1 quart*

*Favorite recipe from **Cherry Marketing Institute, Inc.***

Italian Celebration Cake

1 frozen loaf pound cake (16 ounces), thawed
3 tablespoons orange flavored liqueur*
1¾ cups (15-ounce container) ricotta cheese, well drained
½ cup HERSHEY₍®₎'S Mini Chips₍®₎ Semi-Sweet Chocolate
3 tablespoons chopped candied fruit Cocoa-Mocha Frosting (recipe follows)

Slice top and end pieces from pound cake to form rectangle; cut slices crosswise to form 3 equal layers. Sprinkle top of each layer with liqueur; set aside. Place sieve over top of medium bowl; using rubber scraper, press ricotta cheese through sieve. Fold in chocolate chips and candied fruit. On heavy duty foil, place bottom cake layer; spread evenly with half of cheese mixture. Place second cake layer over cheese mixture; spread with remaining cheese mixture. Top with third cake layer. Press down lightly on layers; wrap tightly in foil. Refrigerate until well chilled, 2 to 3 hours. Prepare Cocoa-Mocha Frosting. Unwrap assembled cake; place on serving plate. Cover top and sides with frosting; cover and refrigerate. Cut into slices. Refrigerate leftovers.
Makes 10 to 12 servings

*Orange juice may be substituted for liqueur.

Cocoa-Mocha Frosting: In small mixer bowl, beat ½ cup margarine or butter, softened, until creamy. Dissolve 2 teaspoons instant coffee in 3 tablespoons warm water. Stir together 2½ cups confectioners' sugar and ⅓ cup Hershey₍®₎'s Premium European Style Cocoa. Add cocoa mixture alternately with coffee mixture to margarine, beating until smooth and creamy. Makes about 2 cups.

San Gennaro Zeppole

1 package active dry yeast
¾ cup warm water (110° to 115°F)
3½ cups all-purpose flour
1 teaspoon salt
¾ cup **FILIPPO BERIO®** Olive Oil
1 cup honey
¼ cup red, white and green
     nonpareils

Dissolve yeast in warm water in small bowl. Combine flour and salt in large bowl; make well in center of mixture. Spoon in yeast mixture; knead mixture until dough is smooth, adding water if necessary.

Shape dough into ball; place in large greased bowl. Cover bowl; let rise in warm place about 1 hour or until doubled.

Turn dough onto lightly floured surface. Punch down dough. Divide dough into 12 equal pieces. Pat each piece into 2½-inch circle; place circles on lightly floured cloth. Cover lightly and let rise about 45 minutes until doubled.

Heat oil in heavy 3-quart saucepan to 360°F on deep-fry thermometer. Fry dough rounds, a few at a time, until puffed and golden on both sides. Remove to paper towels to drain. Repeat with remaining dough.

Place honey in large bowl. Dip fried dough into honey to coat completely. Place on plate; sprinkle with nonpareils.

Makes 6 servings

Cappuccino Bon Bons

1 package **DUNCAN HINES®** Fudge
     Brownie Mix, Family Size
2 eggs
⅓ cup water
⅓ cup **CRISCO®** Oil or **CRISCO®**
     PURITAN® Oil
1½ tablespoons **FOLGERS®** Coffee
     Crystals
1 teaspoon ground cinnamon
     Whipped topping, for garnish
     Additional ground cinnamon, for
     garnish

1. Preheat oven to 350°F. Place 40 (2-inch) foil cupcake liners on baking sheets.

2. Combine brownie mix, eggs, water, oil, coffee and 1 teaspoon cinnamon in large bowl. Stir with spoon until well blended, about 50 strokes. Fill each liner with 1 measuring tablespoonful batter.

3. Bake at 350°F 12 to 15 minutes or until toothpick inserted in center comes out clean. Cool completely. Garnish with whipped topping and a dash of cinnamon. Refrigerate until ready to serve.   *Makes 40 bon bons*

Tip: To make larger bon bons, use twelve 2½-inch foil liners and fill with ¼ cup batter. Bake for 28 to 30 minutes.

Cappuccino Bon Bons

Florentine Cookies

¼ **cup sliced blanched almonds**
¼ **cup walnuts**
5 **red candied cherries**
1 **tablespoon golden or dark raisins**
1 **tablespoon diced candied lemon peel**
1 **tablespoon crystallized ginger**
¼ **cup unsalted butter**
¼ **cup sugar**
1 **tablespoon heavy cream**
3 **tablespoons all-purpose flour**
4 **ounces semisweet chocolate**

Finely chop almonds, walnuts, cherries, raisins, lemon peel and ginger; combine in small bowl. Set aside.

Preheat oven to 350°F. Grease 2 large baking sheets. Combine butter, sugar and cream in small, heavy saucepan. Cook, uncovered, over medium heat until sugar dissolves and mixture boils, stirring constantly. Cook and stir 1 minute more. Remove from heat. Stir in reserved nut-fruit mixture. Add flour; mix well. Spoon heaping teaspoon batter onto prepared baking sheet. Repeat, placing 4 cookies on each baking sheet to allow room for spreading.

Bake cookies, 1 baking sheet at a time, 8 to 10 minutes until deep brown. Remove baking sheet from oven to wire rack. If cookies have spread unevenly, push in edges with metal spatula to round out shape. Cool cookies 1 minute or until firm enough to remove from sheet, then quickly but carefully remove cookies with wide metal spatula to wire racks. Cool completely. Repeat with remaining batter, allowing baking sheets to cool between batches.

Finely chop chocolate. Bring water in bottom of double boiler just to a boil; remove from heat. Place chocolate in top of double boiler and place over water. Stir chocolate until melted; immediately remove from water. Let chocolate cool slightly. Line large baking sheet with waxed paper. Turn cookies over; spread chocolate on bottoms. Place cookies, chocolate sides up, on prepared baking sheet; let stand until chocolate is almost set. Score chocolate in zig-zag pattern with tines of fork. Let stand until completely set or refrigerate until firm. Store in airtight container in refrigerator.

Makes about 2 dozen cookies

Florentine Cookies

Chocolate Tortoni

8 **squares (1 ounce *each*) semi-sweet chocolate**
⅔ **cup KARO® Light or Dark Corn Syrup**
2 **cups heavy cream, divided**
1½ **cups broken chocolate wafer cookies**
1 **cup coarsely chopped walnuts**
Chocolate, nuts and whipped cream (optional)

Line 12 (2½-inch) muffin pan cups with paper or foil liners. In large heavy saucepan, combine chocolate and corn syrup; stir over low heat just until chocolate melts. Remove from heat. Stir in ½ cup cream until blended. Refrigerate 25 to 30 minutes or until cool. Stir in cookies and walnuts. In small bowl with mixer at medium speed, beat remaining 1½ cups cream until soft peaks form; gently fold into chocolate mixture just until combined. Spoon into prepared muffin pan cups. Freeze 4 hours or until firm. Let stand at room temperature several minutes before serving. If desired, garnish with chocolate, nuts or whipped cream. Store covered in freezer for up to 1 month.   *Makes 12 servings*

Cassata alla Bread Crumbs
(Almond Trifle)

Cassata alla Bread Crumbs

1½ cups PROGRESSO® Plain Bread
    Crumbs
 ½ cup all-purpose flour
 1 tablespoon baking powder
 ¼ teaspoon salt
 1 cup sugar
 ½ cup butter, softened
 3 eggs
 1 cup milk
 1 teaspoon vanilla extract
 5 tablespoons amaretto, divided
 ½ cup maraschino cherry halves
 1 container (8 ounces) LA CREME®
    Whipped Topping, thawed
 ½ cup plus 1 tablespoon sliced
    almonds

1. Preheat oven to 350°F.

2. In small bowl, combine bread crumbs, flour, baking powder and salt.

3. In large bowl, beat together sugar and butter on medium speed of electric mixer until light and fluffy. Add eggs, one at a time, beating well after each addition. With mixer on low speed, alternately add bread crumb mixture and milk to sugar mixture. Blend in vanilla.

4. Pour batter evenly into two greased and floured 8-inch square baking dishes.

5. Bake 20 to 25 minutes or until cake tester inserted in centers comes out clean. Cool on wire racks.

6. Sprinkle 1 tablespoon amaretto over each cake; cut into ½-inch cubes.

7. Reserve a few cherries for garnish, if desired. In large glass serving bowl, spoon one fourth of the whipped topping. Top with layers of one third each of the cake cubes, remaining cherries and almonds; sprinkle with 1 tablespoon amaretto. Repeat layers of whipped topping, cake cubes, cherries, almonds and amaretto two more times. Top with remaining whipped topping. Garnish with reserved cherries.

8. Chill at least 2 hours before serving.
                    Makes 10 servings

Prep time: 30 minutes
Baking time: 25 minutes
Chilling/cooling time: 3 hours

Chocolate Hazelnut Pie

Chocolate Hazelnut Crust
(recipe follows)
1 envelope unflavored gelatin
¼ cup cold water
2 cups whipping cream, divided
1½ cups semisweet chocolate chips
2 eggs*
3 tablespoons hazelnut-flavored
liqueur
1 teaspoon vanilla extract
24 caramels, unwrapped
Caramel Flowers, for garnish
(recipe follows)

Prepare Chocolate Hazelnut Crust; set aside.

Sprinkle gelatin over water in small saucepan. Let stand 3 minutes to soften. Heat over low heat, stirring constantly, about 5 minutes or until gelatin is completely dissolved.

Stir 1 cup whipping cream into gelatin mixture. Heat just to a boil; remove from heat. Add chocolate chips. Stir until chocolate is melted. Stir in ½ cup whipping cream, eggs, liqueur and vanilla until blended. Pour into large bowl; refrigerate about 15 minutes or until thickened.

Combine caramels and remaining ½ cup whipping cream in small saucepan. Simmer over low heat, stirring occasionally, until completely melted and smooth. Pour caramel mixture into prepared crust; let stand about 10 minutes.

Beat thickened gelatin mixture with electric mixer at medium speed until smooth. Pour over caramel layer; refrigerate 3 hours or until firm. Garnish, if desired.   *Makes 6 to 8 servings*

*Use clean uncracked eggs.

Chocolate Hazelnut Crust

¾ cup hazelnuts
30 chocolate cookie wafers
½ cup melted butter or margarine

Preheat oven to 350°F. To toast hazelnuts, spread hazelnuts in single layer on baking sheet. Bake 10 to 12 minutes or until toasted and skins begin to flake off; let cool slightly. Wrap hazelnuts in kitchen towel; rub towel to remove as much of the skins as possible.

Combine cookies and hazelnuts in food processor or blender; process with on/off pulses until finely crushed. Combine cookie crumbs, nuts and butter in medium bowl. Press firmly onto bottom and up side of 9-inch pie plate, forming high rim. Bake 10 minutes; cool completely on wire rack.

Caramel Flowers: Place 1 fresh, soft caramel between 2 sheets of waxed paper. With rolling pin, roll out caramel to 2-inch oval (press down hard with rolling pin). Starting at 1 corner, roll caramel into a cone to resemble a flower. Repeat with 5 to 7 more caramels. Before serving, place 1 Caramel Flower on each piece of pie.

Chocolate Hazelnut Pie

Mocha Cannoli Pie

2 cups (15 ounces) light ricotta
    cheese
½ cup sugar
1 tablespoon instant coffee powder
1 teaspoon vanilla extract
1 envelope unflavored gelatine
¼ cup water
½ cup mini semisweet chocolate
    chips
1 cup heavy cream, whipped
1 (9-inch) HONEY MAID® Honey
    Graham Pie Crust
Additional whipped cream,
    chocolate-covered coffee beans
    and mint sprigs, for garnish

In large bowl, with mixer at medium speed, beat ricotta, sugar, coffee powder and vanilla until light, about 3 minutes. Meanwhile, in small saucepan, sprinkle gelatine over water; let stand to soften 1 minute. Cook over medium-low heat, stirring constantly, until gelatine completely dissolves. Stir gelatine mixture and chocolate chips into ricotta mixture; fold in whipped cream. Pour mixture into crust. Refrigerate until set, about 3 hours. To serve, garnish with whipped cream, coffee beans and mint sprigs if desired. *Makes 8 servings*

Chocolate-Amaretto Ice

¾ cup sugar
½ cup HERSHEY'S Cocoa
2 cups (1 pint) light cream or
    half-and-half
2 tablespoons amaretto
    (almond-flavored) liqueur
Sliced almonds (optional)

In small saucepan, stir together sugar and cocoa; gradually stir in light cream. Cook over low heat, stirring constantly, until sugar dissolves and mixture is smooth and hot; do not boil. Remove from heat; stir in liqueur. Pour into 8-inch square pan. Cover; freeze until firm, stirring several times before mixture freezes. Scoop into dessert dishes. Serve frozen. Garnish with sliced almonds, if desired.
Makes about 4 servings

Lemon Ricotta Cheesecake

Cheesecake
2 cups (15 ounces) light ricotta
    cheese
½ cup half-and-half or light cream
½ cup sugar
2 tablespoons all-purpose flour
1 tablespoon lemon juice
1 teaspoon grated lemon peel
¼ teaspoon salt
2 eggs
1 (9-inch) NILLA® Pie Crust

Topping
½ cup light sour cream
1 tablespoon sugar
½ teaspoon vanilla extract

Preheat oven to 350°F. In bowl of electric mixer, combine ricotta cheese, half-and-half, sugar, flour, lemon juice, lemon peel and salt; blend until smooth. Add eggs, one at a time; blend until smooth. Pour into pie crust. Bake 50 minutes or until center is just set. Remove from oven. Beat sour cream with sugar and vanilla. Gently spoon onto warm cheesecake; spread evenly over surface. Return to oven for 10 minutes. *Turn off oven;* cool in oven with door propped open for 30 minutes. Remove to wire rack; cool completely. Refrigerate at least 3 hours before serving. *Makes 8 servings*

Biscotti di Mandorle
(Italian Almond Biscuits)

1 cup finely chopped blanched
    almonds
1 cup finely chopped walnuts
4½ teaspoons anise seeds
2 sticks (1 cup) unsalted butter,
    softened
2 cups granulated sugar
5 eggs
1 tablespoon vanilla extract
1 teaspoon almond extract
¼ teaspoon grated lemon peel
5 cups unsifted all-purpose flour
1 tablespoon baking powder
1 teaspoon salt

Preheat oven to 325°F. Place almonds,
walnuts and anise seeds in large skillet.
Cook over low heat about 5 minutes or
until golden, stirring frequently. Remove
from skillet; place on large plate to cool.

Set aside. Beat butter and sugar in large
bowl with electric mixer until light and
fluffy. Beat in eggs, 1 at a time, until
smooth. Beat in vanilla and almond
extracts, and lemon peel. Add flour,
baking powder and salt to reserved nut
mixture; stir to combine. Gradually add
to butter mixture, mixing until combined.
Divide dough into 4 equal pieces. Roll
each piece into log about 1½ inches in
diameter. Place logs on 2 large ungreased
baking sheets.

Bake about 30 minutes or until golden
brown. Remove logs to wire rack; cool
about 30 minutes. *Reduce oven temperature
to 250°F.* Cut logs diagonally into ½-inch-
thick slices; arrange, cut sides down, on
baking sheets. Bake 8 to 10 minutes until
dry. Cool completely on wire racks. Store
in airtight container.

Makes about 6½ dozen cookies

Favorite recipe from **American Spice Trade Association**

Biscotti di Mandorle

Pecan Florentines

¾ **cup pecan halves, pulverized***
½ **cup all-purpose flour**
⅓ **cup packed brown sugar**
¼ **cup light corn syrup**
¼ **cup butter or margarine**
2 **tablespoons milk**
⅓ **cup semisweet chocolate chips**

Preheat oven to 350°F. Line baking sheets with foil; lightly grease foil. Combine pecans and flour in small bowl. Combine sugar, syrup, butter and milk in medium saucepan. Stir over medium heat until mixture comes to a boil. Remove from heat; stir in flour mixture. Drop batter by teaspoonfuls about 3 inches apart onto prepared baking sheets. Bake 10 to 12 minutes or until lacy and golden brown. (Cookies are soft when hot, but become crispy as they cool.) Cool completely on foil.

Place chocolate chips in small heavy-duty plastic bag; close securely. Set bag in bowl of hot water until chips are melted, being careful not to let any water into bag. (Knead bag lightly to check that chips are completely melted.) Pat bag dry. With scissors, snip off a small corner from one side of bag. Squeeze melted chocolate over cookies to decorate. Let stand until chocolate is set. Peel foil off cookies. Store between layers of waxed paper in airtight container. *Makes about 3 dozen cookies*

*To pulverize pecans, place in food processor or blender. Process until thoroughly ground with a dry, not pasty, texture.

Double-Dipped Hazelnut Crisps

¾ **cup semisweet chocolate chips**
1¼ **cups all-purpose flour**
¾ **cup powdered sugar**
⅔ **cup whole hazelnuts, toasted, hulled and pulverized***
¼ **teaspoon instant espresso coffee powder**
Dash salt
½ **cup butter or margarine, softened**
2 **teaspoons vanilla extract**
4 **squares (1 ounce *each*) bittersweet or semisweet chocolate**
4 **ounces white chocolate**
2 **teaspoons shortening, divided**

Preheat oven to 350°F. Lightly grease baking sheets or line with parchment paper. Melt chocolate chips in top of double boiler over hot, not boiling, water. Remove from heat; cool. Blend flour, sugar, hazelnuts, coffee powder and salt in large bowl. Blend in butter, melted chocolate and vanilla until dough is stiff but smooth. (If dough is too soft to handle, cover and refrigerate until firm.) Roll out dough, one fourth at a time, to ⅛-inch thickness on lightly floured surface. Cut out with 2-inch scalloped round cutters. Place 2 inches apart on

Pecan Florentines and Double-Dipped Hazelnut Crisps

prepared baking sheets. Bake 8 minutes or until not quite firm. (Cookies should not brown. They will puff up during baking and then fall again.) Remove to wire racks to cool.

Place bittersweet and white chocolates into separate small bowls. Add 1 teaspoon shortening to each bowl. Place bowls over hot water; stir until chocolate is melted and smooth. Dip cookies, one at a time, halfway into bittersweet chocolate. Place on waxed paper; refrigerate until chocolate is set. Dip other halves of cookies into white chocolate; refrigerate until set. Store cookies in airtight container in cool place. (If cookies are frozen, chocolate may discolor.)

Makes about 4 dozen cookies

*To pulverize hazelnuts, place in food processor or blender. Process until thoroughly ground with a dry, not pasty, texture.

Orange Cappuccino Brownies

¾ **cup butter**
2 **squares (1 ounce *each*) semisweet chocolate, coarsely chopped**
2 **squares (1 ounce *each*) unsweetened chocolate, coarsely chopped**
1¾ **cups sugar**
1 **tablespoon instant espresso powder or instant coffee granules**
3 **eggs**
¼ **cup orange-flavored liqueur**
2 **teaspoons grated orange peel**
1 **cup all-purpose flour**
1 **package (12 ounces) semisweet chocolate chips**
2 **tablespoons shortening**
1 **orange, for garnish**

Orange Cappuccino Brownies

Preheat oven to 350°F. Grease 13×9-inch baking pan.

Melt butter, chopped semisweet chocolate and unsweetened chocolate in large heavy saucepan over low heat, stirring constantly. Stir in sugar and espresso powder. Remove from heat. Cool slightly.

Beat in eggs, 1 at a time, with wire whisk. Whisk in liqueur and orange peel. Beat flour into chocolate mixture until just blended. Spread batter evenly into prepared pan.

Bake 25 to 30 minutes until center is just set. Remove pan to wire rack. Meanwhile, melt chocolate chips and shortening in small heavy saucepan over low heat, stirring constantly. Immediately after removing brownies from oven, spread hot chocolate mixture over warm brownies. Cool completely in pan on wire rack. Cut into 2-inch squares.

To make orange peel garnish, remove thin strips of peel from orange using citrus zester. Tie strips into knots or twist into spirals. Garnish, if desired.

Makes about 2 dozen brownies

Italian Ice

1 cup fruity white wine
1 cup water
1 cup sugar
1 cup fresh lemon juice
2 egg whites*
Fresh berries (optional)
Mint leaves, for garnish

Place wine and water in small saucepan; add sugar. Cook over medium-high heat until sugar has dissolved and syrup boils, stirring frequently. Cover; boil 1 minute. Uncover; adjust heat to maintain simmer. Simmer 10 minutes without stirring. Remove from heat. Refrigerate 1 hour or until syrup is completely cool.

Stir lemon juice into cooled syrup. Pour into 9-inch round cake pan. Freeze 1 hour. Quickly stir mixture with fork breaking up ice crystals. Freeze 1 hour more or until firm but not solid. Meanwhile, place medium bowl in freezer to chill. Beat egg whites in small bowl with electric mixer at high speed until stiff peaks form. Remove lemon ice mixture from cake pan to chilled bowl. Immediately beat ice with whisk or fork until smooth. Fold in egg whites; mix well. Spread egg mixture evenly into same cake pan. Freeze 30 minutes. Immediately stir with fork; cover cake pan with foil. Freeze at least 3 hours or until firm.

To serve, scoop Italian Ice into fluted champagne glasses or dessert dishes. Serve with berries. Garnish with mint leaves. *Makes 4 servings*

*Use clean uncracked eggs.

Orange Almond Biscotti

3½ cups all-purpose flour
2 tablespoons sliced almonds, chopped
1½ teaspoons baking powder
¼ teaspoon salt
1½ cups sugar
2 tablespoons margarine, softened
3 egg whites
⅓ cup MOTT'S® Apple Sauce
1 tablespoon grated orange peel
2 teaspoons almond extract

Preheat oven to 350°F. Spray 15½×10½×2-inch baking pan with cooking spray.

In medium bowl, combine flour, almonds, baking powder and salt.

In large bowl, beat together sugar and margarine until creamy. Whisk in egg whites, Mott's® Apple Sauce, orange peel and almond extract; add flour mixture and mix until stiff dough is formed. Divide dough in half and shape into two 15×2-inch logs. Place in prepared baking pan.

Bake 30 minutes. Remove from oven. *Decrease oven temperature to 325°F.* Cut logs diagonally into ¼-inch slices. Arrange slices in baking pan and bake for 20 minutes more. Cool and serve.
Makes 36 servings (72 biscotti slices)

Note: These cookies are great for dunking in coffee, tea or any other beverage.

Tiramisu with Galbani® Mascarpone

Tiramisu with Galbani® Mascarpone

24 ladyfingers, split lengthwise
¾ cup espresso coffee, cooled
6 eggs,* separated
6 tablespoons sugar
1 pound GALBANI® Mascarpone
   Cheese
2 tablespoons brandy
8 ounces bittersweet chocolate,
   chopped or coarsely grated

Preheat oven to 375°F. Arrange
ladyfingers on baking sheet. Bake 5 to
10 minutes until toasted; arrange half in
2- or 2½-quart serving dish. Brush lightly
with espresso. In large bowl, beat egg
whites with electric mixer until stiff. In
small bowl, beat egg yolks and sugar
until thick and lemon-colored. Add
Mascarpone and brandy. Stir gently.
Gently fold egg whites into Mascarpone
mixture. Spread half the mixture on
ladyfingers. Sprinkle with half the
chocolate. Repeat layers. Cover;
refrigerate at least 1 hour before serving.
Refrigerate leftovers.   *Makes 12 servings*

*Use clean uncracked eggs

Spumoni Bars

¾ cup butter or margarine, softened
⅔ cup sugar
3 egg yolks
1 teaspoon vanilla
¼ teaspoon baking powder
⅛ teaspoon salt
2 cups all-purpose flour
12 maraschino cherries, well drained
   and chopped
¼ cup chopped walnuts
¼ cup mint-flavored or plain
   semisweet chocolate chips
2 teaspoons water, divided

Preheat oven to 350°F. Beat butter and
sugar in large bowl until blended. Beat in
egg yolks, vanilla, baking powder and
salt. Stir in flour to make stiff dough.
Divide into 3 equal parts; place each part
in small bowl. Add cherries and walnuts
to one part, blending well. Melt chocolate
chips in small bowl over hot water. Stir
until smooth. Stir melted chocolate and 1
teaspoon water into second part. Stir
remaining 1 teaspoon water into third
part. (If doughs are soft, refrigerate 10
minutes.)

Divide each color dough into 4 equal
parts. Shape each into 6-inch rope by
rolling on lightly floured surface. Place 1
rope of each color side by side on
ungreased baking sheet. Flatten ropes so
they attach together making 1 strip of 3
colors. With rolling pin, roll strip directly
on baking sheet until it measures 12×3
inches. Score strip crosswise at 1-inch
intervals. Repeat with remaining ropes to
make a total of 4 tri-colored strips of
dough. Bake 12 minutes or until set but
not browned; remove from oven. *While
cookies are still warm,* trim lengthwise
edges to make even and cut into
individual cookies along score marks.
Cool on baking sheets. Store in airtight
containers.   *Makes 4 dozen cookies*

Raspberry-Filled Chocolate Ravioli

Squares of rich chocolate dough encase a surprise filling of raspberry jam.

2 squares (1 ounce *each*) bittersweet or semisweet chocolate
1 cup butter or margarine, softened
½ cup granulated sugar
1 egg
1 teaspoon vanilla
½ teaspoon chocolate extract
¼ teaspoon baking soda
Dash salt
2½ cups all-purpose flour
1 to 1¼ cups seedless raspberry jam
Powdered sugar

Melt chocolate in top of double boiler over hot, not boiling, water. Remove from heat; cool. Beat butter and granulated sugar in large bowl until blended and creamy. Add egg, vanilla, chocolate extract, baking soda, salt and melted chocolate; beat until light. Blend in flour to make stiff dough. Divide dough in half. Cover; refrigerate until firm.

Preheat oven to 350°F. Lightly grease baking sheets or line with parchment paper. Roll out dough, half at a time, ⅛ inch thick between 2 sheets of plastic wrap. Remove top sheet of plastic. (If dough gets too soft and sticks to plastic, refrigerate until firm.) Cut dough into 1½-inch squares. Place half the squares 2 inches apart on prepared baking sheets. Place about ½ teaspoon jam in center of each square; top with another square. Using fork, press edges of squares together to seal, then pierce center of each square. Bake 10 minutes or just until edges are browned. Remove to wire racks; cool completely. Dust lightly with powdered sugar. Store in airtight containers.   *Makes about 6 dozen cookies*

Strawberry-Banana Granité

2 ripe medium bananas, peeled and sliced (about 2 cups)
2 cups unsweetened frozen strawberries (do not thaw)
¼ cup no sugar added strawberry pourable fruit
Whole fresh strawberries (optional)
Fresh mint leaves (optional)

Place banana slices in plastic bag; freeze until firm. Place frozen banana slices and frozen strawberries in food processor. Let stand 10 minutes for fruit to soften slightly. Add pourable fruit. Remove plunger from top of food processor to allow air to be incorporated. Process until smooth, scraping down sides of container frequently. Serve immediately. Garnish with fresh strawberries and mint leaves, if desired. Freeze leftovers.

Makes 5 servings

Raspberry-Filled Chocolate Ravioli

Sparkling Lemon Ice

1 package (4-serving size) JELL-O®
    Brand Lemon Flavor Sugar Free
    Gelatin
1 cup boiling water
1 cup cold lemon-lime seltzer
3 tablespoons fresh lemon juice
½ teaspoon grated lemon peel

• Completely dissolve gelatin in boiling
water. Add seltzer, lemon juice and peel.
Pour into 8- or 9-inch square pan; cover.
Freeze until firm, about 3 hours.

• Remove from freezer; let stand at room
temperature 10 minutes to soften slightly.
Beat at medium speed with electric mixer
or process with food processor until
smooth. Spoon or scoop into individual
dishes. Serve immediately.

Makes 6 servings

Sparkling Lemon Ice

Espresso Praline Ice Cream

Praline

¾ cup sugar
1 tablespoon *plus* 2 teaspoons water
1½ cups BLUE DIAMOND® Sliced
    Natural Almonds, toasted

Ice Cream

2 cups whipping cream
2 cups half-and-half
¾ cup sugar
5 egg yolks, beaten
1 tablespoon vanilla extract
1 teaspoon almond extract
2 tablespoons instant espresso
    powder
2 tablespoons brandy

To prepare praline, grease baking sheet.
Mix sugar and water in heavy saucepan.
Cook over medium-low heat about 5
minutes or until water evaporates and
sugar turns golden brown. Working
rapidly, add almonds and stir until all
almonds are lightly coated. Spread
immediately on prepared baking sheet.
Cool. Process in food processor or crush
with rolling pin until the size of small
peas. Set aside.

To prepare ice cream, combine cream,
half-and-half and sugar in another
saucepan. Cook and stir over medium
heat until sugar is dissolved and mixture
is hot. Gradually add 1 cup cream
mixture to beaten egg yolks, whisking
constantly. When mixture is smooth,
strain into double boiler. Gradually pour
in remaining cream mixture, whisking
constantly. Cook over simmering water
about 8 minutes, stirring until mixture
thickens slightly and coats back of spoon.
Do not boil. Stir in vanilla and almond
extracts.

Combine espresso powder and brandy in large bowl. Strain cream mixture into bowl, stirring to dissolve espresso. Cool. Stir in almond praline. Pour into ice cream freezer container. Freeze according to manufacturer's instructions.

Makes about 1 quart

Frozen Amaretto Torte

1 (8½-ounce) package chocolate wafers, finely crushed (2½ cups crumbs)
½ cup slivered almonds, toasted and chopped
⅓ cup margarine or butter, melted
1 (6-ounce) package butterscotch-flavored chips (1 cup)
1 (14-ounce) can EAGLE® Brand Sweetened Condensed Milk (NOT evaporated milk)
1 (16-ounce) container BORDEN® or MEADOW GOLD® Sour Cream
⅓ cup amaretto liqueur
1 cup (½ pint) BORDEN® or MEADOW GOLD® Whipping Cream, whipped

Combine crumbs, almonds and margarine. Reserving 1¼ cups crumb mixture, press remainder firmly on bottom of 9-inch springform pan. In small saucepan, over medium heat, melt chips with sweetened condensed milk. In large bowl, combine sour cream and amaretto; stir in butterscotch mixture. Fold in whipped cream. Pour half the cream mixture over prepared crust; top with 1 cup reserved crumb mixture, then remaining cream mixture. Top with remaining ¼ cup crumb mixture; cover. Freeze 6 hours or until firm. Garnish as desired. Freeze leftovers.

Makes 12 to 15 servings

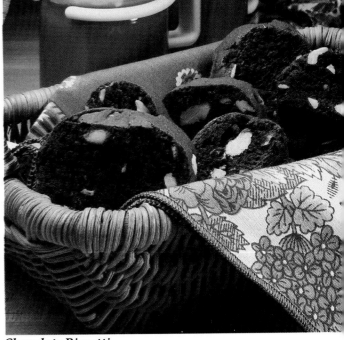
Chocolate Biscotti

Chocolate Biscotti

1½ cups all-purpose flour
½ cup NESTLÉ® Cocoa
1½ teaspoons baking powder
½ teaspoon baking soda
⅔ cup sugar
3 tablespoons butter, softened
2 eggs
½ teaspoon almond extract
½ cup almonds, coarsely chopped

Preheat oven to 350°F. Grease 15½×10½×1-inch baking pan. In small bowl, combine flour, cocoa, baking powder and baking soda; set aside.

In large mixer bowl, beat sugar, butter, eggs and almond extract until creamy. Gradually beat in flour mixture. Stir in almonds. Divide dough in half. Shape into two 12-inch-long logs; flatten slightly. Place in prepared pan.

Bake 25 minutes. Cool in pan on wire rack 5 minutes. Cut into ½-inch-thick slices; return slices to pan, cut sides down. Bake 20 minutes longer. Cool completely.

Makes 4 dozen cookies

Cannoli Pastries

18 to 20 Cannoli Pastry Shells (recipe
  follows)
2 pounds ricotta cheese
1½ cups sifted powdered sugar
2 teaspoons ground cinnamon
¼ cup diced candied orange peel,
  minced
1 teaspoon grated lemon peel
  Powdered sugar
2 ounces semisweet chocolate, finely
  chopped

Prepare Cannoli Pastry Shells; set aside.

For cannoli filling, beat cheese in large
bowl with electric mixer at medium
speed until smooth. Add 1½ cups
powdered sugar and cinnamon; beat at
high speed 3 minutes. Add candied
orange peel and lemon peel to cheese
mixture; mix well. Cover and refrigerate
until ready to serve.

To assemble, spoon cheese filling into
pastry bag fitted with large plain tip. Pipe
about ¼ cup filling into each reserved
Cannoli Pastry Shell.* Roll Cannoli
Pastries in additional powdered sugar to
coat. Dip ends of pastries into chocolate.
Arrange pastries on serving plate.
Garnish as desired.

Makes 18 to 20 pastries

*Do not fill Cannoli Pastry Shells ahead
of time or shells will become soggy.

Cannoli Pastry Shells

1¾ cups all-purpose flour
2 tablespoons granulated sugar
1 teaspoon grated lemon peel
2 tablespoons butter or margarine
1 egg
6 tablespoons Marsala
  Vegetable oil

Mix flour, granulated sugar and lemon
peel in medium bowl; cut in butter with
pastry blender or 2 knives until mixture
resembles fine crumbs. Beat egg and
Marsala in small bowl; add to flour
mixture. Stir with fork to form ball.
Divide dough in half; shape into two
1-inch-thick square pieces. Wrap in
plastic wrap and refrigerate at least 1
hour.

Heat 1½ inches oil in large saucepan to
325°F. Working with 1 piece of dough at a
time, roll out on lightly floured surface to
¹⁄₁₆-inch thickness. Cut dough with knife
into 9 or 10 (4×3-inch) rectangles. Wrap
each rectangle around a greased metal
cannoli form or an uncooked cannelloni
pasta shell. Brush one edge of rectangle
lightly with water; overlap with other
edge and press firmly to seal.

Fry 2 or 3 cannoli pastry shells at a time,
1 to 1½ minutes until light brown,
turning once. Remove; drain on paper
towels. Cool until easy to handle.
Carefully remove fried pastries from
cannoli forms or pasta shells; cool
completely. Repeat with remaining piece
of dough.

Cannoli Pastries

Tiramisu

Tiramisu

1½ cups cold 2% lowfat milk, divided
1 container (8 ounces) pasteurized
   process cream cheese product
2 tablespoons MAXWELL HOUSE®
   or YUBAN® Instant Coffee or
   SANKA® Brand 99.7% Caffeine
   Free Instant Coffee
1 tablespoon hot water
2 tablespoons brandy (optional)
1 package (4-serving size) JELL-O®
   Vanilla Flavor Sugar Free Instant
   Pudding and Pie Filling
2 cups thawed COOL WHIP LITE®
   Whipped Topping
1 package (3 ounces) ladyfingers,
   split
1 square (1 ounce) BAKER'S® Semi-
   Sweet Chocolate, grated

• Pour ½ cup of the milk into blender
container. Add cream cheese product;
cover. Blend until smooth. Blend in the
remaining 1 cup milk.

• Dissolve coffee in water; add to blender
with brandy. Add pudding mix; cover.
Blend until smooth, scraping down sides
occasionally; pour into large bowl. Gently
stir in whipped topping.

• Cut ladyfingers in half crosswise. Cover
bottom of 8-inch springform pan with
ladyfinger halves. Place remaining
halves, cut ends down, around sides of
pan. Spoon pudding mixture into pan.
Chill until firm, about 3 hours. Remove
side of pan. Sprinkle with grated
chocolate.   *Makes 12 servings*

Kahlúa® Cappuccino Almond Pie

1 (9-inch) prepared chocolate cookie
   or graham cracker crumb crust
1 teaspoon espresso instant coffee
   powder
6 tablespoons KAHLÚA®, divided
2 cups French vanilla or vanilla ice
   cream, softened
2 cups mocha almond fudge ice
   cream, softened
3 cups dairy whipped topping
¼ cup toasted sliced almonds
   Heavenly Kahlúa® Fudge Sauce
   (recipe follows) (optional)

Place crust in freezer. Stir coffee powder
and 2 tablespoons Kahlúa® into softened
vanilla ice cream until well mixed.
Remove crust from freezer. Spoon ice
cream mixture quickly into crust; freeze
until firm. Stir 2 tablespoons Kahlúa® into
mocha almond fudge ice cream; spoon
over vanilla layer. Freeze until firm. Stir
remaining 2 tablespoons Kahlúa® into
whipped topping until blended. Spread
over top of pie; sprinkle with almonds
just before serving. Serve with Heavenly
Kahlúa® Fudge Sauce.

Makes 1 (9-inch) pie

Heavenly Kahlúa® Fudge Sauce

1 (16-ounce) can chocolate fudge topping
¼ cup KAHLÚA®

In saucepan (or microwavable bowl), heat fudge topping (or microwave on HIGH) until melted; stir in Kahlúa®. Serve warm. To store, cover and refrigerate; reheat as needed.   *Makes 1⅔ cups*

Chocolate Chip Almond Biscotti

1 cup sliced almonds
2¾ cups all-purpose flour
1½ teaspoons baking powder
¼ teaspoon salt
½ cup butter or margarine, softened
1 cup sugar
3 eggs
3 tablespoons almond-flavored liqueur
1 tablespoon water
1 cup mini semisweet chocolate chips

Preheat oven to 350°F. To toast almonds, spread on baking sheet. Bake 8 to 10 minutes or until golden brown, stirring frequently. Remove almonds from baking sheet and cool. Coarsely chop almonds to measure ¾ cup.

Place flour, baking powder and salt in medium bowl; stir to combine. Beat butter and sugar in large bowl with electric mixer at medium speed until light and fluffy, scraping down side of bowl once. Beat in eggs, 1 at a time, scraping down side of bowl after each addition. Beat in liqueur and water. Gradually add flour mixture. Beat at low speed, scraping down side of bowl occasionally. Stir in chips and almonds with spoon.

Divide dough into fourths. Shape each quarter evenly into 15-inch-long log. Wrap in plastic wrap. Refrigerate about 2 hours or until firm.

Preheat oven to 375°F. Lightly grease baking sheet. Unwrap and place each log on prepared baking sheet. With floured hands, shape each log 2 inches wide and ½ inch thick.

Bake 15 minutes. Remove baking sheet from oven. Cut each log with serrated knife into 1-inch-thick diagonal slices. Place slices, cut sides up, on baking sheet; bake 7 minutes. Turn cookies over; bake 7 minutes or until cut surfaces are golden brown and cookies are dry. Remove cookies with spatula to wire racks; cool completely. Store tightly covered at room temperature or freeze up to 3 months.
Makes about 4 dozen cookies

Chocolate Chip Almond Biscotti

Acknowledgments

The publishers would like to thank the companies and organizations listed below for the use of their recipes in this book.

American Lamb Council
American Spice Trade
 Association
Bel Paese Sales Company
Best Foods, a Division of
 CPC International Inc.
Blue Diamond Growers
Boboli Co.
Bongrain Cheese U.S.A.
Borden Kitchens, Borden,
 Inc.
California Olive Industry
California Poultry
 Industry Federation
California Table Grape
 Commission
Castroville Artichoke
 Festival
Chef Paul Prudhomme's
 Magic Seasoning Blends
Cherry Marketing
 Institute, Inc.
Christopher Ranch of
 Gilroy
Clear Springs Trout
 Company
The Creamette Company

Cucina Classica Italiana,
 Inc.
The Dannon Company,
 Inc.
Delmarva Poultry
 Industry, Inc.
Del Monte Foods
Dole Food Company, Inc.
Filippo Berio Olive Oil
Florida Department of
 Citrus
Heinz U.S.A.
Hershey Chocolate U.S.A.
Hudson Foods, Inc.
Hunt–Wesson, Inc.
The HVR Company
Kahlúa Liqueur
The Kingsford Products
 Company
Kraft General Foods, Inc.
The Larsen Company
Lawry's® Foods, Inc.
Thomas J. Lipton Co.
McIlhenny Company
Mott's U.S.A., A division of
 Cadbury Beverages Inc.
Nabisco Foods Group

National Fisheries Institute
National Live Stock &
 Meat Board
National Pasta Association
Nestlé Food Company
New Jersey Department of
 Agriculture
Newman's Own, Inc.
Norseland Foods, Inc.
North Dakota Wheat
 Commission
Perdue Farms
Pet Incorporated
The Procter & Gamble
 Company
Red Star Yeast Products
Riviana Foods Inc.
Sargento Cheese
 Company, Inc.
StarKist Seafood Company
Uncle Ben's Rice
USA Rice Council
Walnut Marketing Board
Washington Apple
 Commission
Wisconsin Milk Marketing
 Board

Photo Credits

The publishers would like to thank the companies and organizations listed below for the use of their photographs in this book.

American Lamb Council
American Spice Trade
 Association
Bel Paese Sales Company
Best Foods, a Division of
 CPC International Inc.
Borden Kitchens, Borden,
 Inc.
California Table Grape
 Commission
Clear Springs Trout
 Company
Cucina Classica Italiana,
 Inc.
The Dannon Company,
 Inc.

Del Monte Foods
Dole Food Company, Inc.
Filippo Berio Olive Oil
Heinz U.S.A.
Hunt–Wesson, Inc.
The HVR Company
Kahlúa Liqueur
Kraft General Foods, Inc.
The Larsen Company
Lawry's® Foods, Inc.
Thomas J. Lipton Co.
Nabisco Foods Group
National Fisheries Institute
National Live Stock &
 Meat Board
National Pasta Association

Nestlé Food Company
Newman's Own, Inc.
Perdue Farms
Pet Incorporated
The Procter & Gamble
 Company
Riviana Foods Inc.
Sargento Cheese
 Company, Inc.
StarKist Seafood Company
Uncle Ben's Rice
USA Rice Council
Washington Apple
 Commission
Wisconsin Milk Marketing
 Board

INDEX

A

Almonds Italiano, 25
Antipasto Platter, 35
Antipasto Rice, 173
Antipasto Salad, 180
Antipasto with Marinated
　Mushrooms, 20
Appetizers (*see also* **Soups**)
　Almonds Italiano, 25
　Antipasto Platter, 35
　Antipasto with Marinated
　　Mushrooms, 20
　Artichoke Puffs, 10
　Baked Garlic Bundles, 8
　Basil & Vegetable Cheese Spread,
　　11
　Bruschetta, 6
　Caponata, 21
　Chicken Fingers Italiano, 14
　Chilled Seafood Lasagna with
　　Herbed Cheese, 25
　Cocktail Meatballs Italian-Style,
　　34
　Creamy Roasted Red Pepper Dip,
　　26
　Crostini, 13
　Deep-Fried Stuffed Shells, 21
　Elegant Antipasto, 13
　Felicia Solimine's Neapolitan-
　　Style Calamari, 18
　Florentine Crescents, 30
　Flounder Ravioli with Mustard-
　　Tomato Sauce, 29
　Fried Pasta with Marinara Sauce,
　　16
　Hot Artichoke Spread, 14
　Italian Baked Frittata, 18
　Marinated Mushrooms, 20
　Mediterranean Frittata, 32
　Pesto Pizza, 16

Appetizers (*continued*)
　Prosciutto Fruit Bundles in
　　Endive, 22
　Shrimp Cocktail Strata Tart, 9
　Sicilian Eggplant Appetizer, 28
　Spicy Cheese and Cappicola
　　Appetizers, 34
　Two Cheese Pesto Dip, 15
　Venetian Canapés, 37
　Winter Pesto Pizza, 16
　Zesty Bruschetta, 26
　Zucchini Frittata, 27
Apple-Cabbage Ravioli with Bacon
　& Thyme Broth, 52
Artichokes
　Antipasto Rice, 173
　Artichoke Puffs, 10
　Artichoke Spinach Salad, 174
　Cream of Artichoke Soup, 27
　Elegant Antipasto, 13
　Herb Stuffed Artichokes, 163
　Hot Artichoke Spread, 14
　Italian Country Chicken, 114
　Pasta Salad in Artichoke Cups,
　　156
　Penne with Artichokes, 43
　Potato Salad Italian-Style, 164
Asparagus with Roasted Peppers,
　187

B

Baked Cheesy Rotini, 47
Baked Garlic Bundles, 8
Baked Halibut with Roasted Pepper
　Sauce, 128
Baked Polenta Jarlsberg, 187
Balsamic Chicken and Peppers, 106
Basil & Vegetable Cheese Spread, 11
Basil-Vegetable Soup, 33

Basil Vinaigrette Dressing, 156
Beef
　Baked Cheesy Rotini, 47
　Beef and Bean Soup with Pesto,
　　33
　Beef Italienne, 82
　Beef, Tomato and Basil Salad, 164
　Chunky Pasta Sauce with Meat,
　　58
　Classic Meatball Soup, 23
　Cocktail Meatballs Italian-Style,
　　34
　Creamy Beef and Macaroni, 60
　Easy Beef Pizza, 144
　Fillet of Beef Andrea, 90
　Four-Meat Ravioli, 64
　Italian Marinated Steak, 87
　Italian Meat Pie, 94
　Italian Stuffed Shells, 57
　Italian-Style Chili, 10
　Italian Wedding Soup, 15
　Johnnie Marzetti, 84
　Meatza Pizza Pie, 149
　Neapolitan Lasagna, 40
　Saucy Meatballs, 82
　Spaghetti alla Bolognese, 38
　Steak di Sicilia, 90
　Stuffed Mushrooms with Tomato
　　Sauce and Pasta, 71
　Tenderloins with Roasted Garlic
　　Sauce, 96
　Tortellini Bake Parmesano, 72
Biscotti di Mandorle, 201
Breaded Veal Piccata, 95
Breads
　Cheesy Onion Focaccia, 137
　Cheesy Tomato Bread, 142
　Dijon Garlic Bread, 146
　Focaccia Spirals, 153
　Grilled Bread, 97
　Herbed Parmesan Muffins, 152

Breads (*continued*)
One Hour Pan Rolls Italiano, 146
Pepperoni Focaccia, 145
Roasted Red Pepper Biscuits, 132
Three-Cheese Focaccia, 140
Toasted Almond Biscuits, 149
Toasted Anise Biscuits, 149
Zucchini Basil Muffins, 138
Broccoli
Broccoli Lasagna, 67
Broccoli-Stuffed Shells, 49
Broiled Shellfish Venetian-Style, 118
Bruschetta, 6

C

Caesar Dressing, 169
Calico Minestrone Soup, 10
Calzones
Calzone, 138
Deli Stuffed Calzone, 145
Easy Calzone, 135
Italian Pizza Calzones, 130
Vegetable Calzone, 150
Cannoli Pastries, 211
Caponata, 21
Caponata-Style Fettuccine, 78
Cappuccino Bon Bons, 195
Carbonara Pizza, 142
Cassata alla Bread Crumbs, 197
Cheese
Antipasto with Marinated
Mushrooms, 20
Artichoke Spinach Salad, 174
Baked Cheesy Rotini, 47
Baked Polenta Jarlsberg, 187
Basil & Vegetable Cheese Spread,
11
Broccoli Lasagna, 67
Broccoli-Stuffed Shells, 49
Calzone, 138
Cannoli Pastries, 211
Cheesy Mushroom Pizza, 137
Cheesy Onion Focaccia, 137
Cheesy Tomato Bread, 142
Cheesy Turkey and Vegetable
Pizza, 140
Chicken and Spinach Manicotti,
79
Chicken Cutlets Parmesan, 98
Chicken Italiano, 110
Chicken Parmesan, 108
Chicken Parmesan Pizza, 132
Chicken Pesto Mozzarella, 102
Chilled Seafood Lasagna with
Herbed Cheese, 25
Classic Fettuccine Alfredo, 74

Cheese (*continued*)
Classic Veal Florentine, 83
Creamy Beef and Macaroni, 60
Creamy Pasta Primavera, 79
Creamy Roasted Red Pepper Dip,
26
Crostini, 13
Deep-Fried Stuffed Shells, 21
Deli Stuffed Calzone, 145
Easy Beef Pizza, 144
Easy Calzone, 135
Eggplant Northern Italian Style,
173
Eggplant Pasta Bake, 60
Elegant Antipasto, 13
Florentine Crescents, 30
Four Cheese Pizza, 133
Fresh Tomato, Basil and Ricotta
Sauce, 76
Fried Eggplant, 190
Hearty Minestrone Gratiné, 8
Herbed Parmesan Muffins, 152
Homemade Pizza, 150
Hot Artichoke Spread, 14
Italian Baked Frittata, 18
Italian Celebration Cake, 194
Italian Garden Medley, 169
Italian Ham Lasagna, 55
Italian Pasta Salad, 165
Italian Pizza Calzones, 130
Italian Scallop Marinade, 175
Italian Stuffed Shells, 57
Johnnie Marzetti, 84
Lamb and Spinach Manicotti, 70
Lasagna Primavera, 61
Lemon Ricotta Cheesecake, 200
Lentil Lasagna, 52
Macaroni Italiano, 50
Marinated Bell Pepper &
Mushroom Pizza, 138
Meatza Pizza Pie, 149
Mocha Cannoli Pie, 200
Neapolitan Lasagna, 40
Parmesan Chicken, 112
Parmesan Potato Slices, 182
Pesto Chicken Pizza, 130
Pizza Rice Casserole, 115
Plum Tomato Basil Pizza, 149
Quick Classic Pizza, 144
Ravioli and Chicken Parmesano,
76
Rice Napoli, 162
Savory Orzo-Zucchini Boats, 186
Shrimp Linguine, 73
Shrimp Milano, 118
Sicilian Pepper and Potato
Gratin, 186
Sicilian Pizza, 141

Cheese (*continued*)
Skinny Eggplant Parmigiana, 166
Sole Primavera en Croûte, 123
Spicy Cheese and Cappicola
Appetizers, 34
Spicy Pepperoni Pizza, 146
Spinach Gnocchi, 181
Spinach Pasta Bake, 47
Stuffed Pizza, 134
Supreme Style Pizza, 151
Surprisingly Simple Chicken
Cacciatore, 114
Tagliatelle, 48
Thick 'n' Cheesy Vegetable Pizza,
152
Three-Cheese Focaccia, 140
Tiramisu, 212
Tiramisu with Galbani®
Mascarpone, 206
Tomato, Mozzarella & Basil
Salad, 178
Tuna & Eggplant Parmigiana, 119
Turkey Rolls Italiano, 100
Two Cheese Pesto Dip, 15
Valley Eggplant Parmigiano, 163
Veal-Almond Shells with Quick
Basil-Tomato Sauce, 77
Veal Parmesan, 92
Vegetable Calzone, 150
Vegetable Pepperoni Pizza, 134
Vegetarian Lasagna, 76
Whitefish with Red Pepper
Sauce, 124
Chicken
Balsamic Chicken and Peppers,
106
Chicken & Pasta Sicilian, 98
Chicken and Roasted Peppers
Pizza, 152
Chicken and Spinach Manicotti,
79
Chicken Cacciatore, 105
Chicken Cutlets Parmesan, 98
Chicken Fingers Italiano, 14
Chicken Italiano, 110
Chicken Marsala, 109
Chicken Milano, 110
Chicken Parmesan, 108
Chicken Parmesan Pizza, 132
Chicken Pesto Mozzarella, 102
Chicken Pomodoro, 110
Chicken Rosemary, 107
Chicken Saltimbocca, 112
Chicken Scaparella, 101
Chicken Tetrazzini, 113
Chicken Tortellini with
Mushroom-Cream Sauce, 62
Creamy Chicken Primavera, 59

Chicken (*continued*)
Drumsticks Confetti, 103
Forty-Clove Chicken Filice, 102
Four-Meat Ravioli, 64
Italian Chicken Pasta, 54
Italian Country Chicken, 114
Italian Vegetable Chicken, 115
Noodle Soup Parmigiano, 22
Parmesan Chicken, 112
Pesto Chicken Pizza, 130
Pollo alla Firenze, 100
Pollo alla Giardiniera, 108
Pollo Pignoli, 103
Ravioli and Chicken Parmesano, 76
Sicilian Skillet Chicken, 113
Surprisingly Simple Chicken Cacciatore, 114
Venetian Pot Luck, 105
Chilled Seafood Lasagna with Herbed Cheese, 25
Chilled Zucchini-Basil Soup, 32
Chocolate
Cappuccino Bon Bons, 195
Chocolate-Amaretto Ice, 200
Chocolate Amaretto Pie, 192
Chocolate Biscotti, 209
Chocolate Chip Almond Biscotti, 213
Chocolate Hazelnut Crust, 199
Chocolate Hazelnut Pie, 199
Chocolate Tortoni, 196
Cocoa-Mocha Frosting, 194
Double-Dipped Hazelnut Crisps, 202
Florentine Cookies, 196
Heavenly Kahlúa® Fudge Sauce, 213
Raspberry-Filled Chocolate Ravioli, 207
Tiramisu with Galbani® Mascarpone, 206
Chunky Pasta Sauce with Meat, 58
Cioppino, 17
Citrus Veal Majorca, 91
Classic Fettuccine Alfredo, 74
Classic Meatball Soup, 23
Classic Pesto with Linguine, 54
Classic Polenta, 141
Classic Veal Florentine, 83
Cocktail Meatballs Italian-Style, 34
Cocoa-Mocha Frosting, 194
Colorful Grape, Pepper and Pasta Salad, 178
Confetti Risotto, 85
Cookies
Biscotti di Mandorle, 201
Chocolate Biscotti, 209

Cookies (*continued*)
Chocolate Chip Almond Biscotti, 213
Double-Dipped Hazelnut Crisps, 202
Florentine Cookies, 196
Orange Almond Biscotti, 204
Orange Cappuccino Brownies, 203
Pecan Florentines, 202
Raspberry-Filled Chocolate Ravioli, 207
Spumoni Bars, 206
Cream of Artichoke Soup, 27
Creamy Beef and Macaroni, 60
Creamy Chicken Primavera, 59
Creamy Italian Pasta Salad, 188
Creamy Pasta Primavera, 79
Creamy Roasted Red Pepper Dip, 26
Crostini, 13

D

Deep-Fried Stuffed Shells, 21
Deli Stuffed Calzone, 145
Desserts (*see also* **Cookies; Frozen Desserts; Pies**)
Cannoli Pastries, 211
Cappuccino Bon Bons, 195
Cassata alla Bread Crumbs, 197
Italian Celebration Cake, 194
Kahlúa® Tiramisu for Two, 192
Lemon Ricotta Cheesecake, 200
San Gennaro Zeppole, 195
Tiramisu, 212
Tiramisu with Galbani® Mascarpone, 206
Dijon Fettuccine, 41
Dijon Garlic Bread, 146
Double-Dipped Hazelnut Crisps, 202
Drumsticks Confetti, 103

E

Easy Beef Pizza, 144
Easy Calzone, 135
Easy Macaroni Salad, 188
Eggplant
Caponata, 21
Caponata-Style Fettuccine, 78
Confetti Risotto, 85
Eggplant Northern Italian Style, 173

Eggplant (*continued*)
Eggplant Pasta Bake, 60
Elsie's Eggplant Supreme, 188
Fried Eggplant, 190
Polenta with Ratatouille Sauce, 170
Ratatouille, 161
Sicilian Eggplant Appetizer, 28
Skinny Eggplant Parmigiana, 166
Tuna & Eggplant Parmigiana, 119
Valley Eggplant Parmigiano, 163
Elegant Antipasto, 13
Elsie's Eggplant Supreme, 188
Espresso Praline Ice Cream, 208

F

Felicia Solimine's Neapolitan-Style Calamari, 18
Fennel
Fennel, Olive and Radicchio Salad, 161
Herbed Fennel with Tomatoes, 177
Fettuccine
Caponata-Style Fettuccine, 78
Classic Fettuccine Alfredo, 74
Dijon Fettuccine, 41
Fettuccine à la Tuna, 66
Fettuccine alla Carbonara, 50
Fettuccine Italiano, 45
Fettuccine Primavera, 49
Fettuccine with Pesto, 43
Fettuccine with Roasted Red Pepper Sauce, 70
Homemade Fettuccine, 74
Milano Shrimp Fettuccine, 64
Pasta Primavera, 42
Veg-All® Pasta & Tuna Salad Italienne, 185
Fillet of Beef Andrea, 90
Fish (*see also* **Shellfish**)
Baked Halibut with Roasted Pepper Sauce, 128
Chilled Seafood Lasagna with Herbed Cheese, 25
Deep-Fried Stuffed Shells, 21
Easy Calzone, 135
Fettuccine à la Tuna, 66
Fish Rolls Primavera, 128
Flounder Ravioli with Mustard-Tomato Sauce, 29
Grilled Fish Steaks with Tomato Basil Butter Sauce, 116
Grilled Rainbow Trout with Italian Butter, 126

Fish (*continued*)
Grilled Swordfish with Garlic-Basil Butter, 129
Nutty Pan-Fried Trout, 119
Rainbow Trout Parmesan, 128
Rainbow Trout with Walnuts and Oregano, 125
Snapper with Pesto Butter, 123
Sole Primavera en Croûte, 123
Spaghetti Squash with Tuna-Vegetable Sauce, 121
Tuna & Eggplant Parmigiana, 119
Tuna in Red Pepper Sauce, 69
Veg-All® Pasta & Tuna Salad Italienne, 185
Whitefish with Red Pepper Sauce, 124
Florentine Cookies, 196
Florentine Crescents, 30
Flounder Ravioli with Mustard-Tomato Sauce, 29
Focaccia Spirals, 153
Forty-Clove Chicken Filice, 102
Four Cheese Pizza, 133
Four-Meat Ravioli, 64
Fresh Seafood and Linguine Salad, 189
Fresh Tomato, Basil and Ricotta Sauce, 76
Fried Calamari with Tartar Sauce, 126
Fried Eggplant, 190
Fried Pasta with Marinara Sauce, 16
Frittatas
Italian Baked Frittata, 18
Mediterranean Frittata, 32
Zucchini Frittata, 27
Frosting, Cocoa-Mocha, 194
Frozen Desserts
Chocolate-Amaretto Ice, 200
Chocolate Tortoni, 196
Espresso Praline Ice Cream, 208
Frozen Amaretto Torte, 209
Italian Ice, 204
Simple Spumoni, 194
Sparkling Lemon Ice, 208
Strawberry-Banana Granité, 206

G

Garden Primavera Pasta, 69
Garden Salad with Basil, 154
Garlic Mushrooms, 175
Glorious Garbanzo Salad, 182
Grape and Hazelnut Pasta, 40
Green Beans with Pine Nuts, 161
Gremolata, 88

Grilled Bread, 97
Grilled Fish Steaks with Tomato Basil Butter Sauce, 116
Grilled Pasta Salad, 168
Grilled Pizza, 147
Grilled Rainbow Trout with Italian Butter, 126
Grilled Swordfish with Garlic-Basil Butter, 129
Grilled Vegetables with Balsamic Vinaigrette, 165

H

Hearty Minestrone Gratiné, 8
Hearty Veal Stew, 89
Heavenly Kahlúa® Fudge Sauce, 213
Herbed Fennel with Tomatoes, 177
Herbed Parmesan Muffins, 152
Herb Stuffed Artichokes, 163
Homemade Fettuccine, 74
Homemade Pizza, 150
Homestyle Zucchini & Tomatoes, 157
Hot Artichoke Spread, 14

I

Insalata di Riso con Basilico, 176
Italian Baked Frittata, 18
Italian Capellini and Fresh Tomato, 45
Italian Celebration Cake, 194
Italian Chicken Pasta, 54
Italian Country Chicken, 114
Italian Garden Medley, 169
Italian Ham Lasagna, 55
Italian Herb Dressing, 181
Italian Ice, 204
Italian Marinated Steak, 87
Italian Meat Pie, 94
Italian Pasta Salad, 165
Italian Pizza Calzones, 130
Italian Pork Cutlets, 80
Italian Scallop Marinade, 175
Italian Stuffed Shells, 57
Italian-Style Chili, 10
Italian Vegetable Chicken, 115
Italian Vegetable Salad, 183
Italian Wedding Soup, 15

J

Johnnie Marzetti, 84

K

Kahlúa® Cappuccino Almond Pie, 212
Kahlúa® Tiramisu for Two, 192

L

Lamb
Confetti Risotto, 85
Lamb and Spinach Manicotti, 70
Lamb Chops with Herbed Peppercorn Sauce, 91
Lamb Tetrazzini, 95
Pasta with Rustic Lamb Tomato Sauce, 66
Wine & Rosemary Lamb Skewers, 97
Lasagna
Broccoli Lasagna, 67
Chilled Seafood Lasagna with Herbed Cheese, 25
Italian Ham Lasagna, 55
Lasagna Primavera, 61
Lentil Lasagna, 52
Neapolitan Lasagna, 40
Vegetarian Lasagna, 76
Legumes
Basil-Vegetable Soup, 33
Beef and Bean Soup with Pesto, 33
Calico Minestrone Soup, 10
Chicken Milano, 110
Glorious Garbanzo Salad, 182
Green Beans with Pine Nuts, 161
Hearty Minestrone Gratiné, 8
Italian Vegetable Salad, 183
Lentil Lasagna, 52
Light Pasta e Fagiole, 9
Marinated Three Bean Salad, 154
Meatless Italian Minestrone, 37
Minestrone, 25
Minestrone alla Milanese, 30
Pasta Hoppin' John, 72
Turkey Cannellini Sauté, 106
Lemon
Italian Ice, 204
Lemon Ricotta Cheesecake, 200
Sparkling Lemon Ice, 208
Lentil Lasagna, 52
Light Alfredo, 57
Light Pasta e Fagiole, 9
Linguine
Classic Pesto with Linguine, 54
Fresh Seafood and Linguine Salad, 189

Linguine (*continued*)
    Linguine with Creamy
      Peppercorn Sauce, 61
    Linguine with White Clam Sauce,
      78
    Linguine with Zesty Clam Sauce,
      45
    Shrimp Linguine, 73
Lobster Mushroom Sauce di Riso,
    125

M

Macaroni Italiano, 50
Marinated Bell Pepper &
    Mushroom Pizza, 138
Marinated Bell Peppers, 139
Marinated Mushrooms, 20, 139
Marinated Shrimp Italiano, 129
Marinated Three Bean Salad, 154
Marinated Vegetable Spinach Salad,
    158
Meatless Italian Minestrone, 37
Meatza Pizza Pie, 149
Mediterranean Frittata, 32
Microwave Recipes
    Antipasto Rice, 173
    Asparagus with Roasted Peppers,
      187
    Chicken and Spinach Manicotti,
      79
    Cocktail Meatballs Italian-Style,
      34
    Fettuccine Italiano, 45
    Homestyle Zucchini & Tomatoes,
      157
    Hot Artichoke Spread, 14
    Marinated Shrimp Italiano, 129
    Spaghetti Squash with Tuna-
      Vegetable Sauce, 121
    Tagliatelle, 48
    Zucchini Frittata, 27
Milano Shrimp Fettuccine, 64
Minestrone, 25
Minestrone alla Milanese, 30
Mocha
    Cappuccino Bon Bons, 195
    Espresso Praline Ice Cream, 208
    Kahlúa® Cappuccino Almond
      Pie, 212
    Kahlúa® Tiramisu for Two, 192
    Mocha Cannoli Pie, 200
    Orange Cappuccino Brownies,
      203
    Tiramisu, 212
    Tiramisu with Galbani®
      Mascarpone, 206

Mushrooms
    Broccoli Lasagna, 67
    Cheesy Mushroom Pizza, 137
    Chicken Marsala, 109
    Chicken Tortellini with
      Mushroom-Cream Sauce, 62
    Easy Calzone, 135
    Garlic Mushrooms, 175
    Italian Pizza Calzones, 130
    Italian Pork Cutlets, 80
    Lobster Mushroom Sauce di Riso,
      125
    Marinated Bell Pepper &
      Mushroom Pizza, 138
    Marinated Mushrooms, 20, 139
    Pasta with Rustic Lamb Tomato
      Sauce, 66
    Pollo alla Firenze, 100
    Risotto Milanese, 174
    Risotto with Peas and
      Mushrooms, 166
    Shrimp Milano, 118
    Sicilian Skillet Chicken, 113
    Sole Primavera en Croûte, 123
    Stuffed Mushrooms with Tomato
      Sauce and Pasta, 71
    Veal Scaloppine, 96
Mustard Tarragon Marinade, 158
Mustard Walnut Vinaigrette, 178

N

Neapolitan Lasagna, 40
Noodle Soup Parmigiano, 22
Nuts
    Almonds Italiano, 25
    Biscotti di Mandorle, 201
    Cassata alla Bread Crumbs,
      197
    Chocolate Amaretto Pie, 192
    Chocolate Chip Almond Biscotti,
      213
    Chocolate Hazelnut Crust, 199
    Chocolate Hazelnut Pie, 199
    Chocolate Tortoni, 196
    Double-Dipped Hazelnut Crisps,
      202
    Espresso Praline Ice Cream, 208
    Grape and Hazelnut Pasta, 40
    Green Beans with Pine Nuts,
      161
    Kahlúa® Cappuccino Almond
      Pie, 212
    Nutty Pan-Fried Trout, 119
    Orange Almond Biscotti, 204
    Pasta Salad with Pesto and
      Almonds, 180

Nuts (*continued*)
    Pecan Florentines, 202
    Pollo Pignoli, 103
    Rainbow Trout with Walnuts and
      Oregano, 125
    Walnut Pesto Sauce, 59

O

One Hour Pan Rolls Italiano, 146
Open-Faced Zucchini and Roasted
    Red Pepper Melts, 133
Orange
    Citrus Veal Majorca, 91
    Italian Celebration Cake, 194
    Orange Almond Biscotti, 204
    Orange Cappuccino Brownies,
      203

P

Parmesan Chicken, 112
Parmesan Potato Slices, 182
Pasta (*see also* **Fettuccine; Lasagna;**
    Linguine; Ravioli; Spaghetti)
    Baked Cheesy Rotini, 47
    Basil-Vegetable Soup, 33
    Beef Italienne, 82
    Broccoli-Stuffed Shells, 49
    Chicken & Pasta Sicilian, 98
    Chicken and Spinach Manicotti,
      79
    Chicken Pesto Mozzarella, 102
    Chicken Tetrazzini, 113
    Chicken Tortellini with
      Mushroom-Cream Sauce, 62
    Chunky Pasta Sauce with Meat,
      58
    Creamy Beef and Macaroni, 60
    Creamy Chicken Primavera, 59
    Creamy Italian Pasta Salad, 188
    Creamy Pasta Primavera, 79
    Deep-Fried Stuffed Shells, 21
    Easy Macaroni Salad, 188
    Eggplant Pasta Bake, 60
    Fresh Tomato, Basil and Ricotta
      Sauce, 76
    Fried Pasta with Marinara Sauce,
      16
    Garden Primavera Pasta, 69
    Grape and Hazelnut Pasta, 40
    Grilled Pasta Salad, 168
    Hearty Veal Stew, 89
    Italian Capellini and Fresh
      Tomato, 45
    Italian Chicken Pasta, 54

Pasta (*continued*)
Italian Pasta Salad, 165
Italian Stuffed Shells, 57
Italian Wedding Soup, 15
Lamb and Spinach Manicotti, 70
Lamb Tetrazzini, 95
Light Alfredo, 57
Light Pasta e Fagiole, 9
Macaroni Italiano, 50
Pasta Hoppin' John, 72
Pasta Marinara, 46
Pasta Primavera, 42, 57
Pasta Salad in Artichoke Cups, 156
Pasta Salad with Pesto and Almonds, 180
Pasta with Rustic Lamb Tomato Sauce, 66
Pasta with Sausage and Spicy Tomato Sauce, 58
Penne with Artichokes, 43
Quick Veal and Pasta Soup, 28
Ranch Italian Pasta Salad, 185
Roasted Red Pepper Pasta with Shrimp, 46
Sausage Pasta Primavera, 73
Savory Orzo-Zucchini Boats, 186
Shrimp Milano, 118
Spinach Tortellini with Bel Paese®, 48
Tagliatelle, 48
Tomato Caper Sauce, 55
Tortellini Bake Parmesano, 72
Tortellini Soup, 6
Veal-Almond Shells with Quick Basil-Tomato Sauce, 77
Pecan Florentines, 202
Penne with Artichokes, 43
Pepperoni
Deli Stuffed Calzone, 145
Italian-Style Chili, 10
Pepperoni Focaccia, 145
Pizza Soup, 18
Potato Salad Italian-Style, 164
Sausage Pizza Rice, 97
Spicy Pepperoni Pizza, 146
Stuffed Pizza, 134
Vegetable Pepperoni Pizza, 134
Peppers
Antipasto Rice, 173
Asparagus with Roasted Peppers, 187
Baked Halibut with Roasted Pepper Sauce, 128
Balsamic Chicken and Peppers, 106
Chicken and Roasted Peppers Pizza, 152

Peppers (*continued*)
Colorful Grape, Pepper and Pasta Salad, 178
Creamy Roasted Red Pepper Dip, 26
Easy Beef Pizza, 144
Easy Macaroni Salad, 188
Elegant Antipasto, 13
Fettuccine with Roasted Red Pepper Sauce, 70
Hearty Veal Stew, 89
Italian Pork Cutlets, 80
Marinated Bell Pepper & Mushroom Pizza, 138
Marinated Bell Peppers, 139
Open-Faced Zucchini and Roasted Red Pepper Melts, 133
Pasta Hoppin' John, 72
Peppers Piemontese, 171
Pollo Pignoli, 103
Pork Chops Roma, 84
Potato Salad Italian-Style, 164
Rice Napoli, 162
Roasted Pepper Sauce, 129
Roasted Red Pepper Biscuits, 132
Roasted Red Pepper Pasta with Shrimp, 46
Sausage, Peppers & Onions with Grilled Polenta, 87
Shrimp fra Diavolo, 124
Shrimp Milano, 118
Sicilian Pepper and Potato Gratin, 186
Surprisingly Simple Chicken Cacciatore, 114
Tuna in Red Pepper Sauce, 69
Tuscany Sausage and Rice Skillet, 92
Venetian Pot Luck, 105
Whitefish with Red Pepper Sauce, 124
Pesto Chicken Pizza, 130
Pesto Pizza, 16
Pesto Sauce, 33
Pies
Chocolate Amaretto Pie, 192
Chocolate Hazelnut Pie, 199
Italian Meat Pie, 94
Kahlúa® Cappuccino Almond Pie, 212
Mocha Cannoli Pie, 200
Pizza Rice Casserole, 115
Pizzas (*see also* **Calzones**)
Carbonara Pizza, 142
Cheesy Mushroom Pizza, 137
Cheesy Turkey and Vegetable Pizza, 140

Pizzas (*continued*)
Chicken and Roasted Peppers Pizza, 152
Chicken Parmesan Pizza, 132
Easy Beef Pizza, 144
Four Cheese Pizza, 133
Grilled Pizza, 147
Homemade Pizza, 150
Marinated Bell Pepper & Mushroom Pizza, 138
Meatza Pizza Pie, 149
Pesto Chicken Pizza, 130
Pesto Pizza, 16
Plum Tomato Basil Pizza, 149
Quick Classic Pizza, 144
Roma Tomato Pizzas, 142
Sicilian Pizza, 141
Spicy Pepperoni Pizza, 146
Stuffed Pizza, 134
Supreme Style Pizza, 151
Thick 'n' Cheesy Vegetable Pizza, 152
Vegetable Garden Pizza, 153
Vegetable Pepperoni Pizza, 134
Winter Pesto Pizza, 16
Pizza Soup, 18
Plum Tomato Basil Pizza, 149
Plum Tomato Sauce, 65
Polenta
Baked Polenta Jarlsberg, 187
Classic Polenta, 141
Polenta with Ratatouille Sauce, 170
Sausage, Peppers & Onions with Grilled Polenta, 87
Pollo alla Firenze, 100
Pollo alla Giardiniera, 108
Pollo Pignoli, 103
Pork (*see also* **Pepperoni; Prosciutto; Sausage, Italian**)
Antipasto Platter, 35
Antipasto Salad, 180
Apple-Cabbage Ravioli with Bacon & Thyme Broth, 52
Artichoke Spinach Salad, 174
Carbonara Pizza, 142
Fettuccine alla Carbonara, 50
Italian Ham Lasagna, 55
Italian Pork Cutlets, 80
Pasta Salad with Pesto and Almonds, 180
Pork Chops Roma, 84
Pork Cutlets Genovese, 91
Pork Medallions Piccata, 88
Ranch Italian Pasta Salad, 185
Savory Orzo-Zucchini Boats, 186
Spicy Cheese and Cappicola Appetizers, 34

Pork (*continued*)
  Supreme Style Pizza, 151
  Veal-Almond Shells with Quick Basil-Tomato Sauce, 77
Potatoes
  Chicken Scaparella, 101
  Parmesan Potato Slices, 182
  Potato Salad Italian-Style, 164
  Sicilian Pepper and Potato Gratin, 186
  Venetian Pot Luck, 105
Poultry (*see* **Chicken; Turkey**)
Prosciutto
  Antipasto with Marinated Mushrooms, 20
  Calzone, 138
  Chicken Tortellini with Mushroom-Cream Sauce, 62
  Four-Meat Ravioli, 64
  Mediterranean Frittata, 32
  Prosciutto Fruit Bundles in Endive, 22
  Spinach Tortellini with Bel Paese®, 48

Q

Quick Basil-Tomato Sauce, 77
Quick Classic Pizza, 144
Quick Pizza Crust, 144
Quick Risotto, 157
Quick Veal and Pasta Soup, 28

R

Rainbow Trout Parmesan, 128
Rainbow Trout with Walnuts and Oregano, 125
Ranch Italian Pasta Salad, 185
Raspberry-Filled Chocolate Ravioli, 207
Ratatouille, 161
Ravioli
  Apple-Cabbage Ravioli with Bacon & Thyme Broth, 52
  Flounder Ravioli with Mustard-Tomato Sauce, 29
  Four-Meat Ravioli, 64
  Ravioli and Chicken Parmesano, 76
Rice
  Antipasto Rice, 173
  Balsamic Chicken and Peppers, 106
  Confetti Risotto, 85

Rice (*continued*)
  Drumsticks Confetti, 103
  Insalata di Riso con Basilico, 176
  Lobster Mushroom Sauce di Riso, 125
  Pizza Rice Casserole, 115
  Quick Risotto, 157
  Rice and Cabbage Italiano, 190
  Rice Napoli, 162
  Risotto alla Milanese, 185
  Risotto Milanese, 174
  Risotto Primavera, 162
  Risotto with Peas and Mushrooms, 166
  Risotto with Sausage and Shrimp, 177
  Risotto with Shellfish Genoa Style, 158
  Sausage Pizza Rice, 97
  Stuffed Tomatoes, 169
  Tomato Risotto Pronto, 182
  Tuscany Sausage and Rice Skillet, 92
  Two-Squash Risotto, 170
Risotto alla Milanese, 185
Risotto Milanese, 174
Risotto Primavera, 162
Risotto with Peas and Mushrooms, 166
Risotto with Sausage and Shrimp, 177
Risotto with Shellfish Genoa Style, 158
Roasted Pepper Sauce, 129
Roasted Red Pepper Biscuits, 132
Roasted Red Pepper Pasta with Shrimp, 46
Roma Tomato Pizzas, 142

S

Salad Dressings
  Basil Vinaigrette Dressing, 156
  Caesar Dressing, 169
  Italian Herb Dressing, 181
  Mustard Tarragon Marinade, 158
  Mustard Walnut Vinaigrette, 178
Salads
  Antipasto Salad, 180
  Artichoke Spinach Salad, 174
  Beef, Tomato and Basil Salad, 164
  Colorful Grape, Pepper and Pasta Salad, 178
  Creamy Italian Pasta Salad, 188
  Easy Macaroni Salad, 188
  Fennel, Olive and Radicchio Salad, 161

Salads (*continued*)
  Fresh Seafood and Linguine Salad, 189
  Garden Salad with Basil, 154
  Glorious Garbanzo Salad, 182
  Grilled Pasta Salad, 168
  Insalata di Riso con Basilico, 176
  Italian Pasta Salad, 165
  Italian Scallop Marinade, 175
  Italian Vegetable Salad, 183
  Marinated Three Bean Salad, 154
  Marinated Vegetable Spinach Salad, 158
  Pasta Salad in Artichoke Cups, 156
  Pasta Salad with Pesto and Almonds, 180
  Pollo alla Giardiniera, 108
  Potato Salad Italian-Style, 164
  Ranch Italian Pasta Salad, 185
  Tomato, Mozzarella & Basil Salad, 178
  Veg-All® Pasta & Tuna Salad Italienne, 185
Sandwiches
  Open-Faced Zucchini and Roasted Red Pepper Melts, 133
  Turkey Picatta on Grilled Rolls, 109
San Gennaro Zeppole, 195
Sauces
  Fresh Tomato, Basil and Ricotta Sauce, 76
  Heavenly Kahlúa® Fudge Sauce, 213
  Light Alfredo, 57
  Pesto Sauce, 33
  Plum Tomato Sauce, 65
  Quick Basil-Tomato Sauce, 77
  Roasted Pepper Sauce, 129
  Savory Zucchini & Olive Sauce, 41
  Spinach Pesto, 60
  Tartar Sauce, 126
  Tomato Basil Butter Sauce, 116
  Tomato Caper Sauce, 55
  Tomato Sauce, 71
  Tuna in Red Pepper Sauce, 69
  Walnut Pesto Sauce, 59
Saucy Meatballs, 82
Sausage, Italian
  Chunky Pasta Sauce with Meat, 58
  Italian Pizza Calzones, 130
  Italian Vegetable Chicken, 115
  Pasta with Sausage and Spicy Tomato Sauce, 58

Sausage, Italian (*continued*)
Risotto with Sausage and Shrimp, 177
Sausage Pasta Primavera, 73
Sausage, Peppers & Onions with Grilled Polenta, 87
Tuscany Sausage and Rice Skillet, 92
Venetian Pot Luck, 105
Sausage Pizza Rice, 97
Savory Orzo-Zucchini Boats, 186
Savory Zucchini & Olive Sauce, 41
Scampi Italienne, 121
Shellfish (*see also* **Fish; Shrimp**)
Broiled Shellfish Venetian-Style, 118
Cioppino, 17
Felicia Solimine's Neapolitan-Style Calamari, 18
Fresh Seafood and Linguine Salad, 189
Fried Calamari with Tartar Sauce, 126
Italian Scallop Marinade, 175
Linguine with White Clam Sauce, 78
Linguine with Zesty Clam Sauce, 45
Lobster Mushroom Sauce di Riso, 125
Risotto with Shellfish Genoa Style, 158
Sole Primavera en Croûte, 123
Squid Mediterranean, 120
Shrimp
Marinated Shrimp Italiano, 129
Milano Shrimp Fettuccine, 64
Risotto with Sausage and Shrimp, 177
Roasted Red Pepper Pasta with Shrimp, 46
Scampi Italienne, 121
Shrimp Cocktail Strata Tart, 9
Shrimp fra Diavolo, 124
Shrimp Linguine, 73
Shrimp Milano, 118
Sicilian Eggplant Appetizer, 28
Sicilian Pepper and Potato Gratin, 186
Sicilian Pizza, 141
Sicilian Skillet Chicken, 113
Side Dishes
Antipasto Rice, 173
Asparagus with Roasted Peppers, 187
Eggplant Northern Italian Style, 173
Elsie's Eggplant Supreme, 188

Side Dishes (*continued*)
Fried Eggplant, 190
Garlic Mushrooms, 175
Green Beans with Pine Nuts, 161
Grilled Vegetables with Balsamic Vinaigrette, 165
Herbed Fennel with Tomatoes, 177
Herb Stuffed Artichokes, 163
Homestyle Zucchini & Tomatoes, 157
Italian Garden Medley, 169
Parmesan Potato Slices, 182
Peppers Piemontese, 171
Quick Risotto, 157
Ratatouille, 161
Rice and Cabbage Italiano, 190
Rice Napoli, 162
Risotto alla Milanese, 185
Risotto Milanese, 174
Risotto Primavera, 162
Risotto with Peas and Mushrooms, 166
Savory Orzo-Zucchini Boats, 186
Sicilian Pepper and Potato Gratin, 186
Skinny Eggplant Parmigiana, 166
Spinach Gnocchi, 181
Stuffed Tomatoes, 169
Tomato Risotto Pronto, 182
Two-Squash Risotto, 170
Valley Eggplant Parmigiano, 163
Vegetables Italiano, 175
Zucchini Italiano, 171
Simple Spumoni, 194
Skinny Eggplant Parmigiana, 166
Snapper with Pesto Butter, 123
Sole Primavera en Croûte, 123
Soups
Basil-Vegetable Soup, 33
Beef and Bean Soup with Pesto, 33
Calico Minestrone Soup, 10
Chilled Zucchini-Basil Soup, 32
Cioppino, 17
Classic Meatball Soup, 23
Cream of Artichoke Soup, 27
Hearty Minestrone Gratiné, 8
Hearty Veal Stew, 89
Italian-Style Chili, 10
Italian Wedding Soup, 15
Light Pasta e Fagiole, 9
Meatless Italian Minestrone, 37
Minestrone, 25
Minestrone alla Milanese, 30
Noodle Soup Parmigiano, 22
Pizza Soup, 18
Quick Veal and Pasta Soup, 28

Soups (*continued*)
Tomato Soup, 35
Tortellini Soup, 6
Veg-All® Italian Soup, 17
Spaghetti
Antipasto Salad, 180
Colorful Grape, Pepper and Pasta Salad, 178
Spaghetti alla Bolognese, 38
Spaghetti Puttanesca, 42
Spinach Pasta Bake, 47
Stuffed Mushrooms with Tomato Sauce and Pasta, 71
Spaghetti Squash with Tuna-Vegetable Sauce, 121
Sparkling Lemon Ice, 208
Spicy Cheese and Cappicola Appetizers, 34
Spicy Pepperoni Pizza, 146
Spinach
Artichoke Spinach Salad, 174
Chicken and Spinach Manicotti, 79
Classic Veal Florentine, 83
Deli Stuffed Calzone, 145
Florentine Crescents, 30
Four-Meat Ravioli, 64
Italian Ham Lasagna, 55
Italian Wedding Soup, 15
Lamb and Spinach Manicotti, 70
Macaroni Italiano, 50
Marinated Vegetable Spinach Salad, 158
Pollo alla Firenze, 100
Spinach Gnocchi, 181
Spinach Pasta Bake, 47
Spinach Pesto, 60
Spinach Tortellini with Bel Paese®, 48
Stuffed Pizza, 134
Tortellini Soup, 6
Spumoni Bars, 206
Squid Mediterranean, 120
Steak di Sicilia, 90
Strawberry-Banana Granité, 206
Stuffed Mushrooms with Tomato Sauce and Pasta, 71
Stuffed Pizza, 134
Stuffed Tomatoes, 169
Supreme Style Pizza, 151
Surprisingly Simple Chicken Cacciatore, 114

T

Tagliatelle, 48
Tartar Sauce, 126

Tenderloins with Roasted Garlic
   Sauce, 96
Thick 'n' Cheesy Vegetable Pizza,
   152
Three-Cheese Focaccia, 140
Tiramisu, 212
Tiramisu with Galbani®
   Mascarpone, 206
Toasted Almond Biscuits, 149
Toasted Anise Biscuits, 149
Tomatoes
   Beef, Tomato and Basil Salad,
      164
   Cheesy Tomato Bread, 142
   Fresh Tomato, Basil and Ricotta
      Sauce, 76
   Glorious Garbanzo Salad, 182
   Herbed Fennel with Tomatoes,
      177
   Homestyle Zucchini & Tomatoes,
      157
   Italian Capellini and Fresh
      Tomato, 45
   Italian Garden Medley, 169
   Plum Tomato Basil Pizza, 149
   Plum Tomato Sauce, 65
   Quick Basil-Tomato Sauce, 77
   Roma Tomato Pizzas, 142
   Stuffed Tomatoes, 169
   Tomato Basil Butter Sauce, 116
   Tomato Caper Sauce, 55
   Tomato, Mozzarella & Basil
      Salad, 178
   Tomato Risotto Pronto, 182
   Tomato Sauce, 71
   Tomato Soup, 35
Tortellini Bake Parmesano, 72
Tortellini Soup, 6
Tuna & Eggplant Parmigiana,
   119
Tuna in Red Pepper Sauce, 69
Turkey
   Cheesy Turkey and Vegetable
      Pizza, 140
   Pizza Rice Casserole, 115
   Turkey Cannellini Sauté, 106
   Turkey Picatta on Grilled Rolls,
      109
   Turkey Rolls Italiano, 100
Tuscany Sausage and Rice Skillet,
   92
Two Cheese Pesto Dip, 15
Two-Squash Risotto, 170

V

Valley Eggplant Parmigiano, 163

Veal
   Breaded Veal Piccata, 95
   Citrus Veal Majorca, 91
   Classic Veal Florentine, 83
   Hearty Veal Stew, 89
   Quick Veal and Pasta Soup, 28
   Veal-Almond Shells with Quick
      Basil-Tomato Sauce, 77
   Veal Cutlets Parma Style, 80
   Veal Meatballs, 28
   Veal Parmesan, 92
   Veal Piccata, 85
   Veal Scaloppine, 96
   Veal Shanks Braised in Herb-
      Tomato Sauce, 88
Veg-All® Italian Soup, 17
Veg-All® Pasta & Tuna Salad
   Italienne, 185
Vegetables (*see also individual types*)
   Antipasto Salad, 180
   Antipasto with Marinated
      Mushrooms, 20
   Apple-Cabbage Ravioli with
      Bacon & Thyme Broth, 52
   Basil & Vegetable Cheese Spread,
      11
   Basil-Vegetable Soup, 33
   Cheesy Turkey and Vegetable
      Pizza, 140
   Chicken Rosemary, 107
   Creamy Chicken Primavera, 59
   Creamy Pasta Primavera, 79
   Fettuccine Primavera, 49
   Fish Rolls Primavera, 128
   Garden Primavera Pasta, 69
   Grilled Vegetables with Balsamic
      Vinaigrette, 165
   Homemade Pizza, 150
   Insalata di Riso con Basilico,
      176
   Italian Baked Frittata, 18
   Italian Pasta Salad, 165
   Italian Scallop Marinade, 175
   Italian Vegetable Chicken, 115
   Italian Vegetable Salad, 183
   Johnnie Marzetti, 84
   Lasagna Primavera, 61
   Marinated Vegetable Spinach
      Salad, 158
   Meatless Italian Minestrone, 37
   Minestrone, 25
   Minestrone alla Milanese, 30
   Pasta Primavera, 42, 57
   Pasta Salad with Pesto and
      Almonds, 180
   Pesto Chicken Pizza, 130
   Ranch Italian Pasta Salad, 185
   Rice and Cabbage Italiano, 190

Vegetables (*continued*)
   Risotto Primavera, 162
   Sausage Pasta Primavera, 73
   Spaghetti Squash with Tuna-
      Vegetable Sauce, 121
   Thick 'n' Cheesy Vegetable Pizza,
      152
   Veg-All® Italian Soup, 17
   Veg-All® Pasta & Tuna Salad
      Italienne, 185
   Vegetable Calzone, 150
   Vegetable Garden Pizza, 153
   Vegetable Pepperoni Pizza, 134
   Vegetables Italiano, 175
   Vegetarian Lasagna, 76
Venetian Canapés, 37
Venetian Pot Luck, 105

W

Walnut Pesto Sauce, 59
Whitefish with Red Pepper Sauce,
   124
Wine & Rosemary Lamb Skewers,
   97
Winter Pesto Pizza, 16

Z

Zesty Bruschetta, 26
Zucchini
   Chicken Pomodoro, 110
   Chilled Zucchini-Basil Soup, 32
   Grilled Pasta Salad, 168
   Homestyle Zucchini & Tomatoes,
      157
   Italian Garden Medley, 169
   Neapolitan Lasagna, 40
   Open-Faced Zucchini and
      Roasted Red Pepper Melts, 133
   Pasta with Rustic Lamb Tomato
      Sauce, 66
   Ratatouille, 161
   Ravioli and Chicken Parmesano,
      76
   Savory Orzo-Zucchini Boats, 186
   Savory Zucchini & Olive Sauce,
      41
   Tortellini Bake Parmesano, 72
   Two-Squash Risotto, 170
   Veal-Almond Shells with Quick
      Basil-Tomato Sauce, 77
   Vegetarian Lasagna, 76
   Zucchini Basil Muffins, 138
   Zucchini Frittata, 27
   Zucchini Italiano, 171

METRIC CONVERSION CHART

VOLUME MEASUREMENTS (dry)

$\frac{1}{8}$ teaspoon = 0.5 mL
$\frac{1}{4}$ teaspoon = 1 mL
$\frac{1}{2}$ teaspoon = 2 mL
$\frac{3}{4}$ teaspoon = 4 mL
1 teaspoon = 5 mL
1 tablespoon = 15 mL
2 tablespoons = 30 mL
$\frac{1}{4}$ cup = 60 mL
$\frac{1}{3}$ cup = 75 mL
$\frac{1}{2}$ cup = 125 mL
$\frac{2}{3}$ cup = 150 mL
$\frac{3}{4}$ cup = 175 mL
1 cup = 250 mL
2 cups = 1 pint = 500 mL
3 cups = 750 mL
4 cups = 1 quart = 1 L

VOLUME MEASUREMENTS (fluid)

1 fluid ounce (2 tablespoons) = 30 mL
4 fluid ounces ($\frac{1}{2}$ cup) = 125 mL
8 fluid ounces (1 cup) = 250 mL
12 fluid ounces ($1\frac{1}{2}$ cups) = 375 mL
16 fluid ounces (2 cups) = 500 mL

WEIGHTS (mass)

$\frac{1}{2}$ ounce = 15 g
1 ounce = 30 g
3 ounces = 90 g
4 ounces = 120 g
8 ounces = 225 g
10 ounces = 285 g
12 ounces = 360 g
16 ounces = 1 pound = 450 g

DIMENSIONS

$\frac{1}{16}$ inch = 2 mm
$\frac{1}{8}$ inch = 3 mm
$\frac{1}{4}$ inch = 6 mm
$\frac{1}{2}$ inch = 1.5 cm
$\frac{3}{4}$ inch = 2 cm
1 inch = 2.5 cm

OVEN TEMPERATURES

250°F = 120°C
275°F = 140°C
300°F = 150°C
325°F = 160°C
350°F = 180°C
375°F = 190°C
400°F = 200°C
425°F = 220°C
450°F = 230°C

BAKING PAN SIZES

Utensil	Size in Inches/Quarts	Metric Volume	Size in Centimeters
Baking or Cake Pan (square or rectangular)	8×8×2	2 L	20×20×5
	9×9×2	2.5 L	22×22×5
	12×8×2	3 L	30×20×5
	13×9×2	3.5 L	33×23×5
Loaf Pan	8×4×3	1.5 L	20×10×7
	9×5×3	2 L	23×13×7
Round Layer Cake Pan	8×1½	1.2 L	20×4
	9×1½	1.5 L	23×4
Pie Plate	8×1¼	750 mL	20×3
	9×1¼	1 L	23×3
Baking Dish or Casserole	1 quart	1 L	—
	1½ quart	1.5 L	—
	2 quart	2 L	—